WELCOME TO COLORFULLY PLAYING THE PIANO

Write in this book.

Color.

Make songs.

Have fun!

This book belongs to _____

This is your book and your COLORFUL musical adventure starts right here!

Printed in the United States of America
First Edition 2021
Colorfully Playing the Piano

 ColorfullyPlayingthePiano

ISBN 978-0-578-24432-7

TABLE OF CONTENTS

Part One – Technique and Theory 1-118

A Note on How to Use This Book 1

Play Something 3

What Does Your Piano Look Like? 5

Supplies 7

Play and Sing Songs 9

What Colors Are the Piano? 11

Songs in Black and White 12

Finger Numbers 14

Finger Techniques 17

High and Low 21

Groups of Two or Three Black Notes 25
Up and Down the Rainbow 28
Butterflies Flying 30
Panda Eats Bamboo 34
Ladybug Goes Up 36
Up the Slide and the Trampoline 38

Songs on Black Notes 39
Hot Cross Buns 41
Rain is Falling Down 42
Bells Are Ringing 43
I Can Ride My Bike 44
Your Three Walking Song 45

Rhythm 47

Finger Number Songs 58
Up We Go 61
Snowflakes 62
Going to the Moon 63
Falling Leaves 64
Sunshine 65
Over the Bridge 66
Your Songs 67

More RH Melody Techniques 69
Extending Finger Number Five 71
I Can Fly 72
Extending Finger Number One 73
Plant a Seed 74
Going Over Mountains 75
Going Down the Mountain 77
Hiking Two Mountains 79
Up and Down and Around I Go 80

Dynamics 81

The Musical Alphabet 83

The 123 ABC Song 94

Sandwiches 95

Improvising 101

Part Two - Our Songbook......120-277

Songs with C G Chords and RH on C.....122
Row Row Row Your Boat..............123
Mary Had a Little Lamb................125
Ring Around the Rosie..................127
Rain, Rain Go Away......................129
London Bridge Is Falling Down......131
Skip to My Lou..............................133
Do Your Ears Hang Low?..............135
Are You Sleeping?........................137
There is Thunder..........................139
Your Song......................................141

Songs with C F Chords and RH on C.....144
The Farmer in the Dell..................145

Songs with C F G Chords and RH on C.....148
Twinkle, Twinkle Little Star............149
The ABC's......................................151
Baa, Baa Black Sheep...................153
Five Little Ducks............................155
The Bear Went Over the Mountain..157
I'm a Little Teapot..........................159
Hickory Dickory Dock.....................161
This Old Man..................................163
He's Got the Whole World.............165
Alice the Camel.............................167
Peas Porridge Hot.........................169
On Top of Spaghetti......................171
Humpty Dumpty............................173
Lavender's Blue.............................175
For He's a Jolly Good Fellow.........177

Songs with RH on G......180
Old MacDonald Had a Farm.........181
I'm Bringing Home a Baby Bumblebee..183
Do You Know the Muffin Man?......185
Six Little Ducks...............................187
Three Little Kittens........................189

Songs with RH on A and B............192
If You're Happy and You Know It........193
Apples and Bananas......................195

Songs That Switch RH Positions......198
A Switcheroo Song........................199
The More We Get Together..........200
Bingo..203
Hey Diddle Diddle..........................205
Yankee Doodle...............................207
Rockabye Baby..............................209
The Ants Go Marching...................212
Skidamarink...................................216
Happy Birthday..............................219

Songs That Switch to G............222
The Wheels on the Bus.................223
Shoo Fly...225
Hush Little Baby.............................227
You Are My Sunshine....................229

Songs That Go Over the Mountain..232
Pop Goes the Weasel....................233
The Itsy Bitsy Spider......................235
Down By the Station......................237
Where Is Thumbkin?......................239
My Bonnie Lies Over the Ocean........241
If All of the Raindrops....................243
Here We Go Looby Loo.................245
She'll Be Coming Round the Mountain...247
I've Been Working on the Railroad..250

Songs that Use Accidentals........254
Chromatic Scale.............................256
Accidentals with Numbers.............259
Head, Shoulders, Knees and Toes...270
Down by the Bay............................272
The Hokey Pokey...........................274
Your Last Song...............................276

Part Three – Resources and Practice........278-335

Let's Make More Sandwiches	279
All Major Thirds	280
All Minor Thirds	281
Different Ways to Play Sandwiches	282
Sandwich Finger Number Patterns	284
More Inside Sandwiches (Intervals)	286
Double Decker Sandwiches (Triads)	290
Diatonic Triads	292
Triad Finger Number Patterns	294
All Major Triads	296
All Minor Triads	297
How Can You Learn More Songs?	298
Introduction to the Musical Staff	299
Warm Ups	313
How to Play Warm Ups	315
Groups of TWO Warm Ups	316
Groups of THREE Warm Ups	317
Warm Ups on White Notes	318
Patterns in Warm Ups	319
Warm Ups with Steps and Jumps	320
Warm Ups with Thirds	321
Warm Ups with Rhythms	322
Warm Ups with Many Notes at a Time	324
Triad Warm Ups	326
Five Finger Scale Warm Ups	328
Over the Mountain Warm Ups	329
Bridge Warm Ups	330
Major Scale Warm Ups	332
Every Day Warm Ups	333
Certificate of Acheivement	335

ALPHABETICAL SONG LIST

The 123 ABC Song......94
The ABC's......151
Alice the Camel......167
The Ants Go Marching......212
Apples and Bananas......195
Are you Sleeping?......137
Baa, Baa Black Sheep......153
The Bear Went Over the Mountain..157
Bells Are Ringing......43
Bingo......203
Down by the Bay......272
Down by the Station......237
Do You Know the Muffin Man?...185
Do Your Ears Hang Low?......135
Falling Leaves......64
The Farmer in the Dell......145
Five Little Ducks......155
For He's a Jolly Good Fellow....177
Going Down the Mountain......77
Going to the Moon......63
Happy Birthday......219
Head, Shoulders, Knees and Toes....270
Here We Go Looby Loo......245
He's Got the Whole World......165
Hey Diddle Diddle......205
Hickory Dickory Dock......161
Hiking Two Mountains......79
The Hokey Pokey......274
Hot Cross Buns......41
Humpty Dumpty......173
Hush Little Baby......227
I Can Fly......72
I Can Ride My Bike......44
If All of the Raindrops......243
If You're Happy and You Know It......193
I'm a Little Teapot......159
I'm Bringing Home a Baby Bumblebee....183
The Itsy Bitsy Spider......235
I've Been Working on the Railroad....250

Lavender's Blue	175
London Bridge Is Falling Down	131
Mary Had a Little Lamb	125
The More We Get Together	200
My Bonnie Lies Over the Ocean	241
Old MacDonald Had a Farm	181
On Top of Spaghetti	171
Over the Bridge	66
Peas Porridge Hot	169
Plant a Seed	74
Pop Goes the Weasel	233
Rain is Falling Down	42
Rain, Rain Go Away	129
Ring Around the Rosie	127
Rockabye Baby	209
Row Row Row Your Boat	123
Six Little Ducks	187
She'll Be Coming Round the Mountain	247
Shoo Fly	225
Skidamarink	216
Skip to My Lou	133
Snowflakes	62
Sunshine	65
A Switcheroo Song	199
Three Little Kittens	189
There is Thunder	139
This Old Man	163
Twinkle, Twinkle Little Star	149
Up Down and Around I Go	80
Up We Go	61
The Wheels on the Bus	233
Where Is Thumbkin?	239
Yankee Doodle	207
You Are My Sunshine	229
Your Last Song	276
Your Song	141
Your Songs	67
Your Three Walking Song	45

A Note on How to Use This Book

MUSIC is a language.

We can
READ music
WRITE music
PLAY music
SING songs
LISTEN to music
and
PRACTICE music.

This book teaches all of those things.

For **reading music**, try going through the book in order or use one of the methods on the next page.

For **writing music**, there are prompts throughout the pages for writing your own music.

For **playing music** and **singing songs**, try the methods on the next page too.

For **listening to music** look for the ear on pages 211, 215, and 249. I will give you the title of some classical music pieces (music without words) for listening practice.

For **practicing music**, you can do WARM UPS. Warm ups are important to get your fingers ready to play. While there are many pages of warm ups on pages 313-333, I would recommend starting with page 333 each time you want to play and practice.

You can see there are hearts and stars next to the page numbers. These are for coloring in to show you've done that page. You can also write the date you learn and play them.

Most pages have a doodle or drawing for you to color and make your own! After you play a song, you can color the doodle to remember what you learned.

If you want to see a video explanation of how to use this book, connect through social media here and join the conversation too:

 ColorfullyPlayingthePiano

Most importantly, HAVE FUN!

Possible Methods for Using This Book

Method 1: The best way to use this book would be to start at the beginning and work your way through it in order and learn everything along the way.

But maybe you already know some techniques, so you want to jump right to learning **how to play and sing songs**. If that's you, it would be important to **first learn the basic techniques used in this book** which would be on page 48 for rhythm, 59-60 for RH melodies and pages 95-100 for sandwiches or chords.

You can also use one of the following methods:

Method 2: Learn techniques for **playing melodies** with your RH on pages 58-80. Then, you can play all the melodies of any song in our songbook with the finger number technique on the right side pages starting on page 120 and play any melodies you want!

Method 3: Learn techniques for playing sandwiches (chords) on pages 95-100 and just use those chords in our songbook on the left side to **play and sing all the songs.**

Method 4: When you're ready and you know how to play both sandwiches and melodies, you can try and play the **sandwiches and melody at the same time!**

Method 5: If you want to play **a DUET**, you can play the sandwiches and someone else can play the melody. Then you can switch and play the melody while they play the sandwiches.

Method 6: **Improvising** is a fun way to learn how to play piano spontaneously without needing written music. You can try improvising as soon as you know how to play sandwiches. Improvising is found on pages 101-118.

Method 7: If you want more **resources and practice**, look at pages 278-335.

Method 8: You can also just use the book as a **SONGBOOK & coloring book** and just go right to page 120 and sing songs with the lyrics.

You'll see. I will help you along the way.

Good luck. Go!

Play Something!

Music is **noise.**

Let's make some NOISE!

Start by just playing SOMETHING.
Anything at all.
Anything you like!

Now, see if you can play what sounds like these things to you:

Or Play THESE Things

birds

a dinosaur

the sky

a starry sky

flowers

a volcano

♡ 4

What Does YOUR Piano Look Like?

Very traditional pianos look like this:

Also, there are many other more modern options for playing the piano like on these:

Truthfully though, you can also play on modern devices as long as you can download a piano app so that you could use a piano on these:

tablet   phone

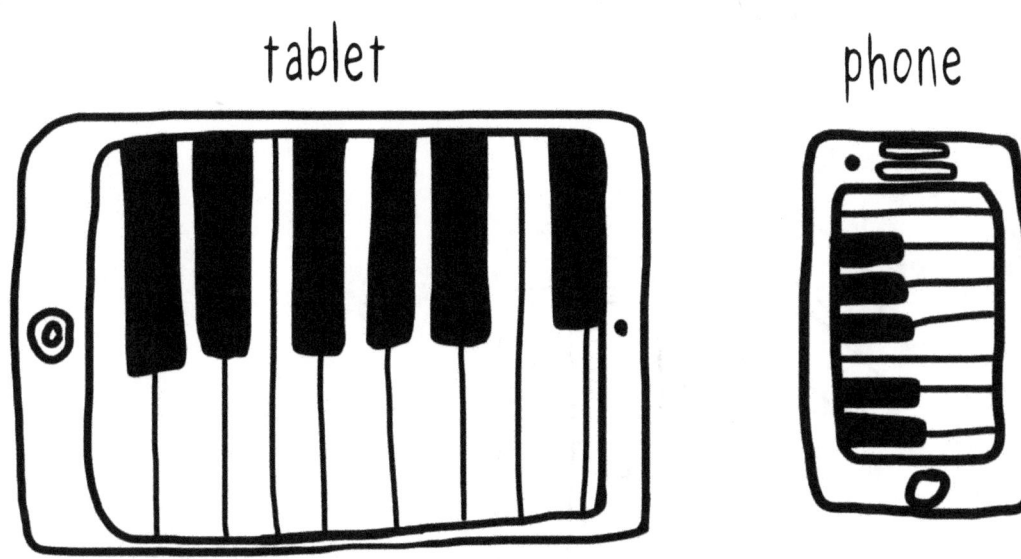

There is even one you can connect to a computer called a MIDI keyboard.

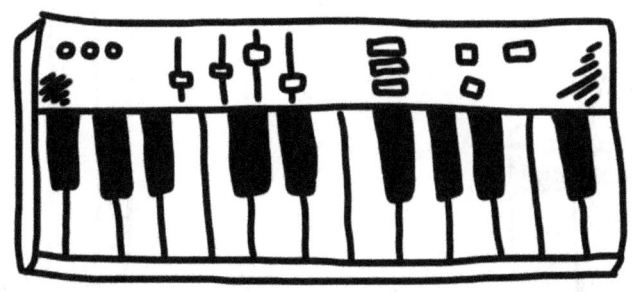

Color what your piano looks like or what you want it to look like! Have fun imagining something new or make it look the same.

Supplies

Other than a piano or keyboard, you will need:

Something to COLOR with.

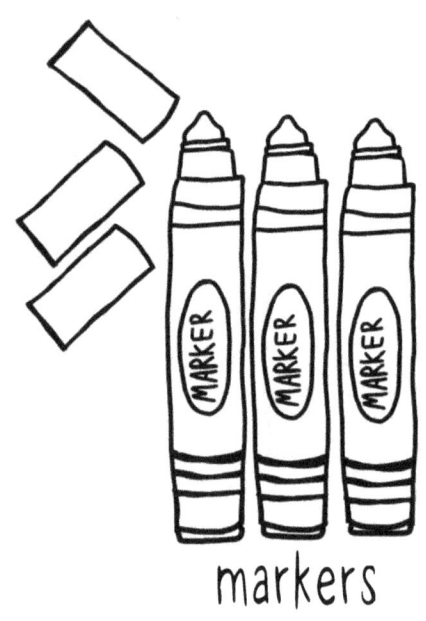
markers

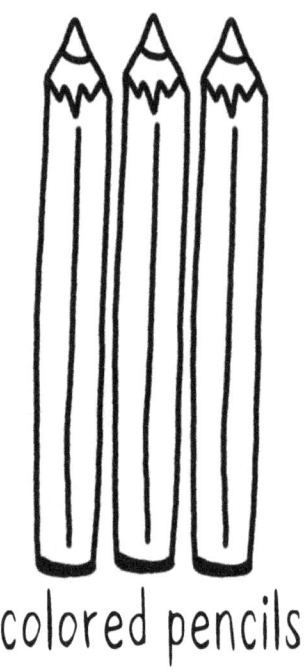
colored pencils

crayons

Something to REWARD yourself for each page, song, or time you play or complete something.

stickers

stamps

Your IMAGINATION and hard work!

Using your imagination, we will use imaginary GLUE to help us keep our fingers on the keys.

your imagination

imaginary glue

What are your favorite songs?
Write some of them here:
1.
2.
3.
4.
5.

What are your favorite singers or groups?
Write some of them here:
1.
2.
3.
4.
5.

What are some of the song titles you remember?
You can look at the Table of Contents for ideas if you like:
1.
2.
3.
4.
5.

Play and Sing a Song

Now, play and sing your favorite song.

To do so at first, just lift your hands up and down to play while you are singing.

Can we learn some other ways to play piano together?

Get your fingers, your imagination, and your coloring supplies ready and let's go!

♡ 10

What Colors Are the Piano?

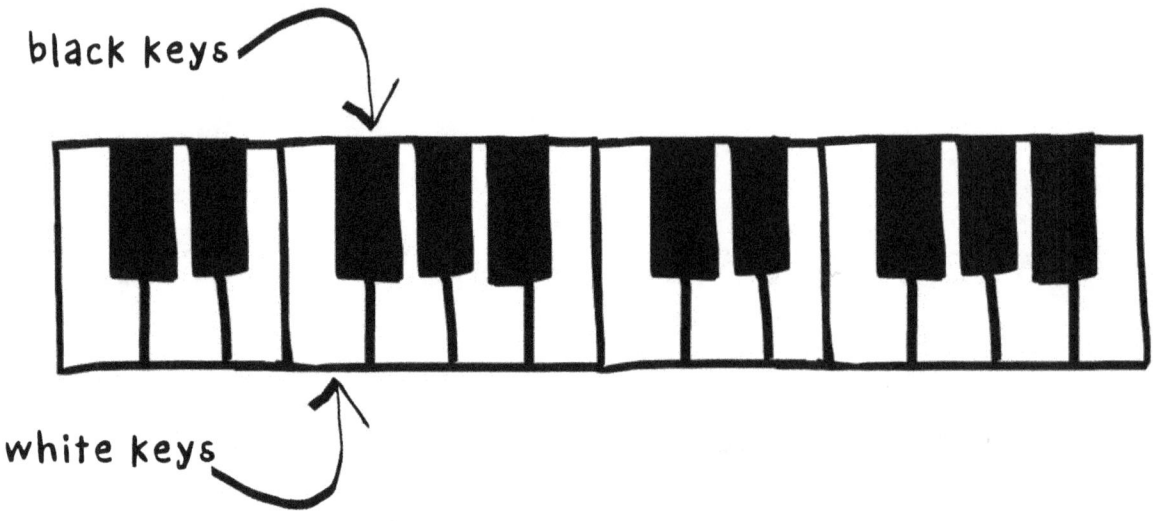

Color in all the black keys:

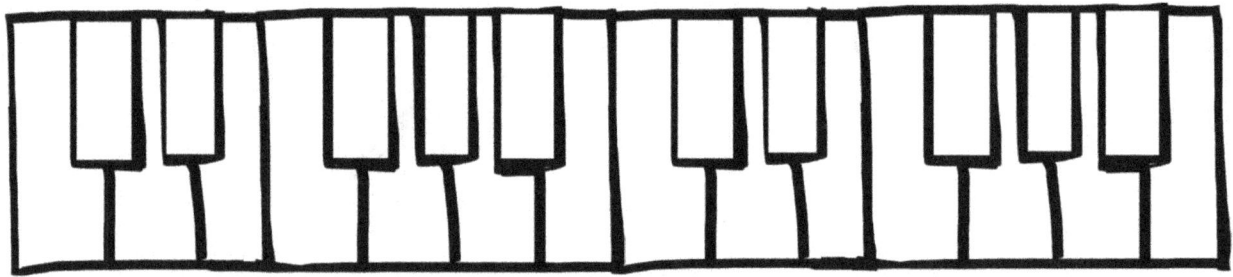

Now, play this many different black keys:

Color in all the white keys (use a different color):

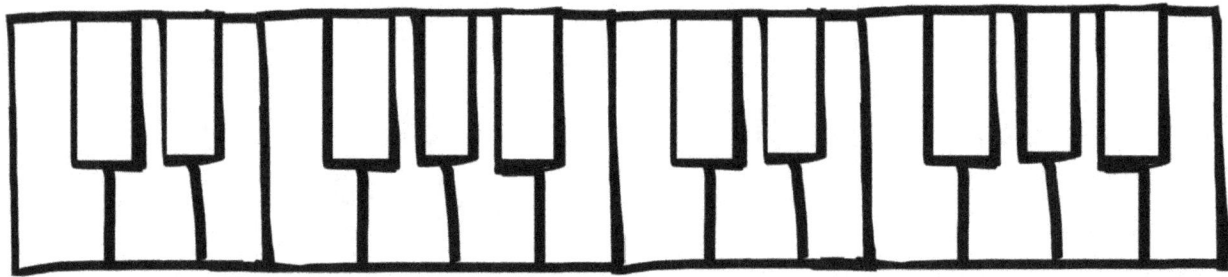

Now, play this many different white keys:

Songs in Black and White

Play these "songs" using a white or black key for each box:

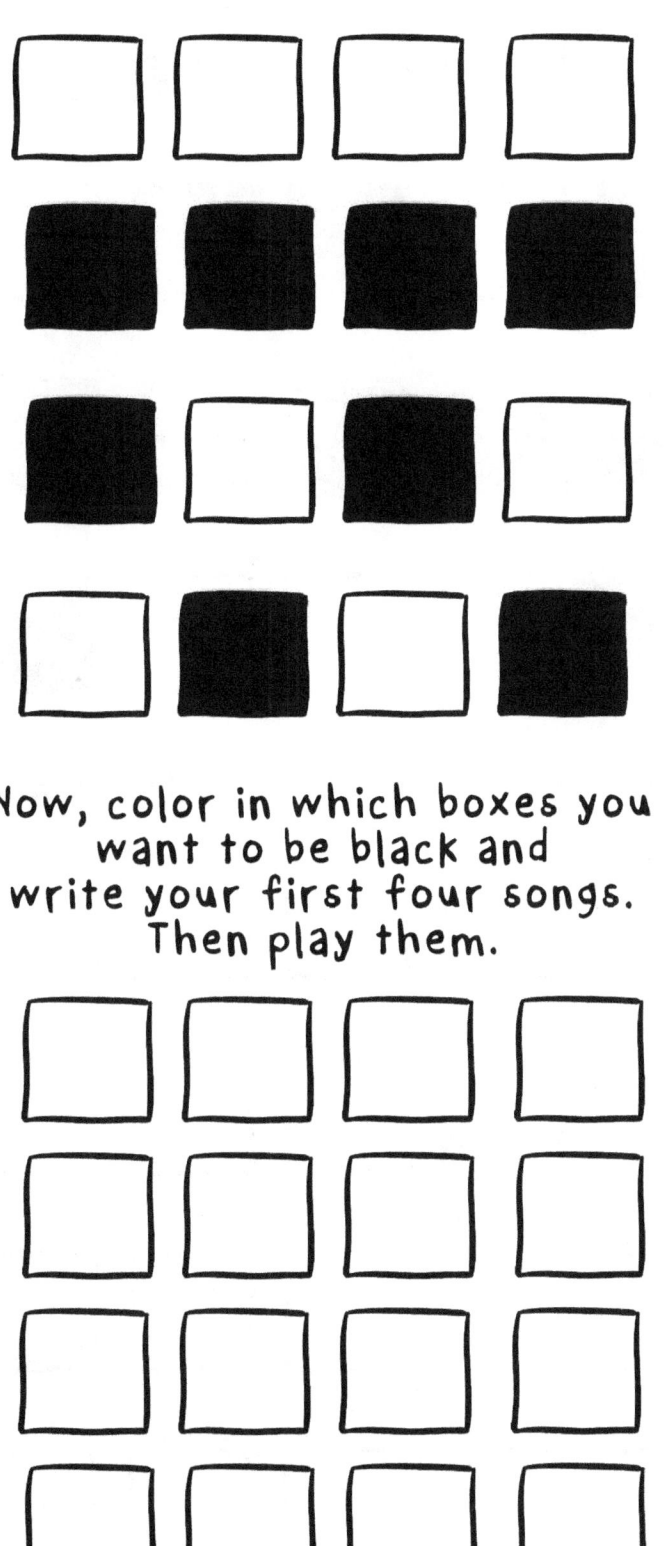

Now, color in which boxes you want to be black and write your first four songs. Then play them.

More Songs in Black and White

Play each line as a song playing ANY black or white key:

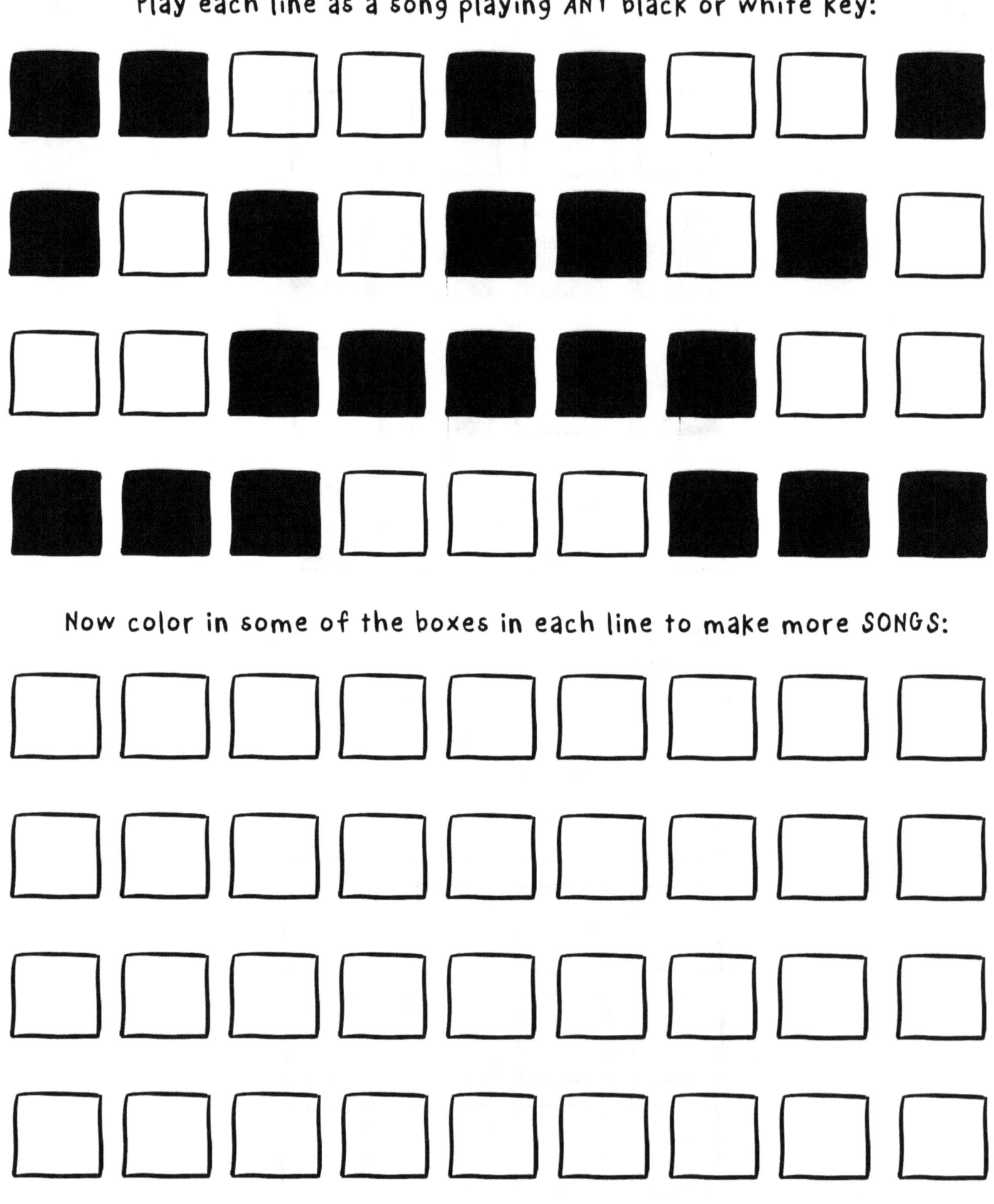

Now color in some of the boxes in each line to make more SONGS:

Finger Numbers

How many fingers do you have on each hand?
Can you count them?

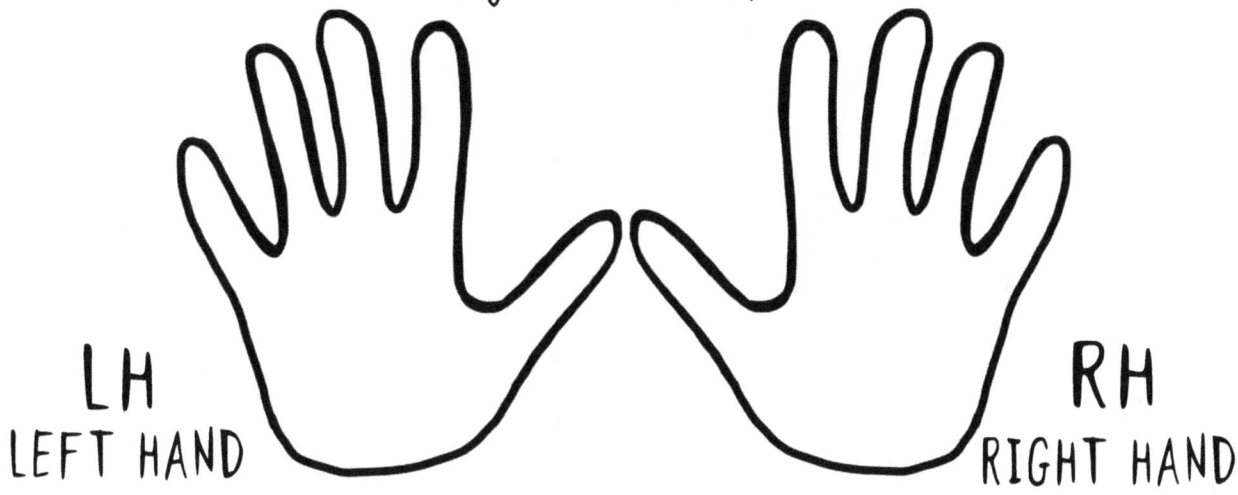

That's right! FIVE! Give me five! Now, give me TWO THUMBS UP.

If we start with our THUMBS as finger number ONE,
we can make all the finger numbers.

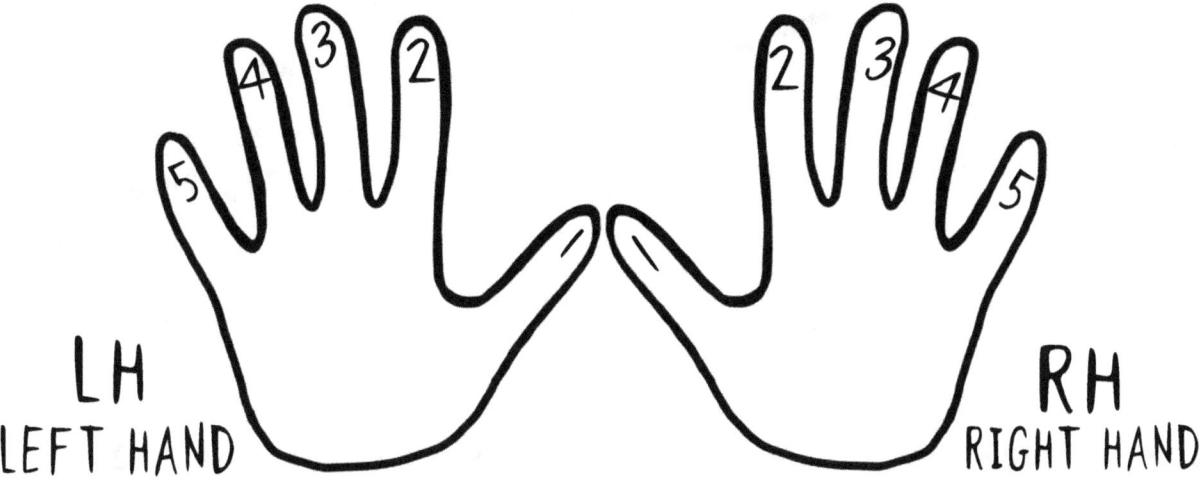

Left Hand

Write the numbers on the LEFT HAND below:

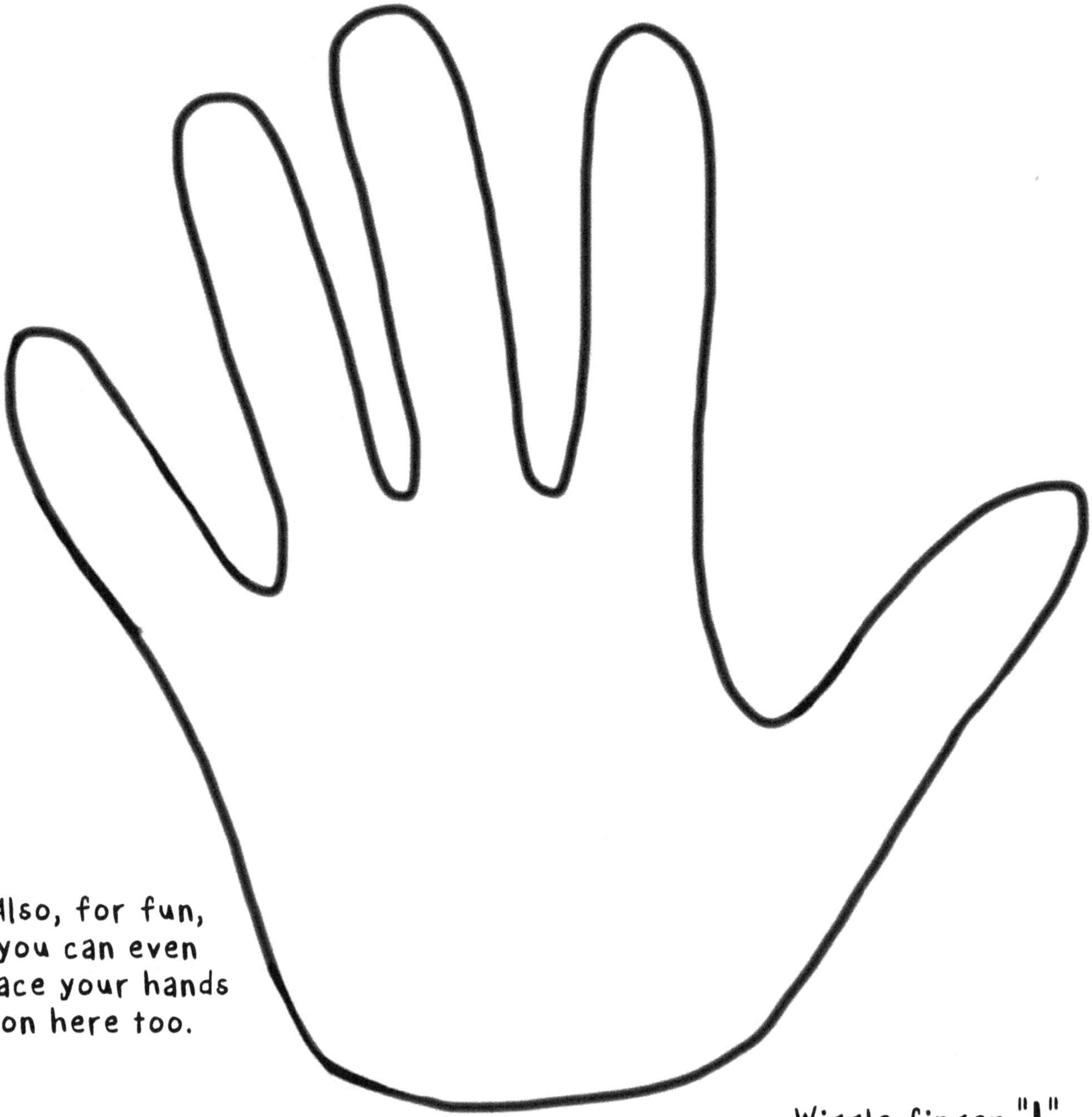

Also, for fun, you can even trace your hands on here too.

Wiggle finger "1"
Now wiggle finger "2"
Try finger "3"
What about finger "4"
Lastly, little finger "5"

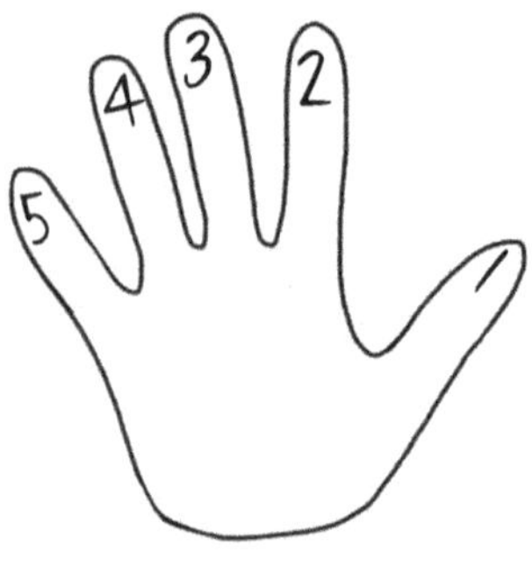

Can you play the piano with each of those fingers, one at a time?

Right Hand

Now, write the numbers on your RIGHT HAND too:

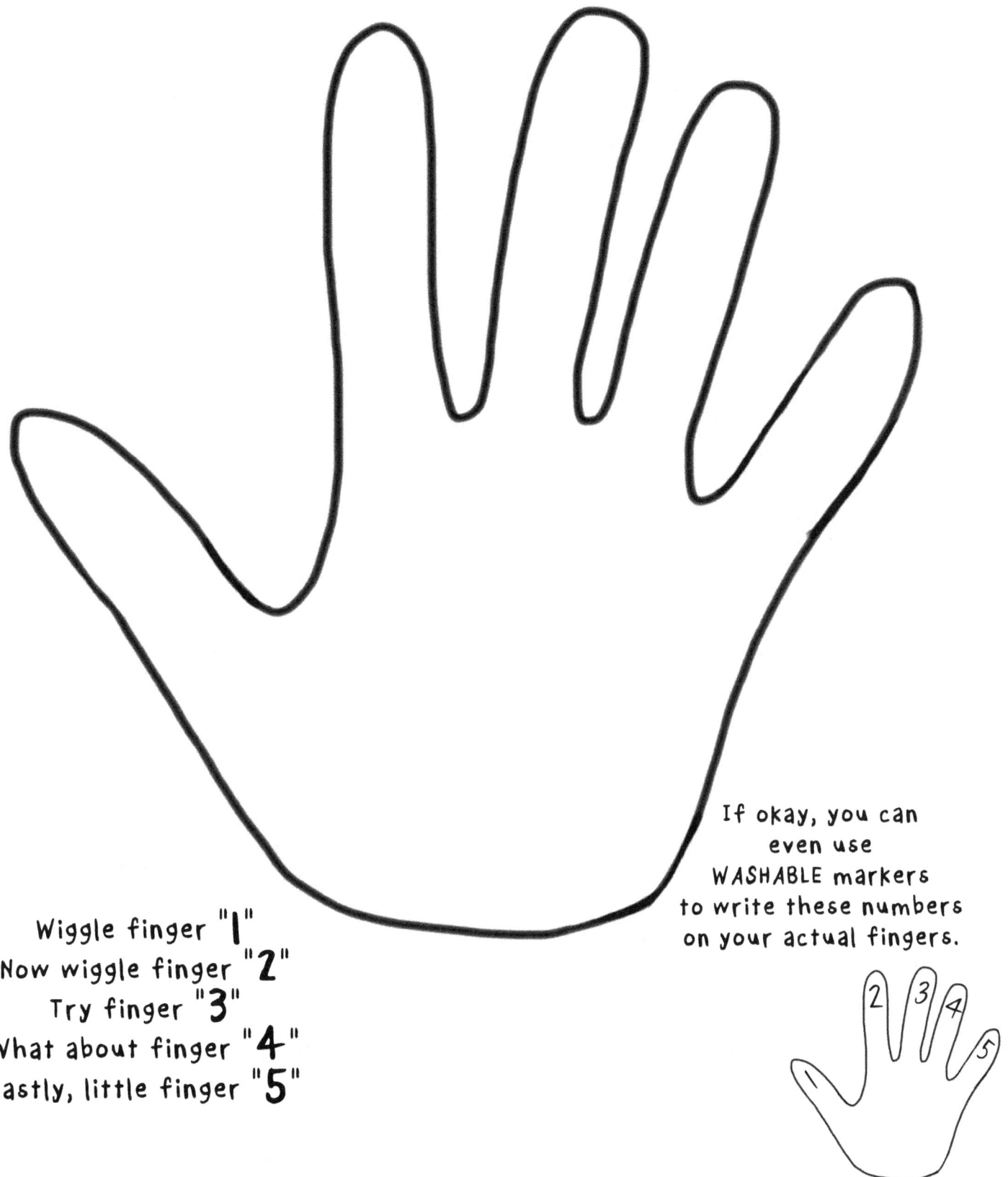

If okay, you can even use WASHABLE markers to write these numbers on your actual fingers.

Wiggle finger "1"
Now wiggle finger "2"
Try finger "3"
What about finger "4"
Lastly, little finger "5"

Can you play the piano with each of those fingers, one at a time?

♡ 16

Who Lives on the Piano?

Maybe a **spider**.

Can you make your fingers into a spider and make him run across the piano?

Keep those fingers curved!

Or a **ladybug**!  Don't smash the ladybug!

Keep your fingers CURVED to give the ladybug space.

Perhaps a **snail** too?

Can you try to move slowly on the piano like a snail?

Keep space under the palm of your hands to give the snail space to move too.

Finger Techniques

Try donut fingers!
NICE AND ROUND

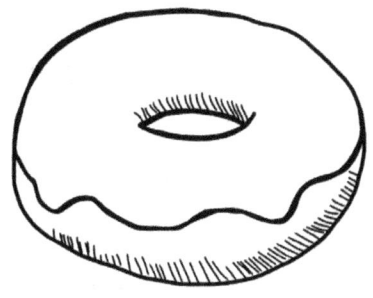

Now use these groups of two fingers at a time to make a circle donut and play some notes:

fingers 1 and 2

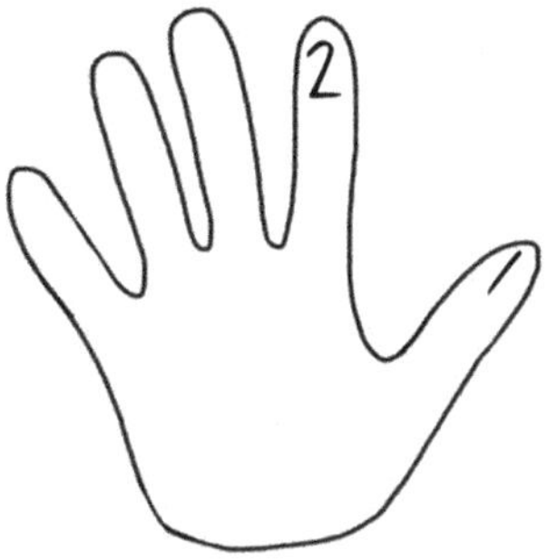

fingers 1 and 4

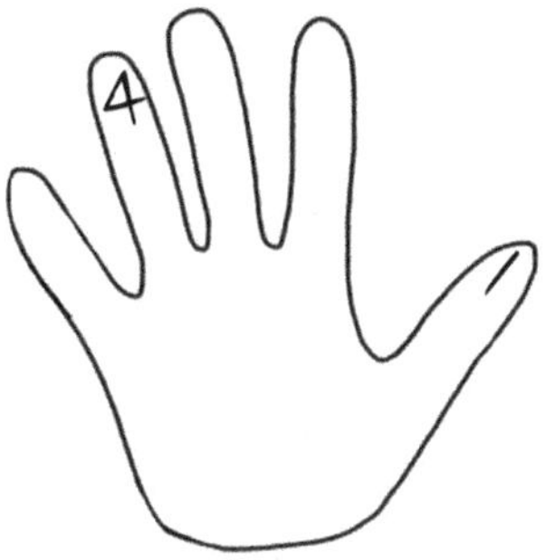

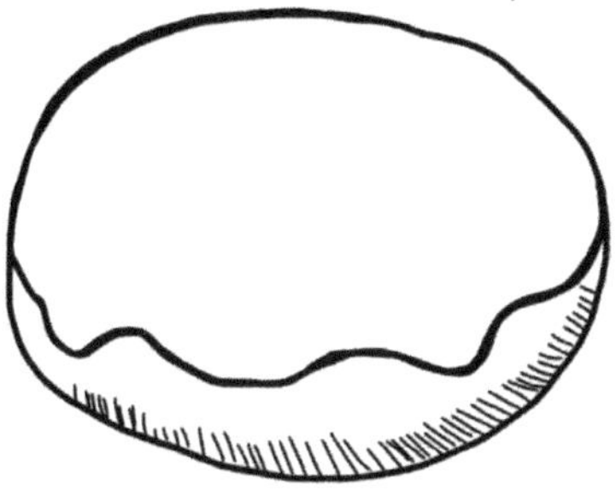

fingers 1 and 3

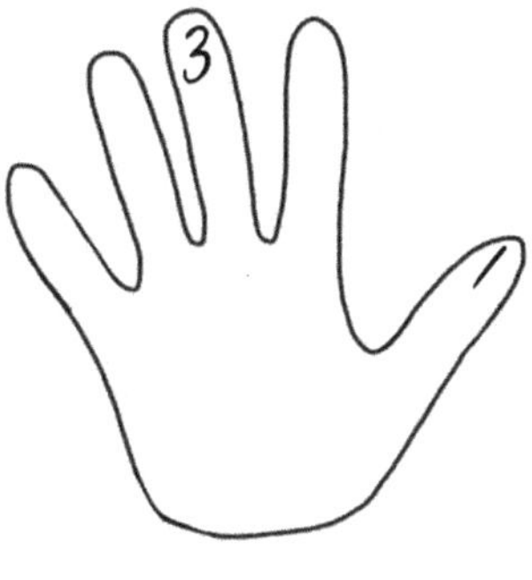

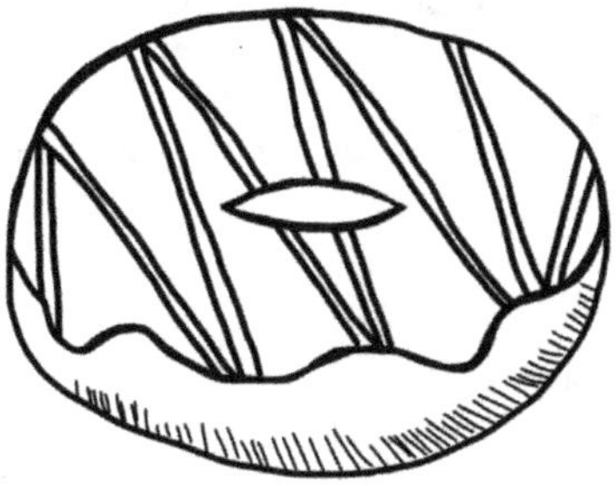

fingers 1 and 5

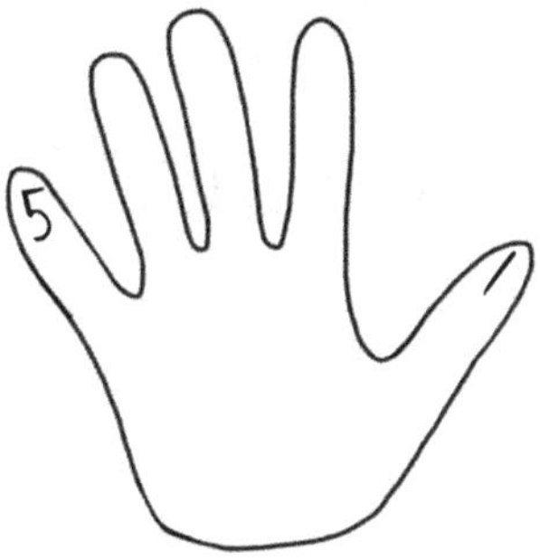

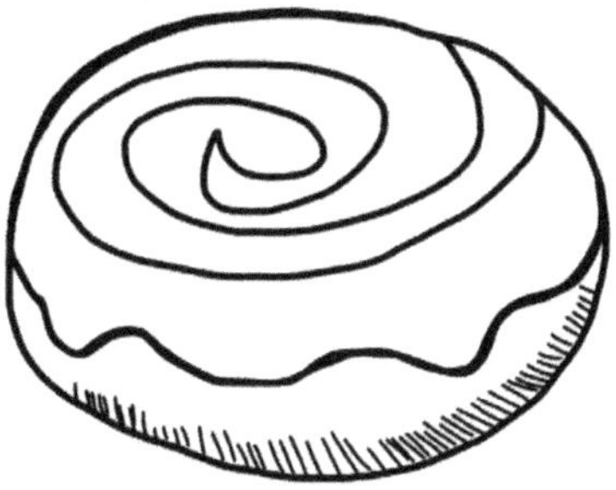

What flavors of donuts are they?

Do not play pizza fingers!
NOT STRAIGHT

More Finger Techniques

Now, roll your fingers on the piano like a rock.

This is the right way to play!
CURVED and round like a rock.

Try playing the WRONG way as stick fingers!
Stick fingers are too straight.

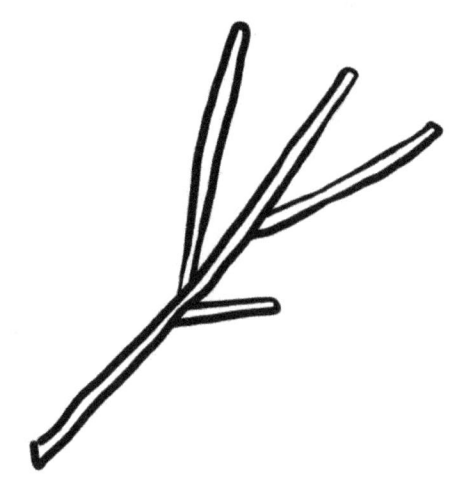

Even More Finger Techniques

Try these too:

Roll a BALL on the piano!
NICE AND ROUND

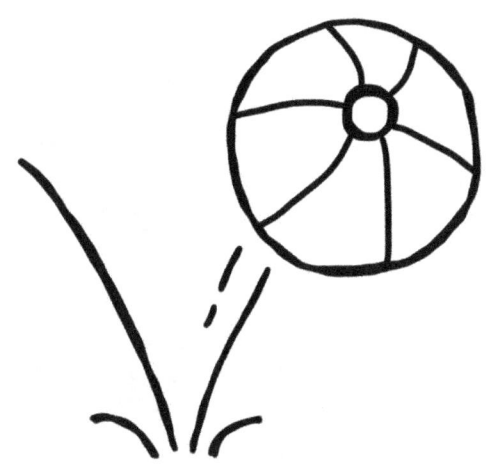

Not a pencil! No pencil fingers!
NOT STRAIGHT

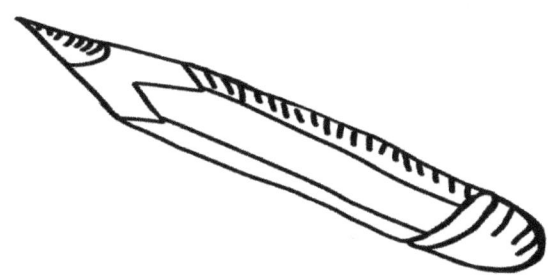

♡20

Up and Down

Let's turn the piano this way to see which way is UP.

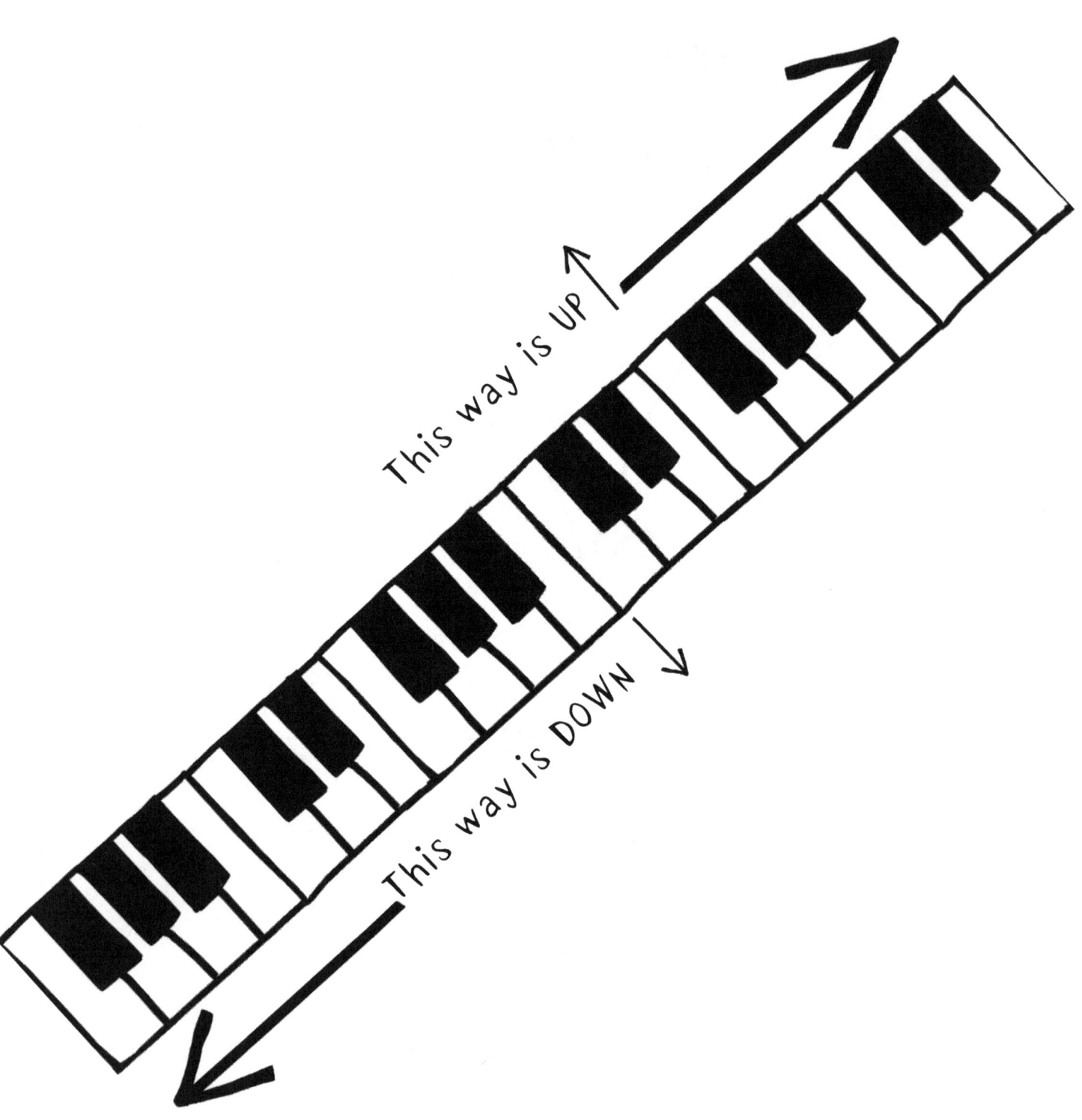

Can you make your voice go **up and down** and follow these lines with your finger to guide you?

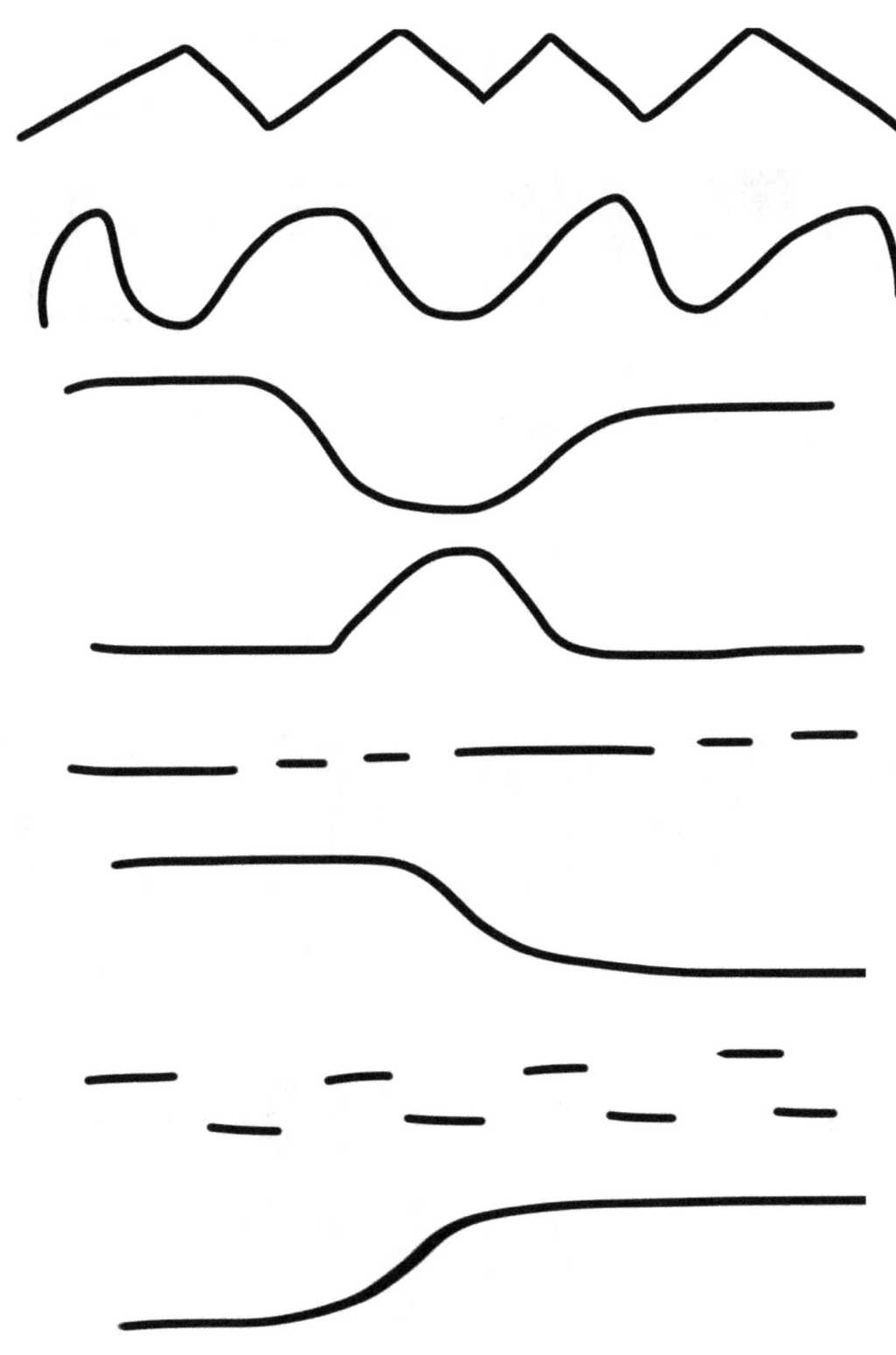

You can even try to play these going **up and down on the piano** too.

Practice Going Up or Down

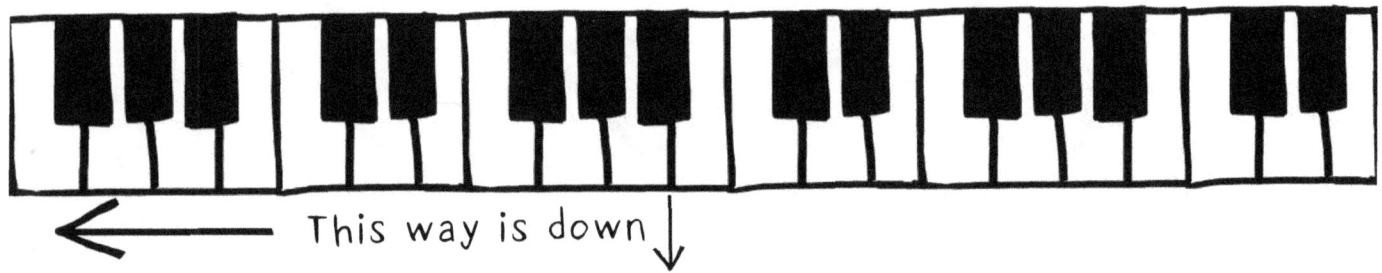

This way is UP ↑ →

These notes are the HIGH notes

← This way is down ↓

These notes are the LOW notes.

black keys

Try sliding all the way up, then all the way down on the black keys.

↑ ↓

Now, try on the white keys.

white keys

↑ ↓

Low and High

Use these two fingers to "walk" on the piano.

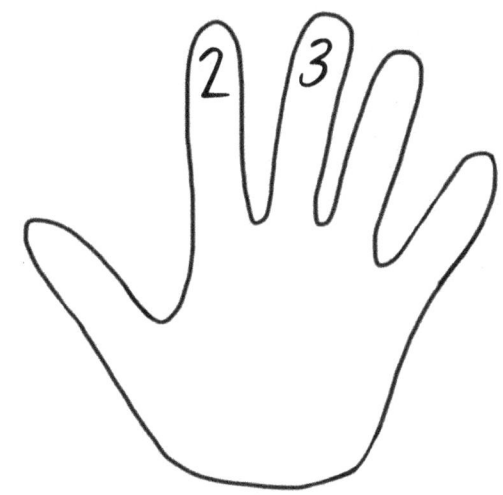

Play some LOW notes walking on the left side of the piano.
Sing, "Walk - ing, walk - ing ele - phant."

Play some IN THE MIDDLE notes walking in the middle of the piano.
Sing, "Walk - ing, walk - ing ca - t."

Play some HIGH notes walking on the right side of the piano.
Sing, "Walk - ing, walk - ing bir - d."

Jump and Hop

Before you learn two and three bounces,
can you think of animals that jump and hop?

Now, hop, jump, or bounce on the piano like these animals.

We will use this swirl ℨ to mean a
jump or bounce on the piano.

Can you draw the swirl too?

25 ☆   Try it on the low notes and high notes too!

Walk, Step, and Climb

Also before you learn two and three walking,
can you think of animals that walk, step, or climb?

Now, walk, step, or climb on the piano like these animals.
We will use this stair ⌐┘ to mean
walking or taking steps on the piano.

Can you draw the stair too?

Try it on the low notes and high notes too!

♡26

Can you find the groups of **TWO (2) BLACK KEYS** on the piano?

Can you circle all the groups of 2 black keys?

Can you bounce on all the groups of 2 with your RIGHT HAND?

2 2 2 2 2

Can you bounce on all the groups of 2 with your LEFT HAND?

2 2 2 2 2

How many 2's are on your piano? Write it in the box:

27☆

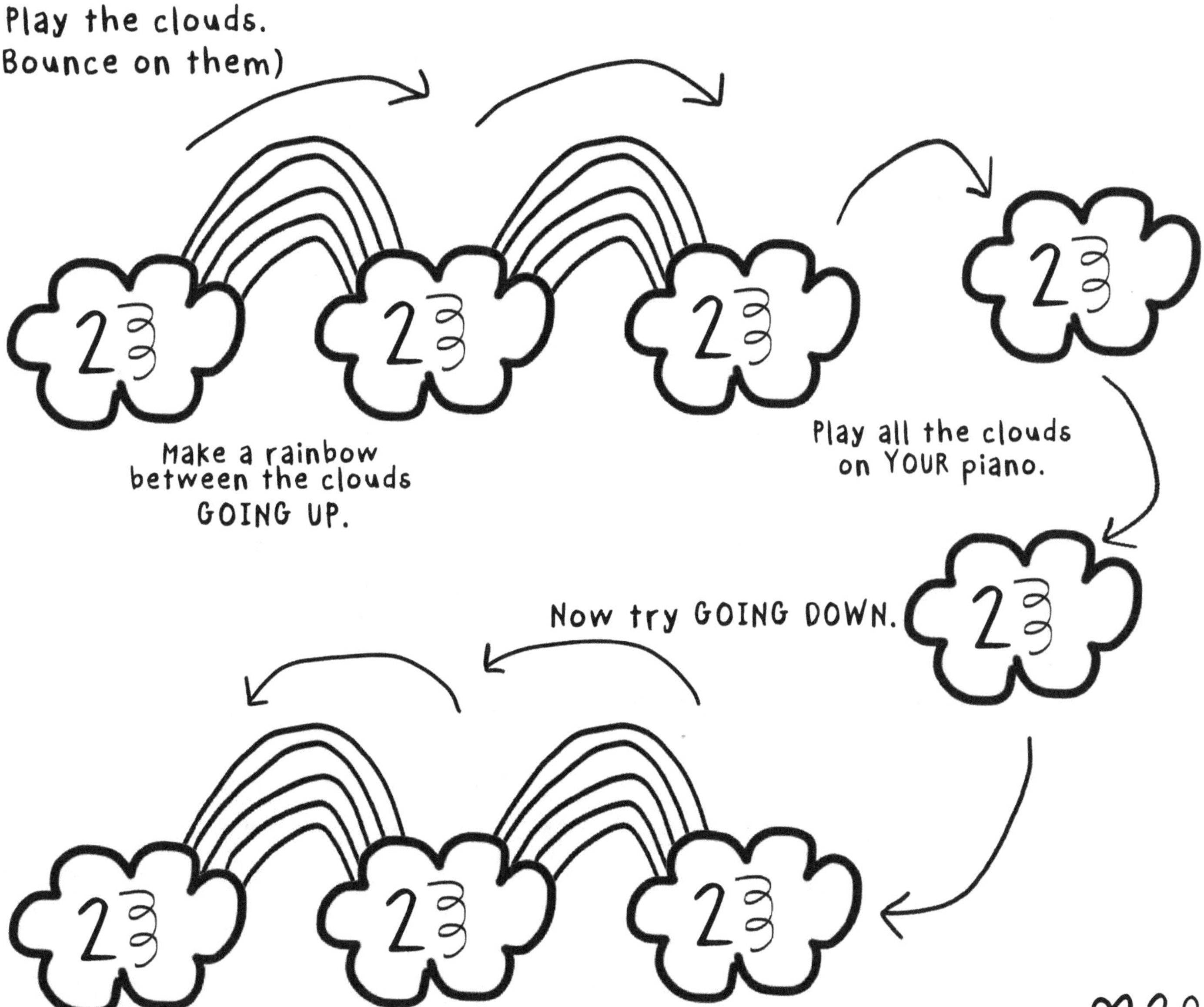

Can you find the groups of **THREE (3) BLACK KEYS** on the piano?

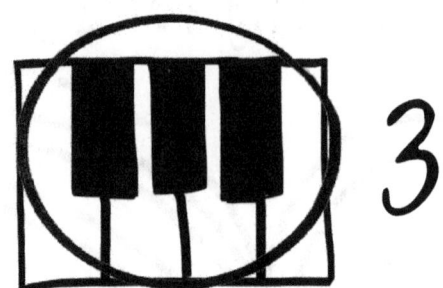 3

Can you circle all the groups of 3 black keys?

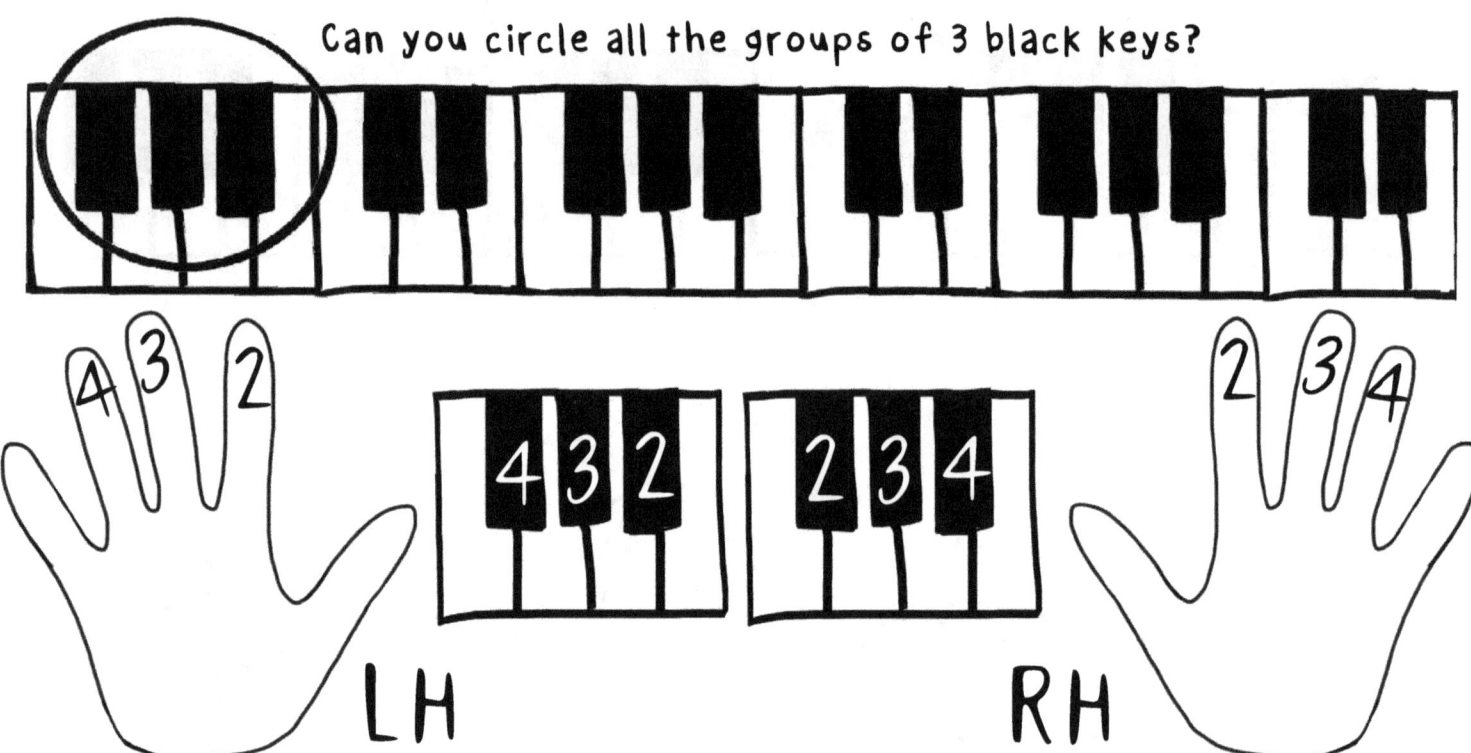

LH   RH

Can you bounce on all the groups of 3 with your RIGHT HAND?

3 3 3 3 3

Can you bounce on all the groups of 3 with your LEFT HAND?

3 3 3 3 3

How many 3's are on your piano? Write it in the box: ☐

Play Some TWO and THREE Bouncing Songs

Play the bounce that you see. Each line is a song.

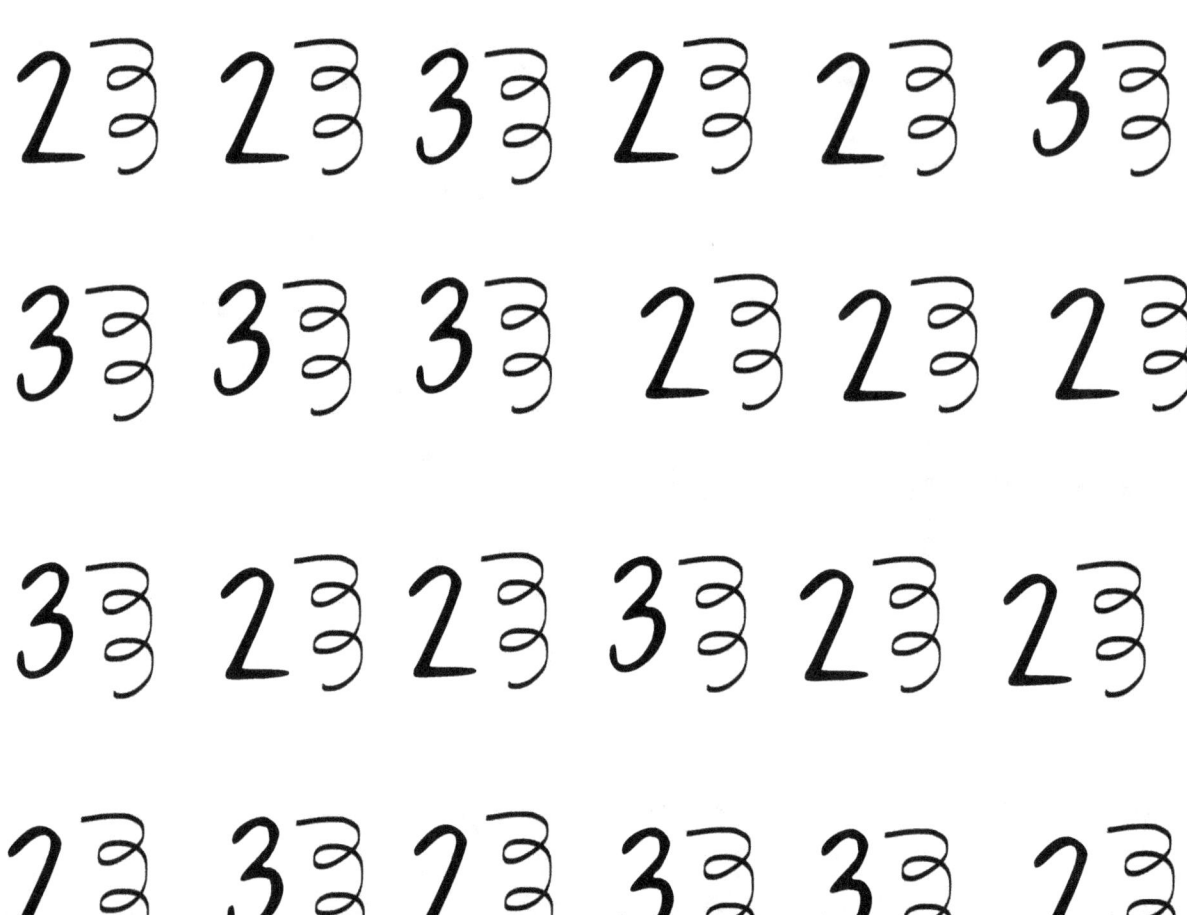

Now, write your own:

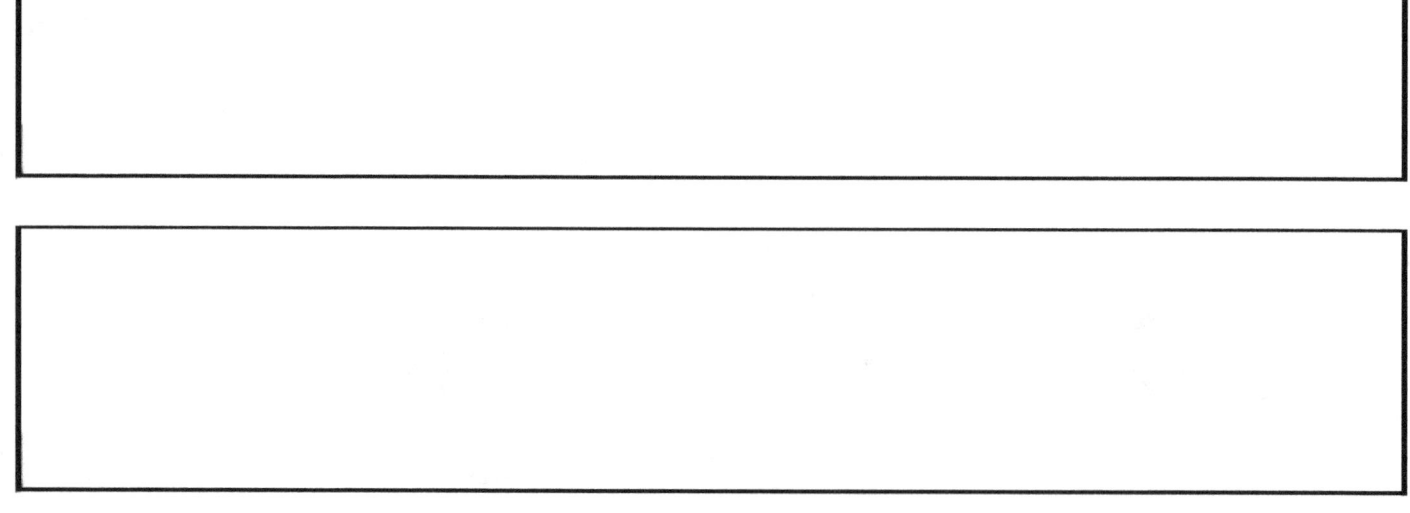

Up and Down the Stairs

Now, we can imagine that the black notes on the piano are steps on a set of stairs.

Can you walk up the stairs like this on your piano and see if you can go all the way to the top?

Now, can you walk down the stairs too?

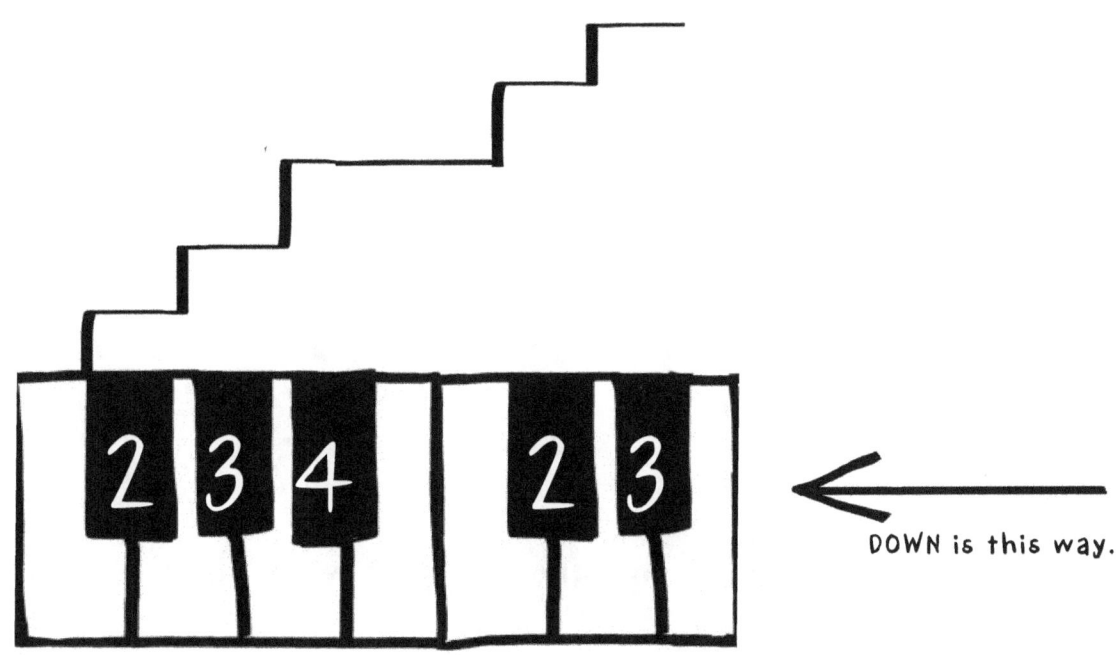

You can try going up and down with your LH too.

♡ 32

Can you find the groups of **TWO (2) BLACK KEYS** for walking?

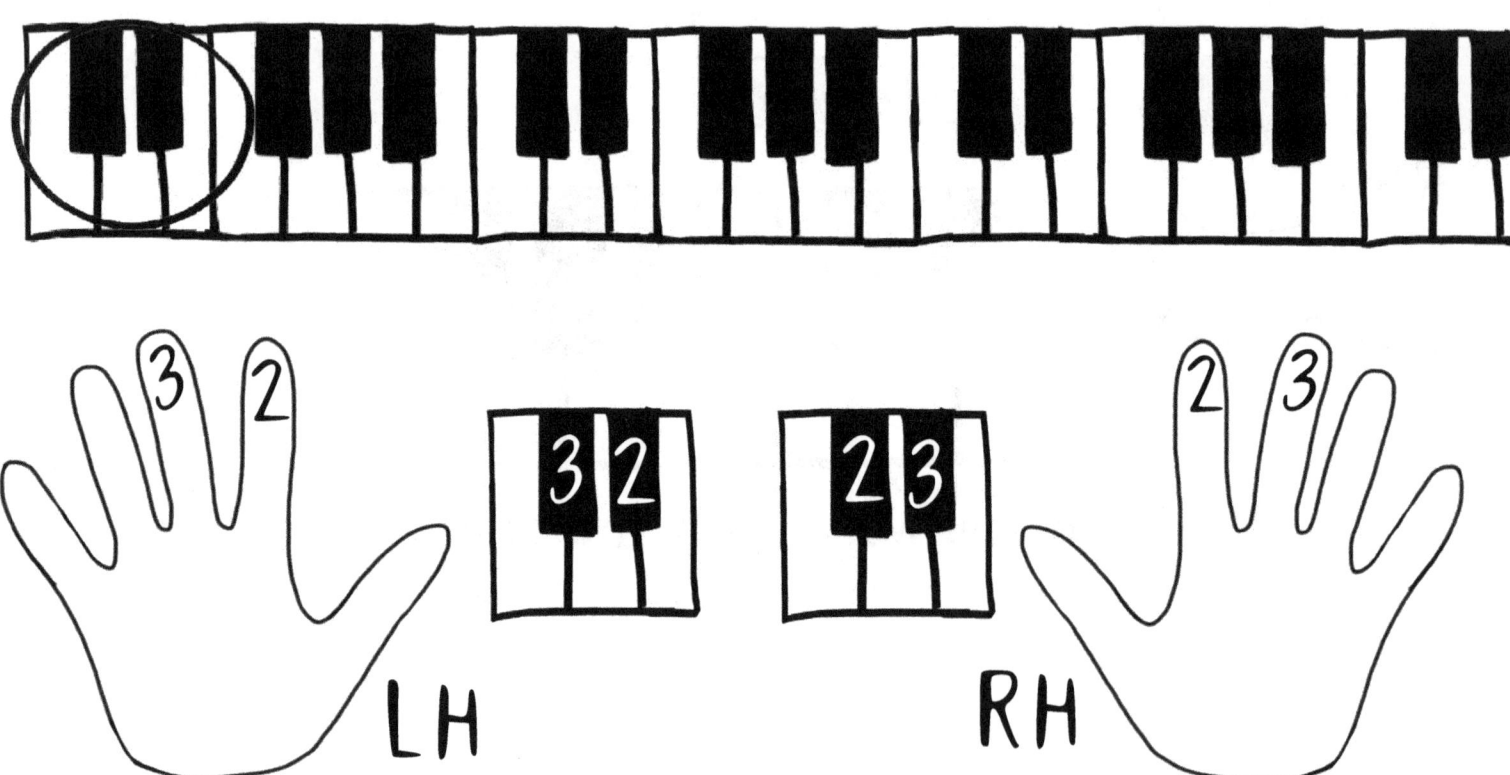

Can you walk on all the groups of 2 with your RIGHT HAND?

2️⃣ 2️⃣ 2️⃣ 2️⃣ 2️⃣

Can you walk on all the groups of 2 with your LEFT HAND?

2️⃣ 2️⃣ 2️⃣ 2️⃣ 2️⃣

Panda Eats Bamboo
A song for 2 ♫

Make the panda walk up two steps then rest and eat bamboo.

Play a 2 ♫

You can say or sing PAN - DA while you play the 2 ♫

Don't play the bamboo. (groups of three)

Help the panda go all the way up.

Now try GOING DOWN.

♡ 34

Can you find the groups of **THREE (3) BLACK KEYS** for walking?

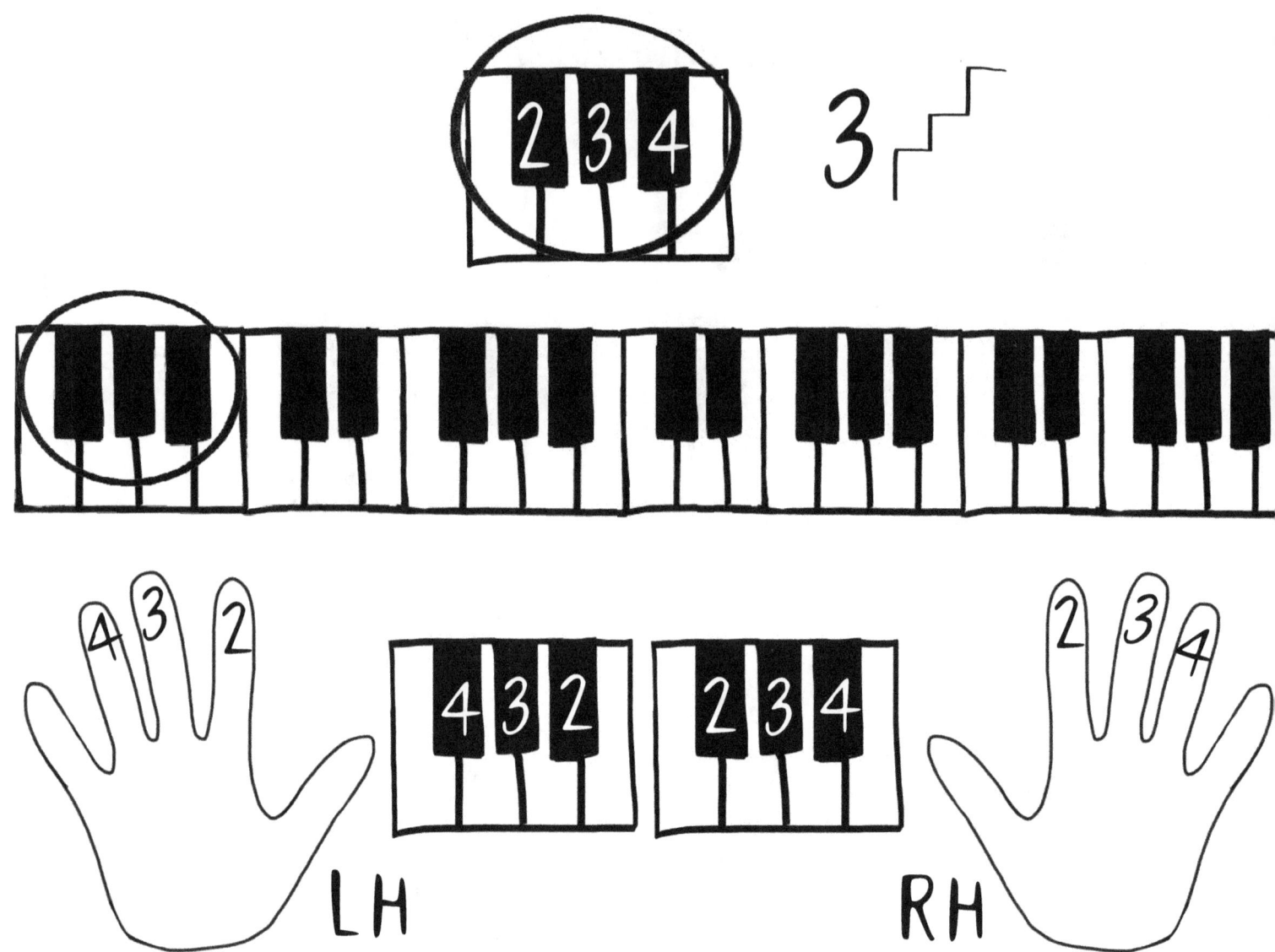

Can you walk on all the groups of 3 with your RIGHT HAND?

3 3 3 3 3

Can you walk on all the groups of 3 with your LEFT HAND?

3 3 3 3 3

Ladybug Goes Up
A song for 3 🎵

Help the ladybug walk up three steps on the leaf.

Play a 3 🎵

Then, she can fly to the next leaf.

You can say or sing LA - DY - BUG while you play the 3 🎵

Make the ladybug walk and fly all the way up the piano.

Now try GOING DOWN.

♡ 36

Can You Walk and Bounce Across the Piano?

Try pointing to a 2♩, 2♫, 3♩, or 3♫
and then play whatever you point to.

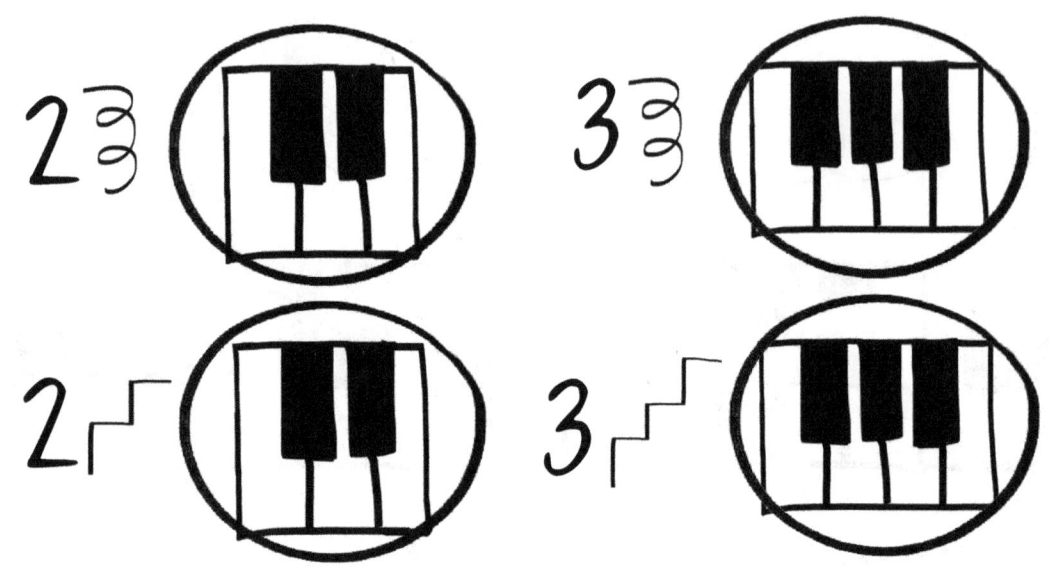

Now, play these three songs that mix these things:

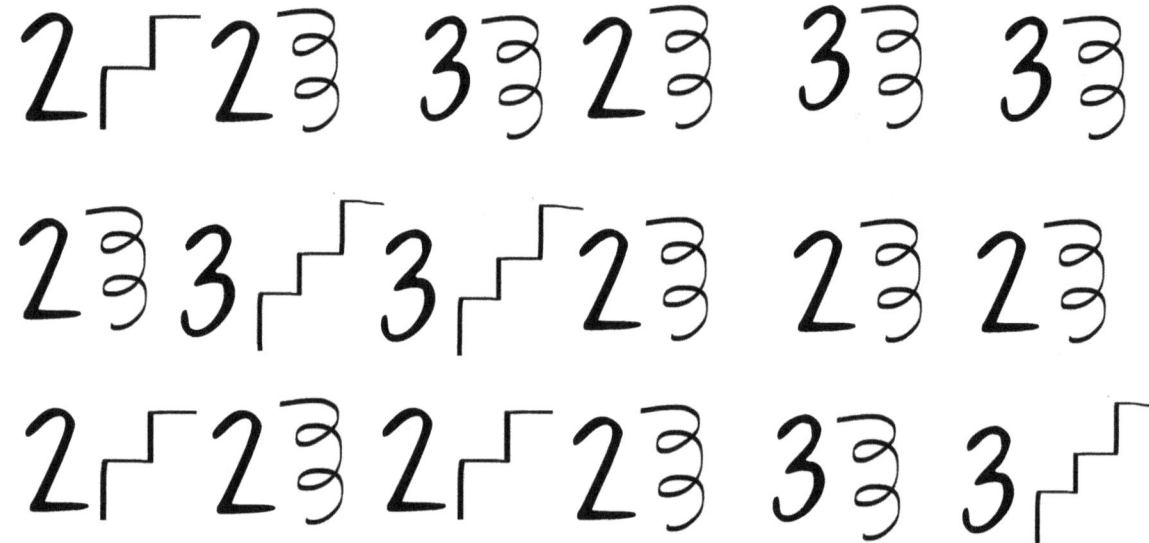

Now, write your own:

Up the Slide and the Trampoline
A song that mixes bounces and walking

3 Up the ladder is 2, 3, 4 walking.   2 The trampoline is a 2 bounce.

Can you go up the ladder, down the slide, and then bounce on the trampolines while you go up the piano?

3   2   3   2

Then can you go down the piano bouncing on the trampolines?

2   2   2   2

Practice with the LEFT HAND
Three Walking Notes

You can use the same 3 walking notes from the stairs to play a melody.
Play one note at a time. You can practice a few here:

2 2 3 3 4 4

2 3 2 3 4 2

4 3 2 2 3 4

Write two short songs below for your left hand using the numbers 2, 3, and 4:

Practice with the RIGHT HAND

You can use these same 3 walking notes with your RH to practice and then we can play different songs with the RH on the next few pages.

These are the same numbers as the LH, but listen to how they sound different.

2 2 3 3 4 4

2 3 2 3 4 2

4 3 2 2 3 4

Write two short songs below for your right hand using the numbers 2, 3, and 4:

♡40

Hot Cross Buns

Can you add an X to make another hot cross bun?

RH [keyboard with 2 3 4 on black keys]

4 3 2
Hot cross buns

4 3 2
Hot cross buns

2 2 2 2
One a pen ney

3 3 3 3
Two a pen ney

4 3 2
Hot cross buns

Rain is Falling Down

4 4 3 3 2 2
Rain is fall ing down, splash!

4 4 3 3 2 2
Rain is fall ing down, splash!

4 4 3 3
Pit ter pat ter

4 4 3 3
Pit ter pat ter

4 4 3 3 2 2
Rain is fall ing down, splash!

♡42

Bells Are Ringing

RH 2 3 4

4   2
Ding   Dong

4   2
Ding   Dong

4   4   4   2
Bells are ring ing

4   4   4   2
Bells are ring ing

4   3   2
Ding Ding Dong

I Can Ride My Bike

4 3 2 3 4 4 4
I can ride my bike to day.

3 3 3
Yes, I can.

4 4 4
Watch me ride.

4 3 2 3 4 4 4
I can ride my bike to day.

3 3 4 3 2
Watch me ride my bike.

♡44

Your Three Walking Song

Write the numbers 2, 3, and 4 to make your own song:

Peter, Peter Pumpkin Eater

This is a very fun song with the black notes, but it's a little different. It's different because we will ONLY USE FINGER NUMBER 2 on both hands

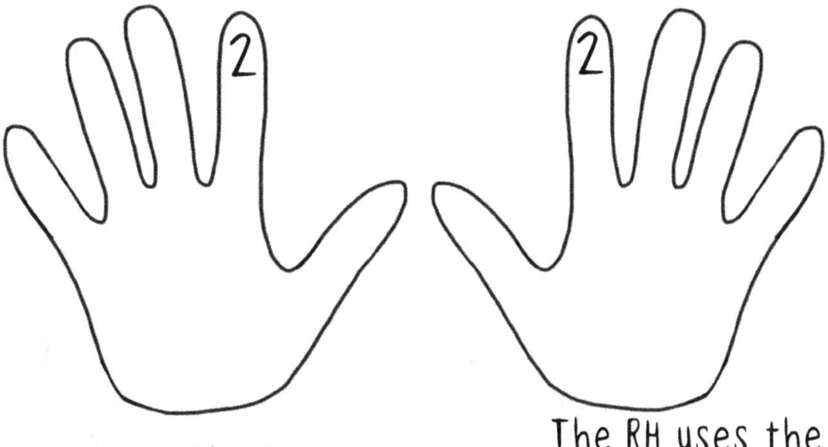

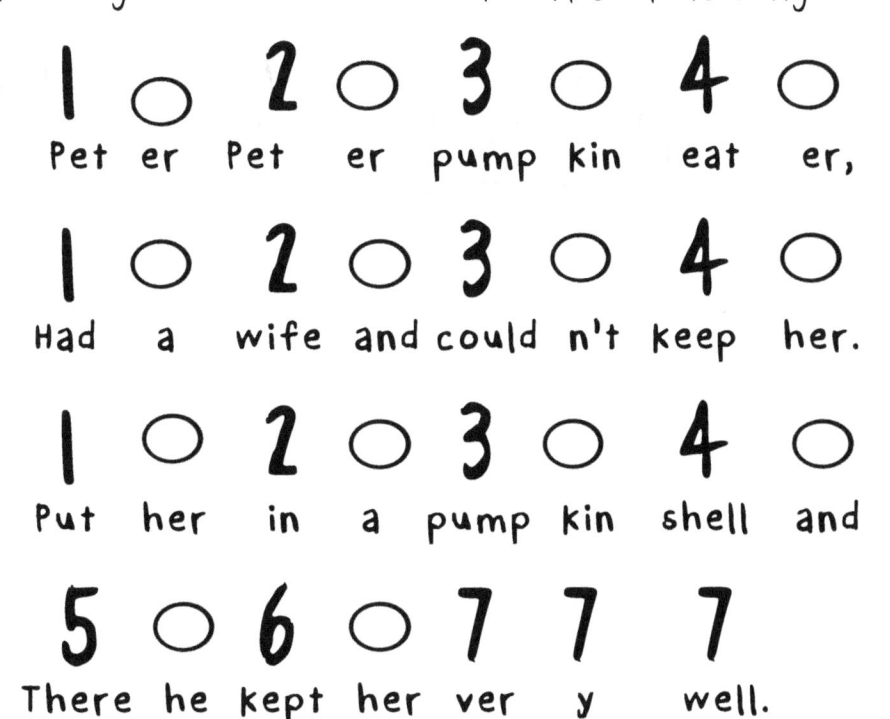

Try playing this on this piano in the book, then on your piano.

The LH uses this ONE NOTE right here.

The RH uses the numbers, moving down to the notes starting here

Keep your LH finger 2 here for the whole song!

Here is the song:

1 ○ 2 ○ 3 ○ 4 ○
Pet er Pet er pump kin eat er,

1 ○ 2 ○ 3 ○ 4 ○
Had a wife and could n't keep her.

1 ○ 2 ○ 3 ○ 4 ○
Put her in a pump kin shell and

5 ○ 6 ○ 7 7 7
There he kept her ver y well.

♡ 46

RHYTHM

This next page is the only page you need on rhythm in this book, as we will only focus on playing the finger numbers either **LONG** or **SHORT**.

After you learn and play page 48, if you want to keep playing songs, you can skip to page 58 and continue playing.

Or, you can look through pages 49-57 to learn and practice more concepts of rhythm and also how rhythm is traditionally written in music.

Rhythm in THIS BOOK

In this book, the only type of rhythm we will use is **long** or **short**.

When a number is by itself like these, it is short:

1   2   3   4   5

When a number has a long line, it is long:

1_   2_   3_   4_   5_

Now, try playing each finger number long or short:

1_1   1   1   1_   1   1
long short short short long short short

3_   3   3   3_   2   2_   2
long short short long short long short

See if you can make a **VERY SHORT** note by playing a note really quick.

Now, can you make a **VERY LONG** note and count how many seconds it lasts?

♡ 48

Musical Counting

One of the best ways to learn RHYTHM is counting.

See if you can play any note 1 time, then 2 times, 3 times, etc.

Also, close your eyes and have your teacher, parent, or friend play a note a certain amount of times and see if you can guess how many times you hear the note.

Basically, point to a number, then play that amount or listen for that number in a guessing game.

Things in Nature

You can also practice rhythm with differents words. Just say the word related to nature you see and play any note as you say each syllable that number of times. It works as a rhythm guide, like counting numbers. Try it:

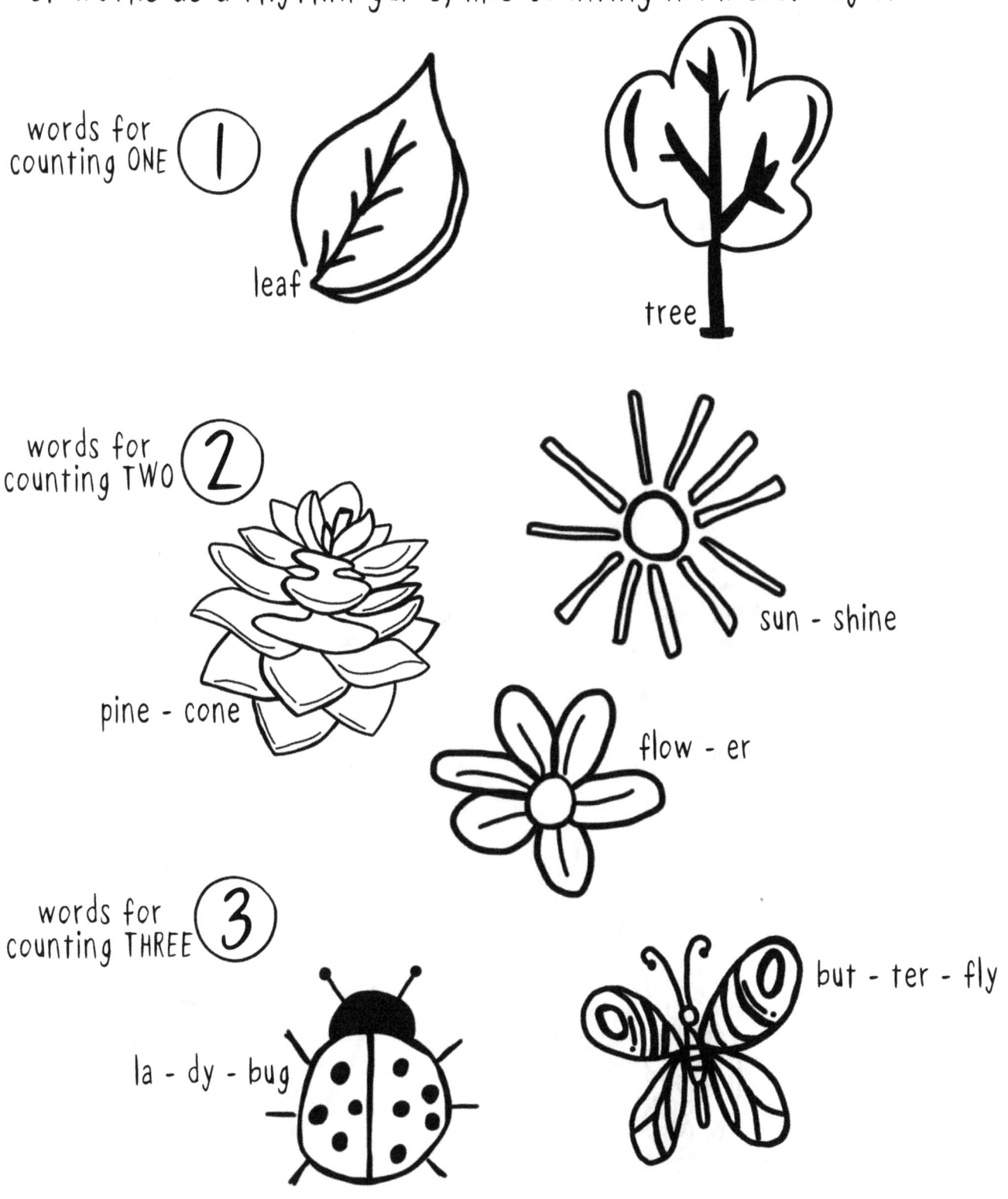

You can say the words in any order you want.

♡50

Fruit

Now, try it saying the names of fruit.

① orange   grapes

② ap -ple   ki - wi

③ straw - ber - ry   ba - na - na   pine - ap - ple

④ pom - e - gran - ate   wa - ter - mel - on

Vegetables
Try it also saying the names of vegetables.

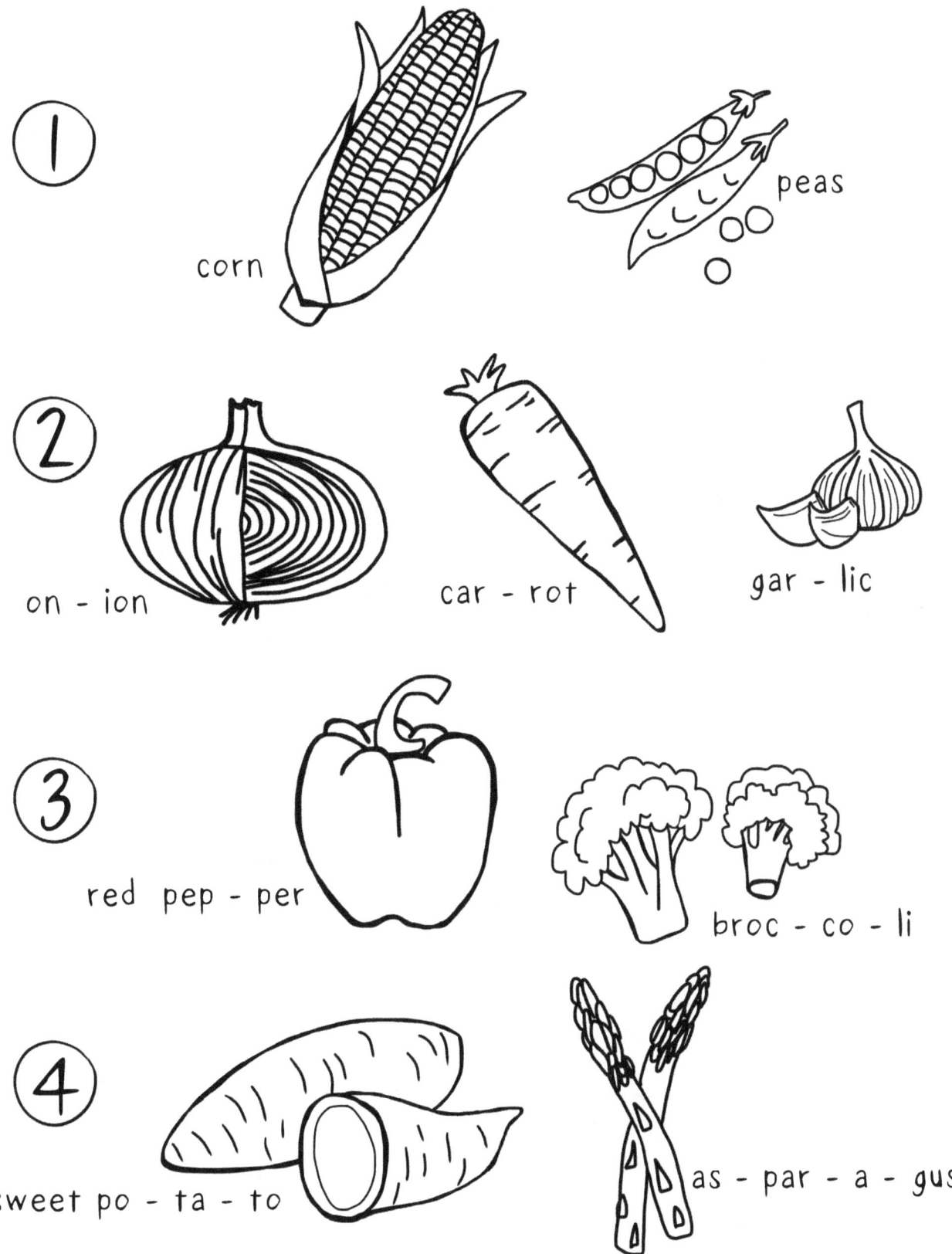

Keep a Steady Beat

Can you count to four and keep the rhythm going?

Count OUTLOUD like this:

1	2	3	4
one	two	three	four

Now, **ACCENT** different beats.

Say the accented note (the circled one) a little louder.

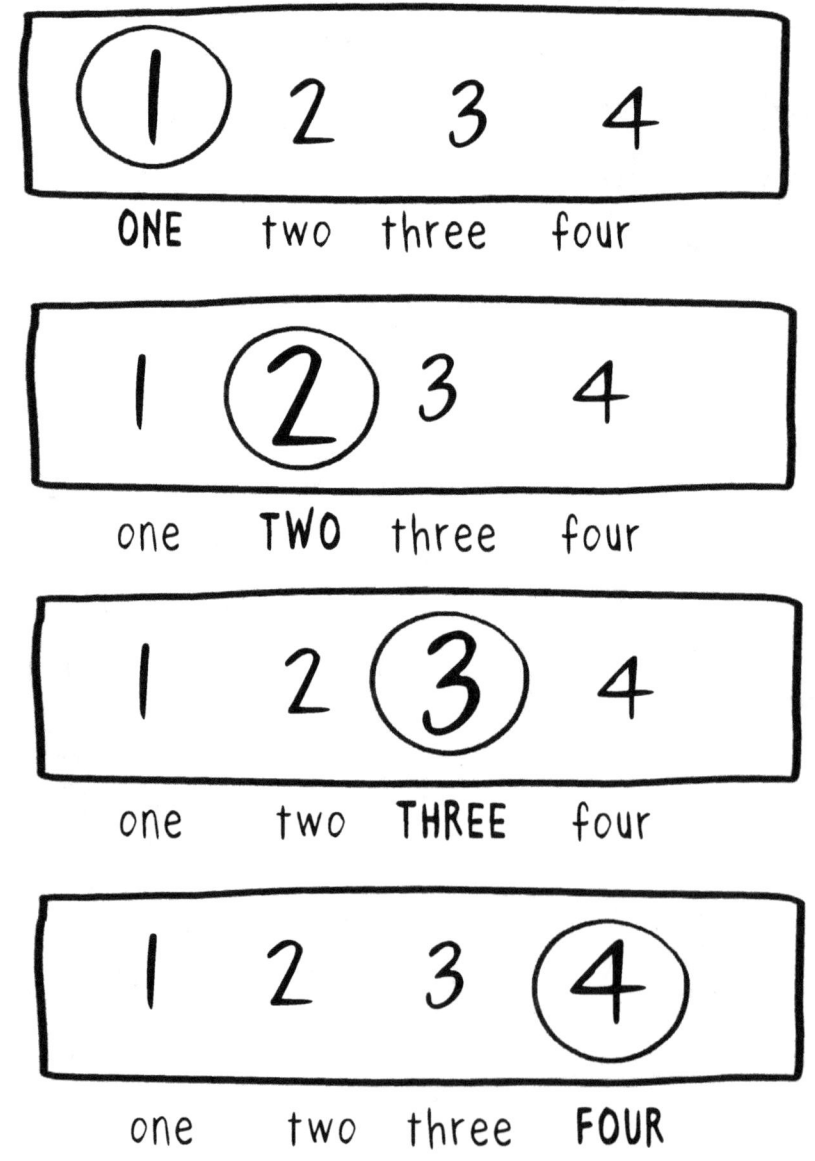

Written Rhythm in Musical Notation

So, we can keep a steady beat. But, how long do we play each beat?

For most music, one beat is written like this with a quarter note. → ♩ When you clap it or play it, you can say: **one** because it is one beat.

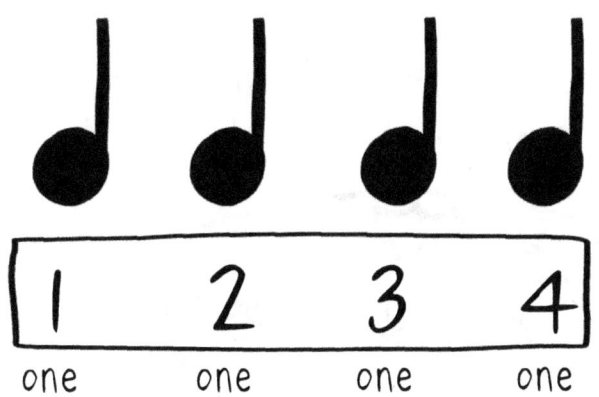

For most music, two beats is written like this with a half note. → 𝅗𝅥 When you clap it, you can hold the clap and say **one - two** because it is two beats.

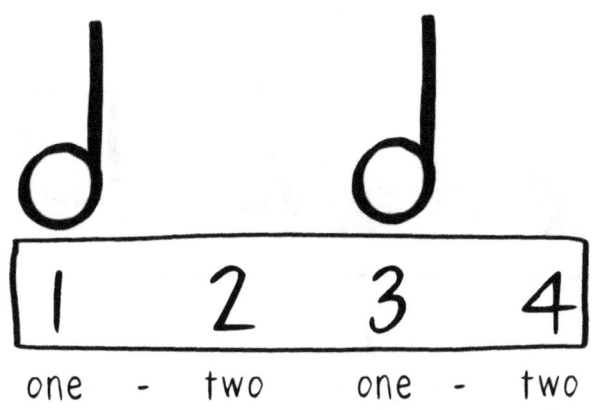

♡54

More Rhythm in Musical Notation

We've already looked at rhythm using ideas from nature, fruit, and vegetables. So, here we will use PIE to get an idea of rhythm in traditional musical notation.

For the word **PIE** with written music we will write it with a quarter note (remember it's ONE beat).

So then, **peach pie** could be written with a half note for the word peach.

Remember to make this one longer.

In music, you can actually divide one beat into two parts with these eighth notes.

ONE and

When you clap it, say **one - and** as it is one beat in two parts.

ONE - and TWO - and THREE - and FOUR - and

More Pie, Please

Apple pie could be written using these notes:

ap   ple   pie

Here's a rhythm to say **strawberry pie**:

straw   ber ry   pie

Give **huckleberry** pie a try:

huck le   ber ry   pie

This is a WHOLE note that gets all four beats. YUM! When you clap it, hold the clap and say one - two - three - four.

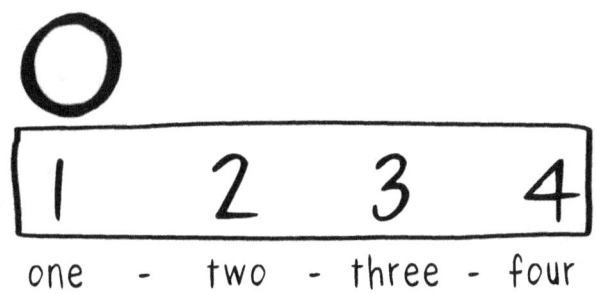

one - two - three - four

A whole note could be used to say a long yum!

Fast and Slow

One of the easiest ways to play with rhythm is to play **fast** or **slow**.

Try playing as if you were these FAST animals on the piano:

Try playing as if you were these SLOW animals on the piano:

You can also say the name of the animals and play them fast or slow.

If you want to try reading more written rhythms and rhythm practice, go to the resources in the back of the book (page 282), but we'll focus on long or short notes from here on out.

Finger Number Songs

Let's get back to playing some simple songs using finger numbers.

Get your imaginary glue ready to keep your finger numbers where they go on the piano.

Practice with the LEFT HAND

First, we will give this idea of long and short a try and practice with left hand numbers.

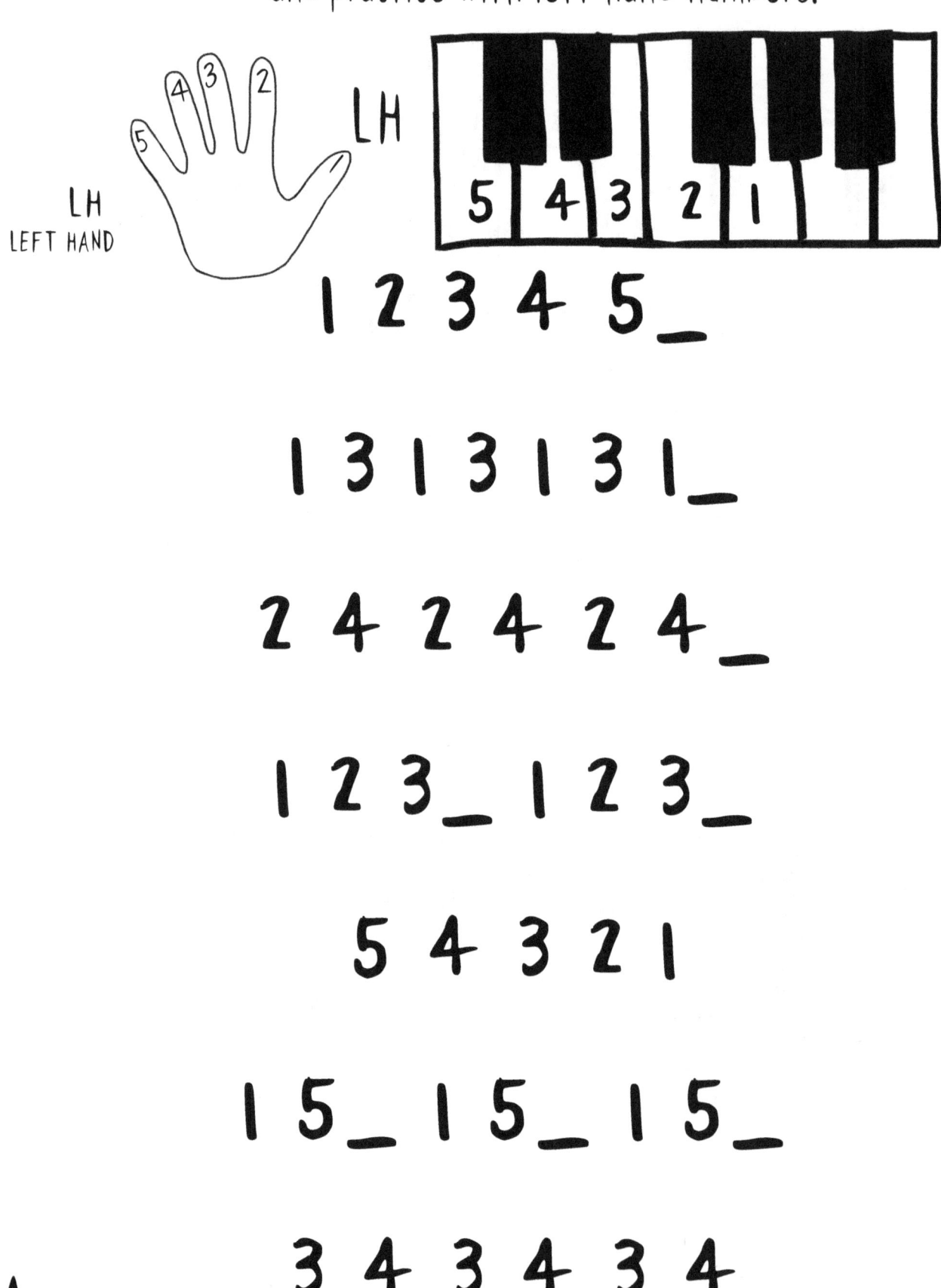

1 2 3 4 5_

1 3 1 3 1 3 1_

2 4 2 4 2 4_

1 2 3_ 1 2 3_

5 4 3 2 1

1 5_ 1 5_ 1 5_

3 4 3 4 3 4

Practice with the RIGHT HAND
Then try with your right hand numbers too.
For more practice like this, see Warm Ups on page 313.

RH

1 2 3 4 5 _

1 3 1 3 1 3 1 _

2 4 2 4 2 4 _

1 2 3 _ 1 2 3 _

5 4 3 2 1

1 5 _ 1 5 _ 1 5 _

3 4 3 4 3 4

♡ 60

Up We Go

Here are some more songs with finger numbers to make a melody. From now on, our songs have words that are called lyrics.

Sing the part of the word while you play the melody finger number.

RH [keyboard diagram: 1 2 3 4 5]

1 1 2 _
Up we go

2 2 3 _
Up we go

3 3 4 _
Up we go

4 4 5 _
Up we go

5 4 3 2 1 _
Now we go back down

Snowflakes

RH [keyboard diagram: 1 2 3 4 5]

1 2_ 1 2_
Snow flakes spark ling

2 3_ 2 3_
Snow flakes shin ing

3 4_ 3 4_
Snow flakes shim mering

4 5_ 4 5_
Snow flakes glit tering

5 4_ 4 3_
Snow flakes fall ing

3 2 1_
Fall ing down

♡62

Going to the Moon

1 1 1 1 1_
Go ing to the moon

2 2 2 2 2_
Go ing to the moon

3_ 3 3 3_
Zoom here I go.

4 4 4 4 4_
Go ing to the moon

5_ 5 5 5_
Zoom, here I go

5_ 4_ 3 2 1
Blast off! Here I go

Falling Leaves

5 _ 5 5 _
Five   leaves fall

4 _ 4 4 _
Four   leaves   fall

3 _ 3 3 _
Three leaves fall

2 _ 2 2 _
Two   leaves fall

1 _ 1 1 _
One   leaf falls

5 4 3 2 1 _
Fall - ing   to the   ground

♡64

Sunshine

1_ 5_
Sun shine

5_ 1_
Sun shine

1 2 3 4 5_
Shi ning on my face

5_ 1_
Sun shine

1_ 5_
Sun shine

5 4 3 2 1_
Shi ing all a round

Over the Bridge

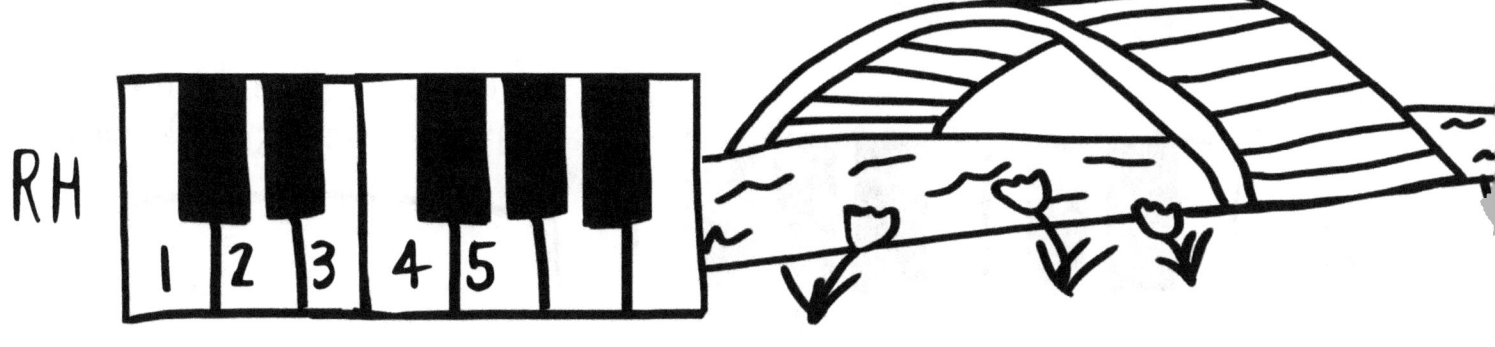

1 1 3 1_
O ver the bridge

2 2 4 2_
Let's go a gain

3 3 5 3_
O ver the bridge

5 5 3_
Down we go

4 4 2_
Down a gain

3 3 1_
Down the bridge

5_ 1_
Big jump

♡ 66

Name of Your Song _____

RH

You can draw a doodle related to your song here.

Now, you can write your own song using numbers 1, 2, 3, 4, or 5:

Name of Your Song ______________________

What doodle can you add here?

RH

Write another song. What is it called? What are the lyrics (words of your song)?

Extending to Play More Songs

WAY TO GO!

You've played some songs and even WROTE YOUR OWN SONGS!

Let's try ways to extend our finger numbers to below and above where we were before.

You can keep your fingers imaginarily glued to the main keys on the guide but then you can stretch finger five (5) up or finger one (1) down.

More RH Melody Techniques

♡70

More Techniques for the RH Melodies
A few more things and techniques to learn

Starting with our finger 5:

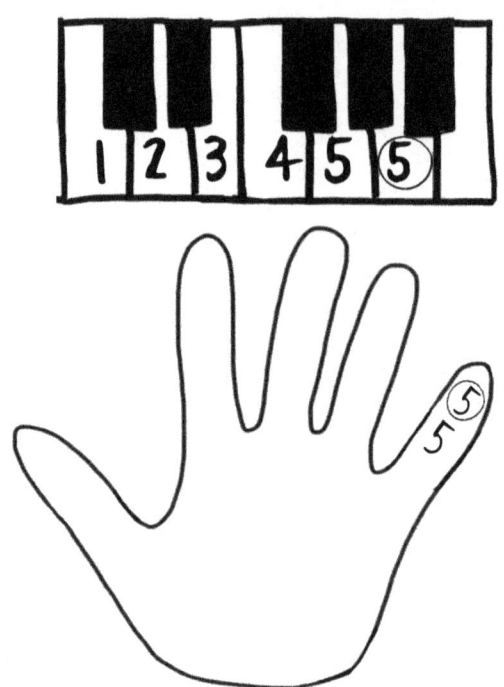

You can stretch finger five to the note above 5, but with the circle around it to play the note ⑤.

Keep your other fingers imaginarily glued to the keys.

1 2 3 4 5 ⑤ 5 ⑤ 5 ⑤ 5

5 ⑤ 5 ⑤ 5 4 3 2 1 ⑤ 5

1 5 ⑤ 5 1 5 ⑤ 5 4 3 2 1 ⑤ 1

A good song for this is Twinkle Twinkle Little Star on page 149.

I Can Fly

1 2 3 4 5 ⑤ 5̲
I have wings and I can fly.

5 ⑤ 5 4 3 2 1̲
I can fly then go back down.

1 5 ⑤̲
Can you fly?

1 5 ⑤̲
I can fly.

⑤ 5 4 3 2 1 1̲
I have wings and I can fly.

♡72

Now, Extending Finger 1

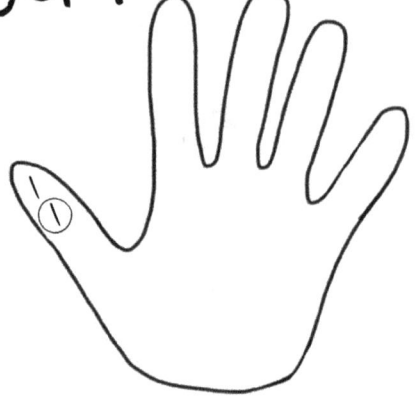

You can stretch finger one to the note below 1, but with the circle around it to play the note ①.

Keep your other fingers imaginary glued to the keys.

5 4 3 2 1 ① 1 ① 1 ① 1 _

1 ① 1 2 _ 1 ① 1 3 _

1 ① 1 4 _ 1 ① 1 5 _

1 2 3 2 1 ① 1 3 2 1 ① 1 3 ① 1

A good song for this is Skip to My Lou on page 133.

Plant a Seed

1 3 2 1 ①
I will plant a seed.

1 5 4 3 ①
I will watch it grow.

1 ① 1 2 3
Give it some wa ter

2 3 4
And sun light.

① 1 ① 2 1
Watch my flow er grow.

① 1 ① 2 1
Watch my flow er grow.

♡74

GOING OVER MOUNTAINS
Another way to stretch our finger one is to:
GO OVER THE MOUNTAIN

We will always use number 1 and then go over one (/\) or two (/\/\) mountains and then always use number ② in a circle to play the note below the mountain(s).

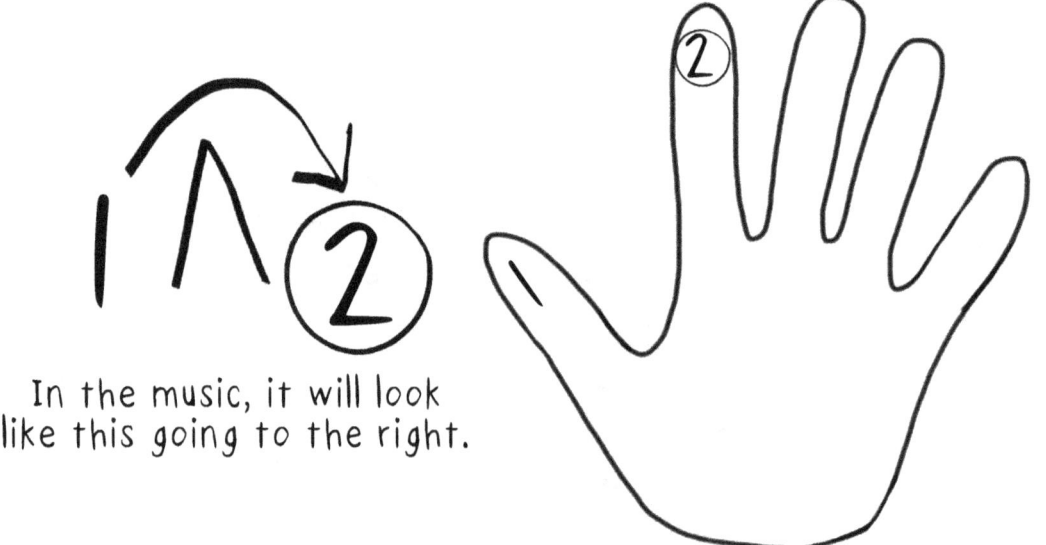

In the music, it will look like this going to the right.

Try these two options on C's around the piano:

When you see these in the music in our songbook, you will go DOWN the piano to play it with those finger numbers.

If you want to specifically practice songs with this method, you can go to page 232 for many in this category.

Try Going Over One Mountain Down the Piano:

Also try doing the same thing going UP the piano with your LEFT HAND.

♡76

Going Down the Mountain

Keep finger 1 imaginarily glued and lift up your other fingers, but let finger 2 play the note below the mountain, then put the rest of your fingers back where they go.

5   4   3   2   1 — ∧ ②
Go ing down the moun   tain.

1   2   3   2   1 — ∧ ②
Walk ing down the moun   tain.

5 —   1 ∧ ②   1
I   will walk and

5 —   1 ∧ ②   1
I   will run   and

2   3   2   1
I will jump and

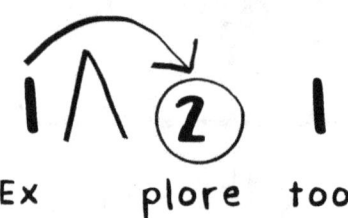

1 ∧ ② 1
Ex plore too.

Try Going Over Two Mountains Down the Piano:

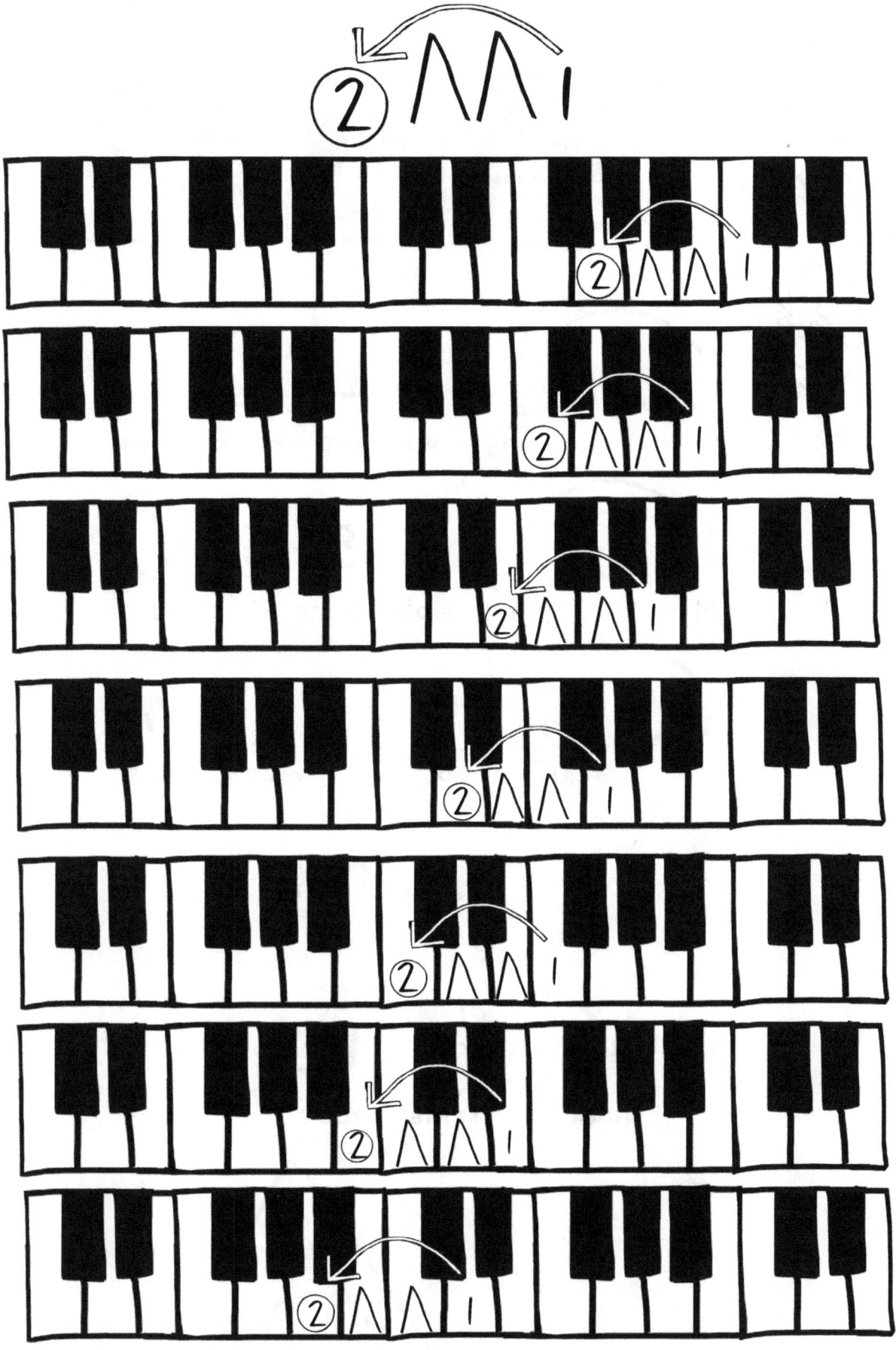

Also try doing the same thing going UP the piano with your LEFT HAND.

Hiking TWO Mountains

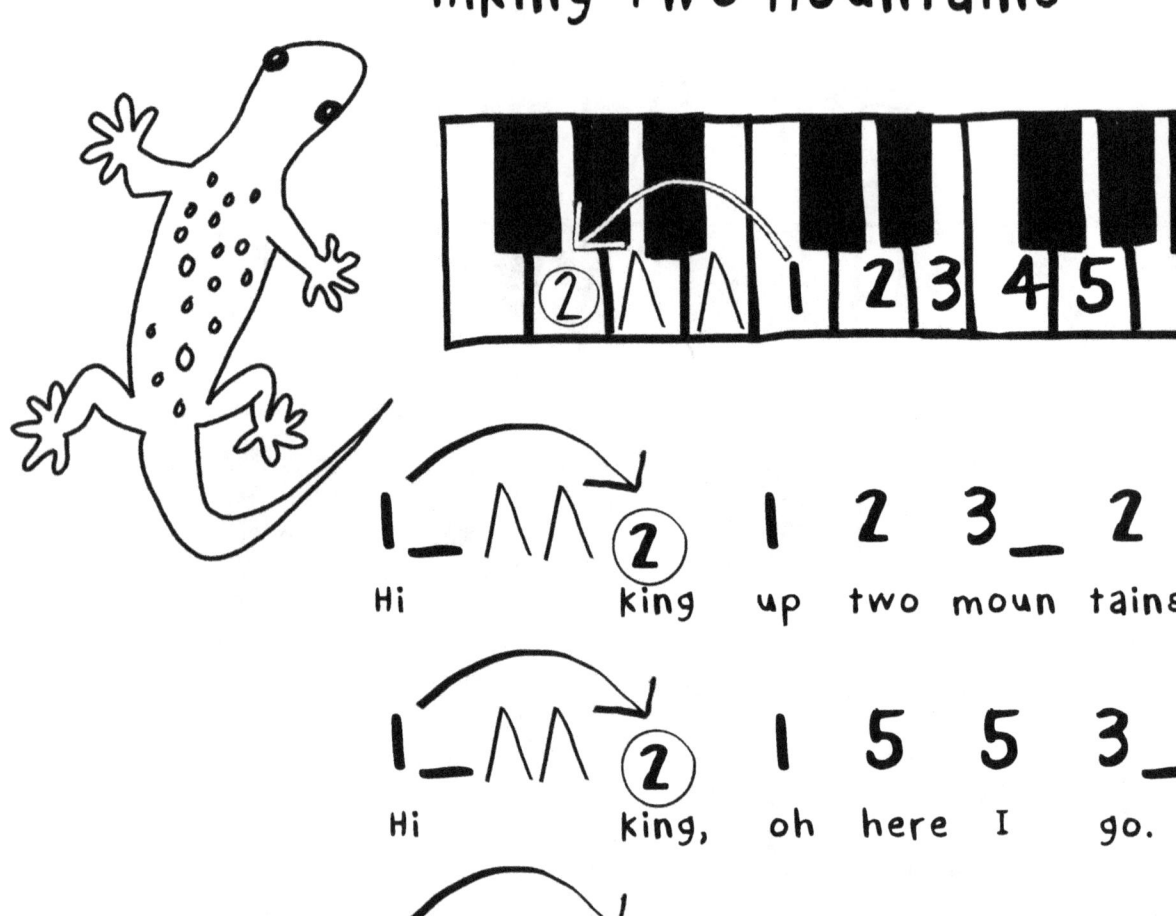

1 ∧∧ ②   1   2   3_ 2
Hi   king   up   two   moun tains.

1 ∧∧ ②   1   5   5   3_
Hi   king,   oh   here   I   go.

1 ∧∧ ②   1   2   3_ 4
Hi   king   up   two   moun tains.

5   4   3   2
Can   you   find   two

1 ∧∧ ②   1_
Moun   tains   too?

Up and Down and Around I Go

In the book, from here on out, we won't show these techniques anymore.
We'll just show you where the right hand fingers 1, 2, 3, 4, and 5 go.
Can you remember how to play all these techniques in this song?

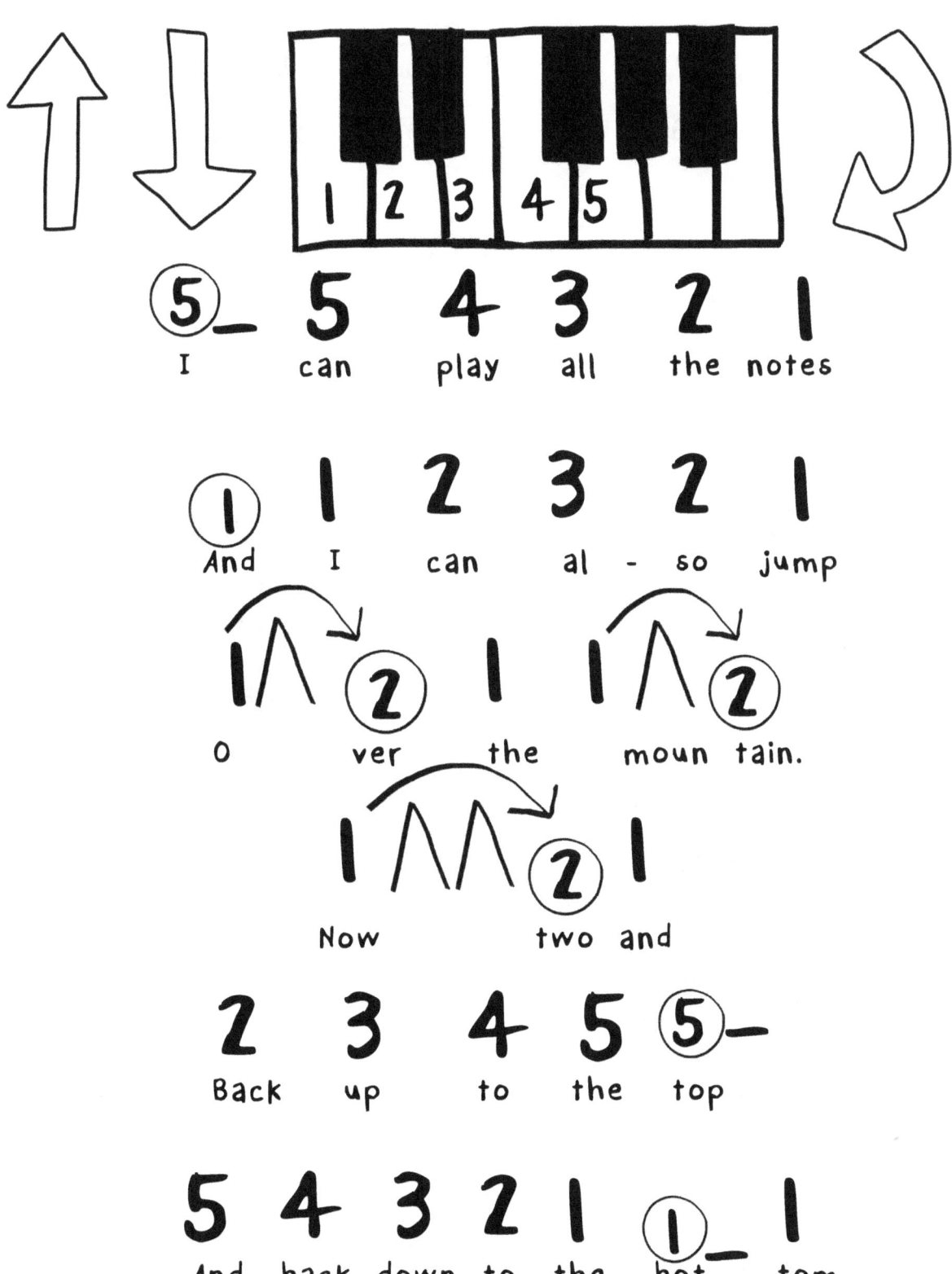

How LOUD or QUIET you play is called
DYNAMICS

Can you play like these **LOUD** animals?

Can you play like these **QUIET** animals?

lion

kitten

wolf

little doggy

dragon

iguana

elephant

hedgehog

Let's imagine dynamics using different
FOOTPRINTS

Play each set of footprints and match the dynamic level (loud or soft) to the size of the animal.

Try changing your dynamics while playing the songs will you learn later in our **songbook** on page 120.

The Musical Alphabet

If you already know these notes on the piano, continue to page 95 to learn how to use these letters to make musical sandwiches (chords).

If you don't know where these are at on the piano yet, continue through pages 84-94 to learn where they are, and to learn ways to remember where they are.

This is the MUSICAL ALPHABET
Can you write the letters too?

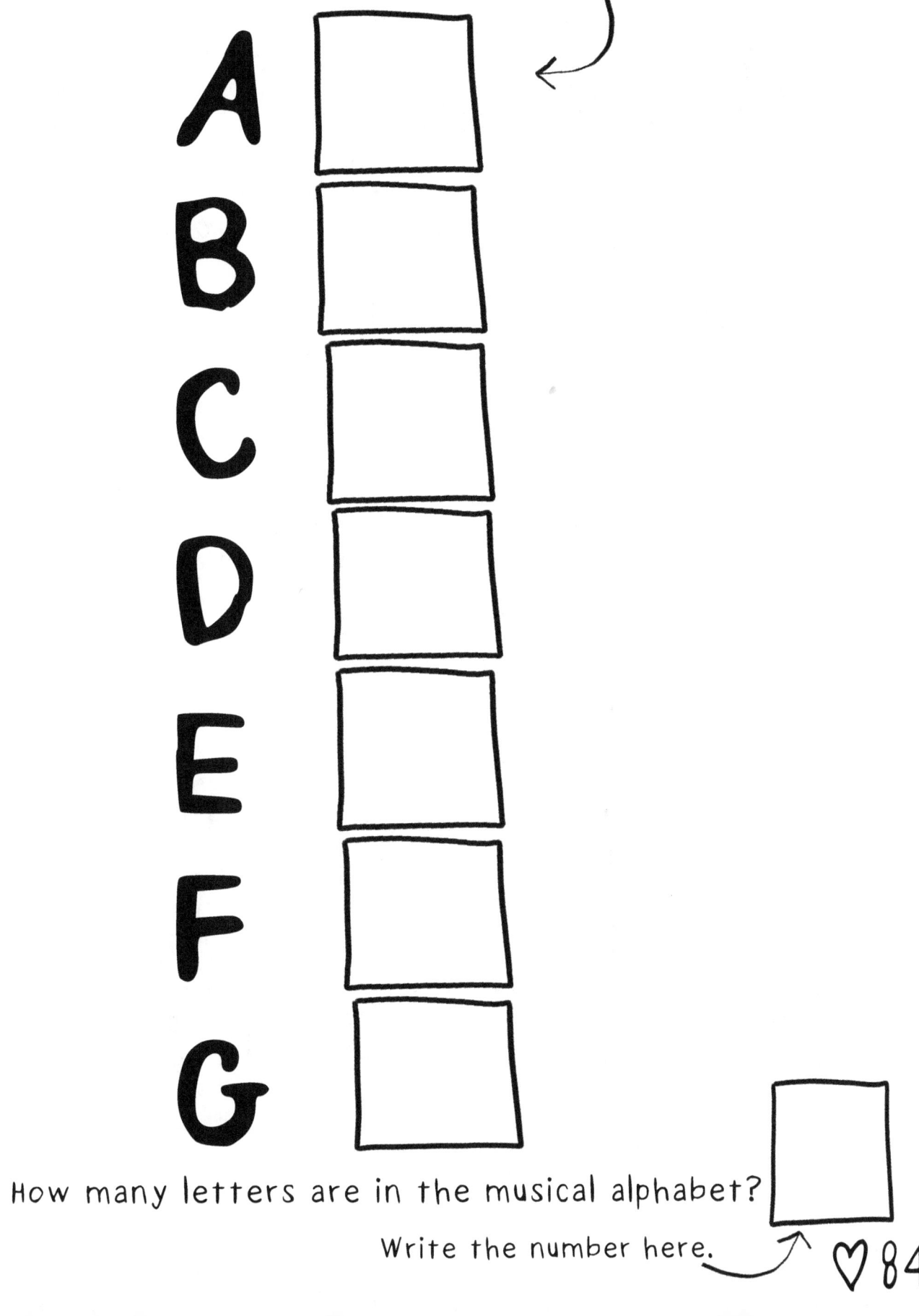

A
B
C
D
E
F
G

How many letters are in the musical alphabet? Write the number here.

♡ 84

Where Does the MUSICAL ALPHABET GO on the Piano?

We can pretend like a group of two is actually a house.

Can you draw more houses on the groups of two?

You can actually fold small pieces of paper in half like this.

Then put them over the black keys to make houses on your piano too, if you like.

So, who lives in the house?

DOG

The dog lives inside the doghouse.

Can you write the rest of the D's above?

CAT
The cat is outside of the doghouse on this side.

Can you write the rest of the C's above?

ELEPHANT
The elephant wouldn't fit in the doghouse, so the elephant is outside the doghouse on this side.

Can you write the rest of the E's above?

♡ 86

Can You Write the Rest of the C's, D's, and E's Below?

Can you also draw houses on the groups of three?

You can put your house papers over the groups of three to make houses too.

So, who lives in the house of 3 notes?

Grandma Georgina and **Grandpa Alfred** live there!

Grandma Georgina and Grandpa Alfred's House

GEORGINA

Grandma Georgina goes in the front door on the left side.

Can you write the rest of the G's above?

ALFRED

Grandpa Alfred goes in the back door on the right side.

Can you write the rest of the A's above?

The Front Door and the Back Door

Grandma Georgina and Grandpa Alfred
have to leave their house somehow.
So, they have a **front door** and a **back door**.

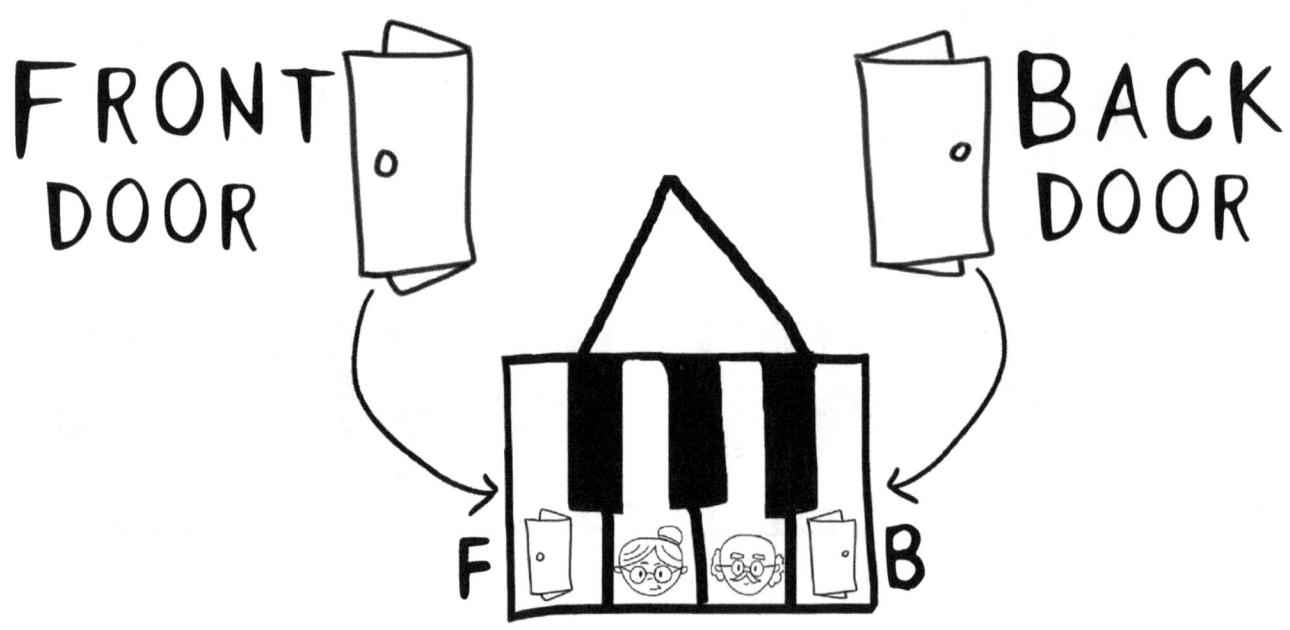

Write in the F's

Write in the B's

This Is All of the PIANO STREET:

This is for when we put the two houses next to each other.

F G A B C D E

Now, can YOU write the musical alphabet (ABCDEFG) on the piano?

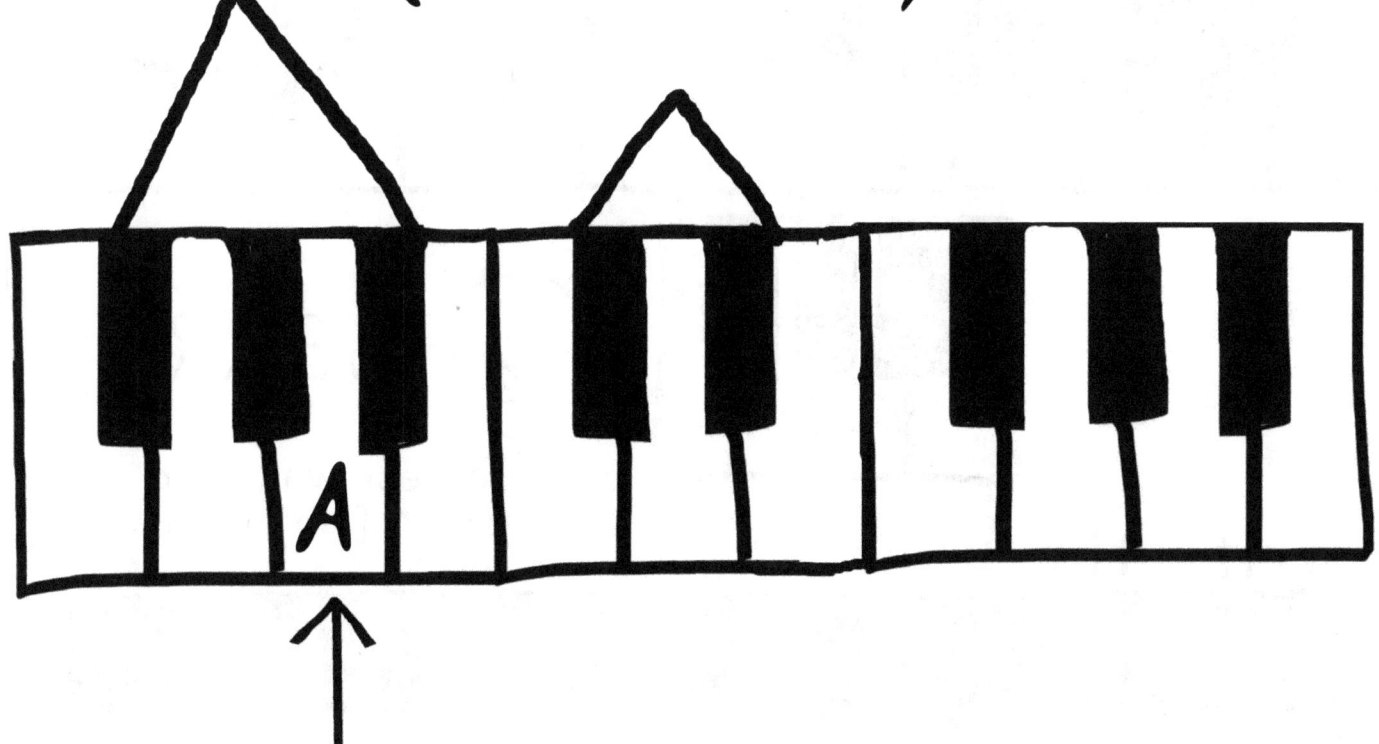

Start writing here.

Who's on Either Side of the Pond?
You could also see the notes in the 3's as a pond.

Can you draw swirled 3 ponds on this piano?

The frog wants to jump into the pond.

Write the F's

The bear wants to look for fish to eat.

Write the B's

The Goldfish and the Alligator in the Pond

GOLDFISH
The goldfish is swimming in the pond.

Write the G's

ALLIGATOR
The alligator is in the pond too. On this side.

Write the A's

Criss Cross Alphabet Notes

Let's play different notes on the piano with criss cross (XX) alphabet notes. Start at the bottom and play one note at a time alternating your hands and criss crossing them. I like to play them with finger 2, but you can with any.

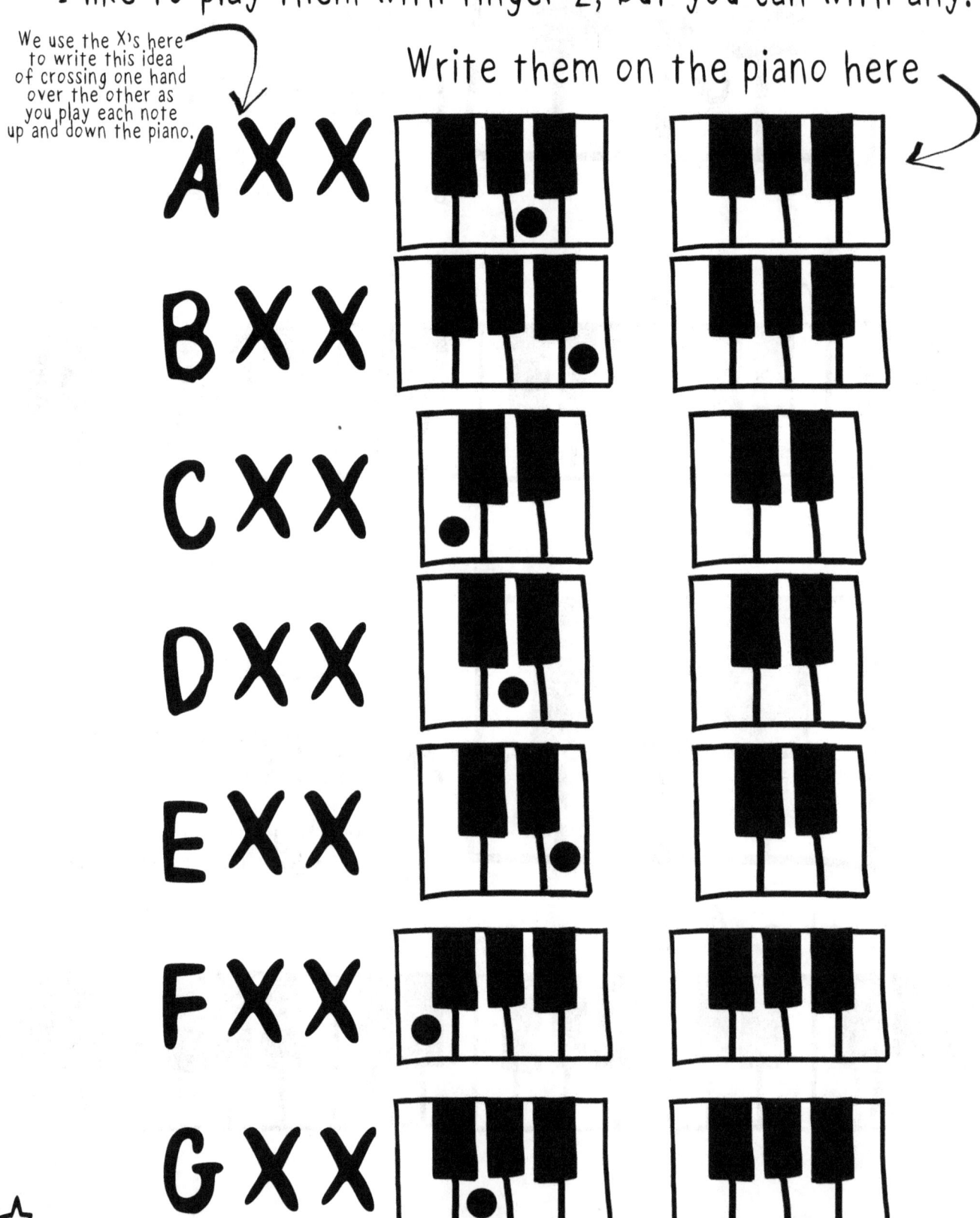

The 123 ABC Song
Try playing this song with numbers or letters.

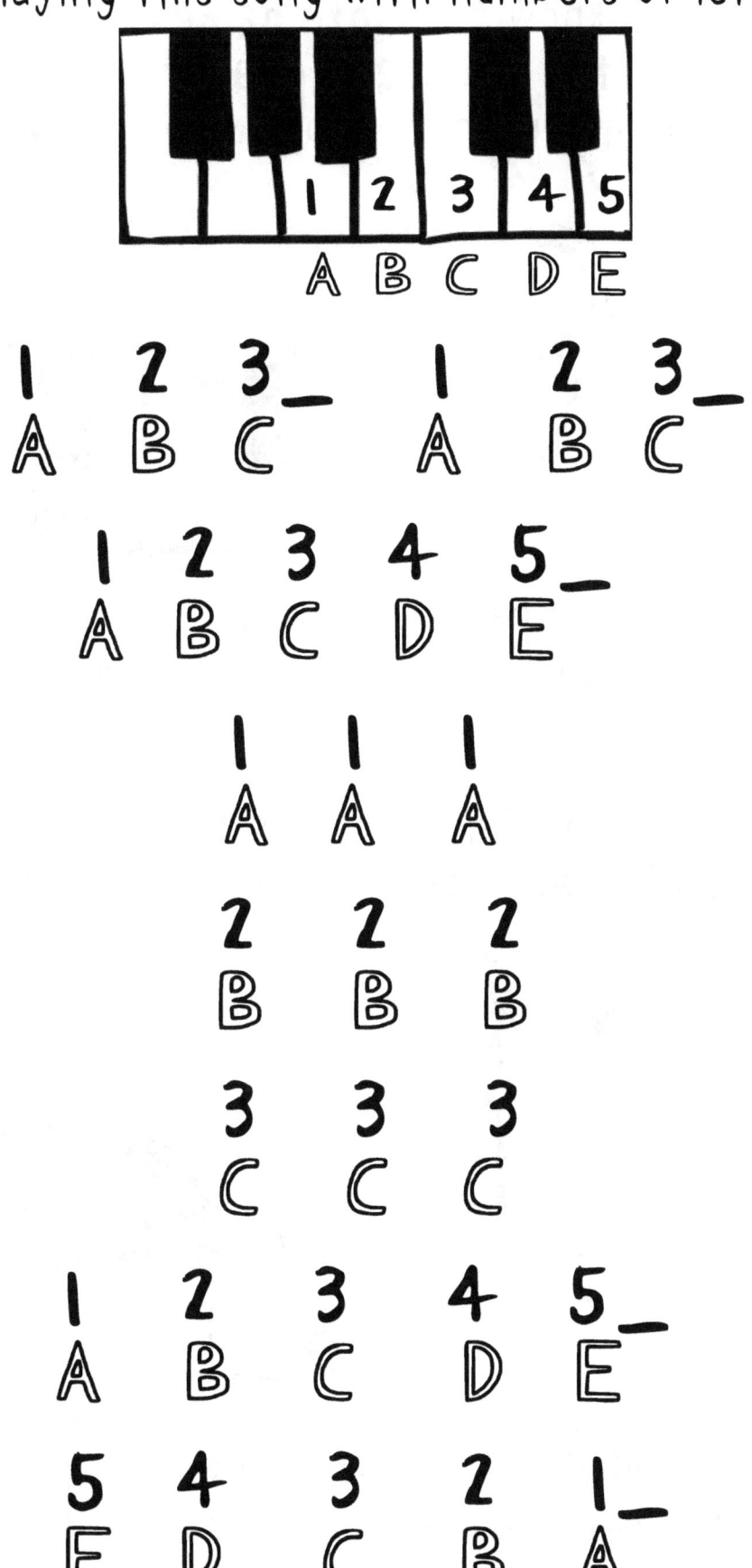

Where To Now?

Now that you know **the note names on the piano**, you will use **the musical alphabet** for where to put your **RH Finger 1** on the piano to **play a melody!**

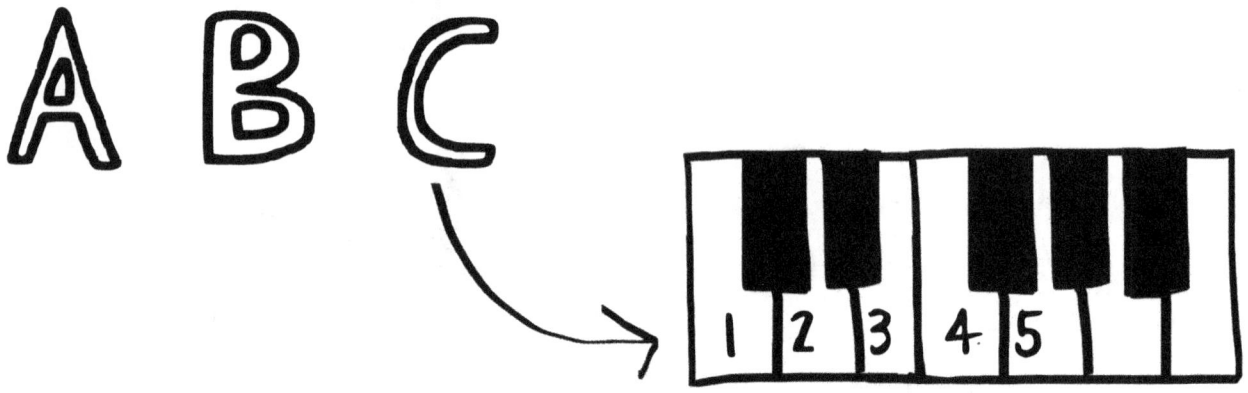

A **melody** is a pattern of one note at a time that is what we sing when we sing a song.

And, you will use the note names to **play SANDWICHES** which we will learn now to play an accompaniment.

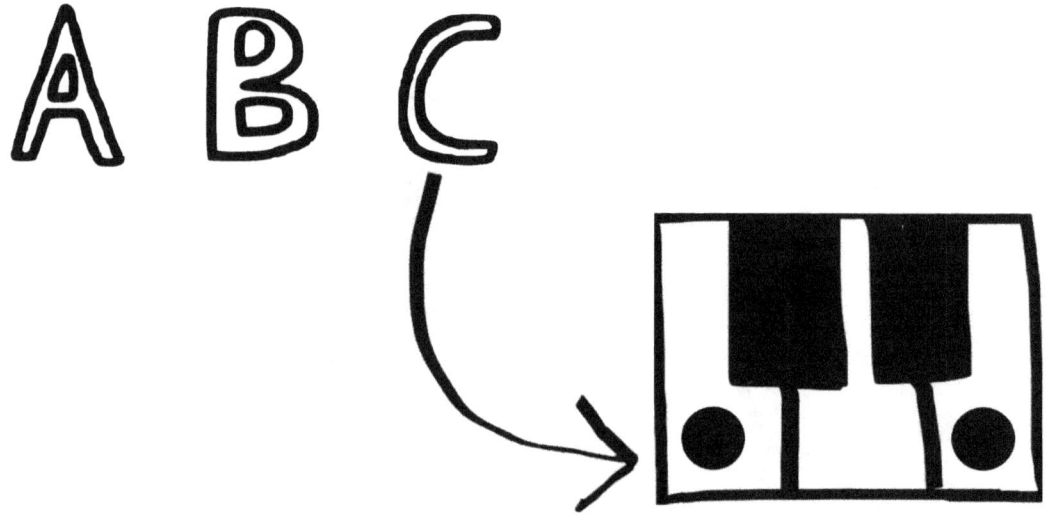

An **accompaniment** is what we use to sing with and it gives the background and support for the melody.

Sandwiches
really called
chords

*What's in your sandwich?
(Try to pick only ONE thing.)*

What I am calling **sandwiches** in this book are also called chords or thirds in music. Continue to page 97 to learn them.

Extended sandwich information is also on pages 274-297.

You can play them to sing a song (starting on page 120), or for improvising (starting on page 101).

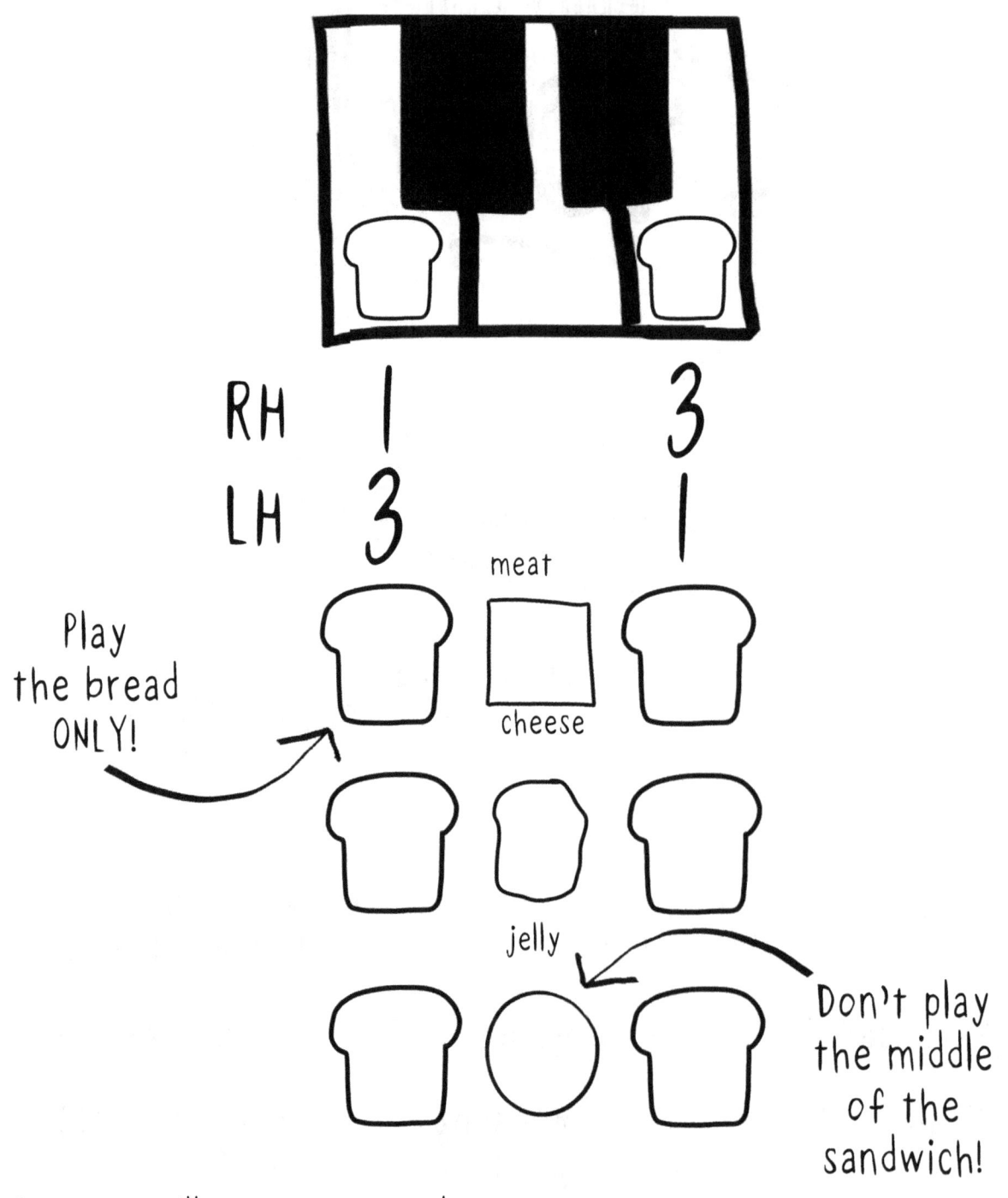

C Sandwiches

Do you remember where the note C is?
You can make a C sandwich by starting with your right hand thumb (finger 1) on C and remember to play only the bread 🍞, but now the bread will be dots to show where to put your fingers:

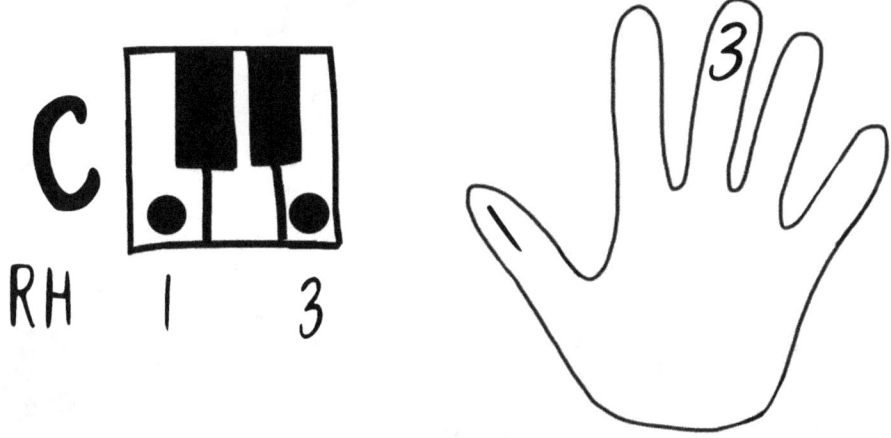

Can you put dots on all the rest of the C sandwiches and play them?

After playing all the C sandwiches going up with your right hand RH, then try with your left hand LH. Just put finger 3 on C.

F and G Sandwiches

Do you remember where the note F is?
Can you make F sandwiches too?

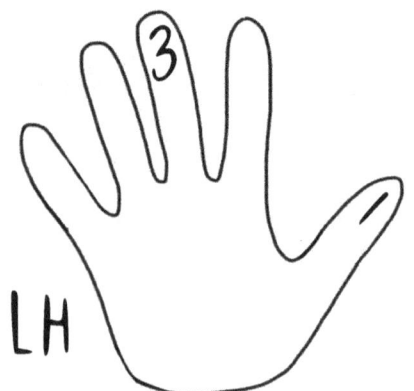 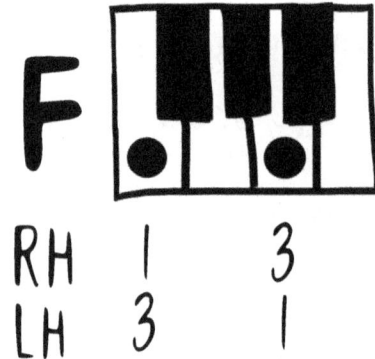 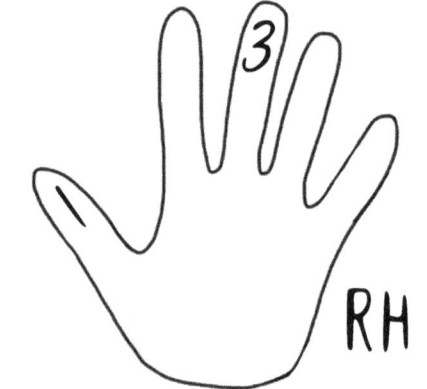

Can you put dots on all the rest of the F sandwiches and play them?

Do you remember where the note G is?
Can you make G sandwiches too?

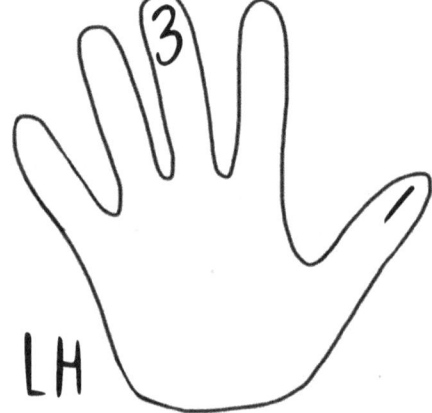 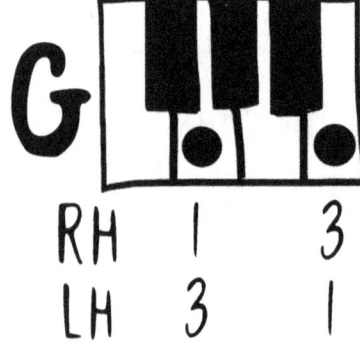 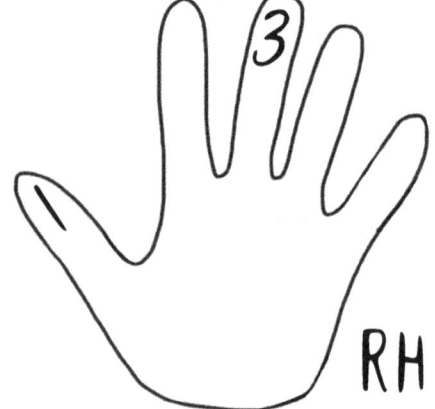

Can you put dots on all the rest of the G sandwiches and play them?

Criss Cross Sandwiches

Can you do each of these sandwiches with two notes and draw dots for each one on the piano beside it? These are actually major or minor sandwiches (more info on pages 280-281), but for now, we'll focus on their first alphabet note.

Then, you can play one of the sandwiches with one hand, then cross the other hand over to make the same sandwich. Go all the way up then all the way down the piano to make criss cross XX's with each of the sandwiches:

How many of each are on your piano?

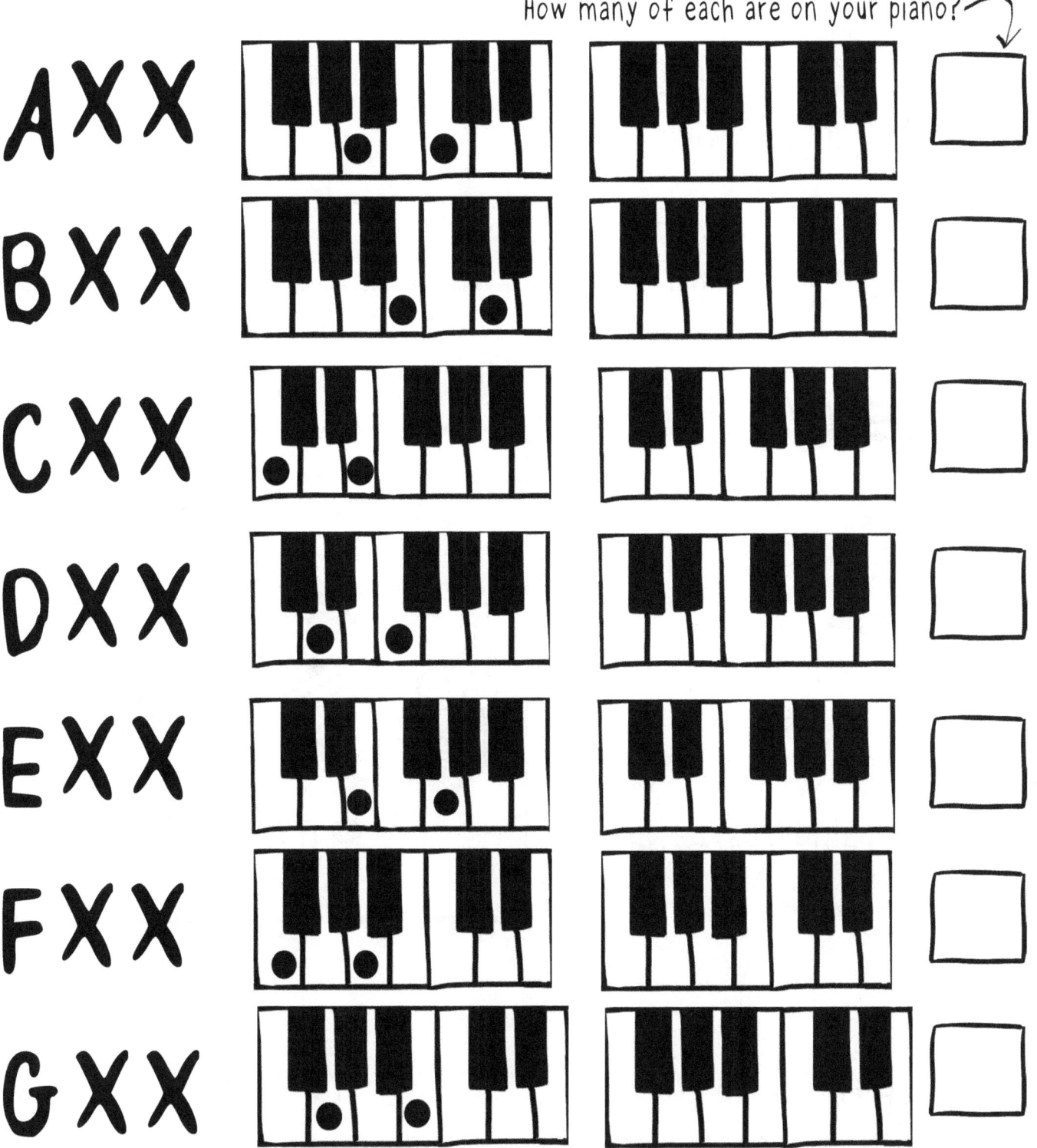

Now that you know these sandwiches, you can use them to improvise. Continue to the next page to see how to play without written music!

♡100

Improvising with DOODLES

To DRAW something new, you can use any shapes, lines, and doodles like these:

 single swirls

 double swirls

 lines

 triangles

 circles

 raindrops/petals

Can you draw your own design with those shapes?

Then put them in a NEW pattern to color like this.

This is IMPROVISING with color, shapes and designs.

Improvising

Improvise: to make up something on the spot
or to make up a song without music!
(**Improv** for short)

Improvising is AWESOME, and you should totally start
to learn this concept a few pages at a time.
You can also go ahead to **Our Songbook** on page 120,
and start playing and singing all sorts of songs first too!

Then, come back to this section on improvising
anytime you want to **play without written music**
and play just for the fun of it, making up something NEW!

Let's start by
IMPROVISING
with sound!

Let's Make a STORM

Make these parts of a storm on the piano in ANY ORDER you want.

You can play each type of weather the way I suggest, or make up your own way to make the sound of each type below:

This can be one note at a time and then make the rain stronger and faster. **rain**

lightning
Slide up and down the piano.

thunder
Make loud boom noises.

tornado
Roll your hands in a fist on the keys.

snow
Lightly let your fingers fall like snowflakes, then softly play notes.

sunshine
Make some sunshine rays wiggling your fingers on the keys.

Play with SHAPES

To improvise with shapes, say and play the word of the shape, while you play one note at a time, using the parts or syllables of the words you say.

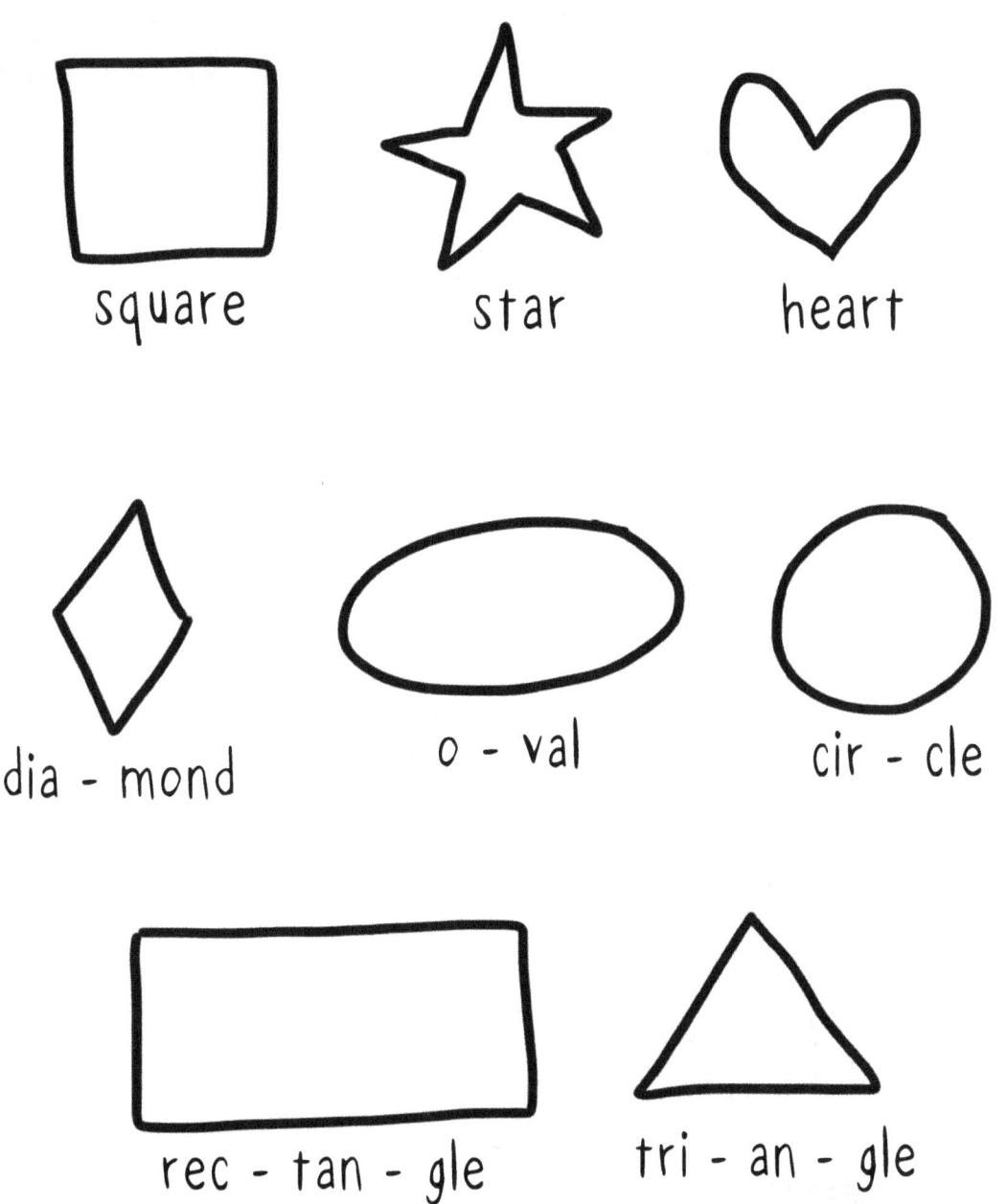

square

star

heart

dia - mond

o - val

cir - cle

rec - tan - gle

tri - an - gle

Improvising TOGETHER on Black Keys

Play **any black keys** to make a melody up!
A melody is one note at a time like a song.

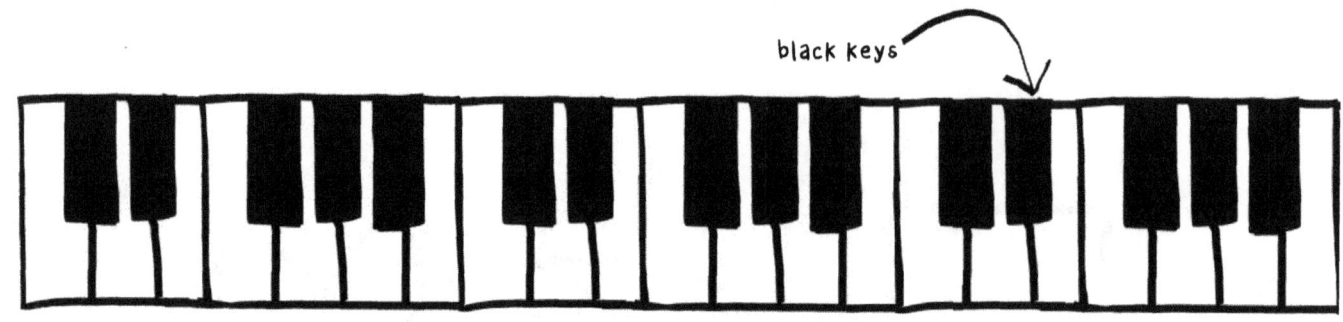

Play these ways to make a melody:

step up or **step down**
repeat a note
jump from note to note
fast or **slow**
loud or **quiet**
long or **short**

The only rule is only black keys for now. Otherwise, HAVE FUN!

Your teacher, grown up, or a friend can play these two sandwiches/triads under your improv if you like:

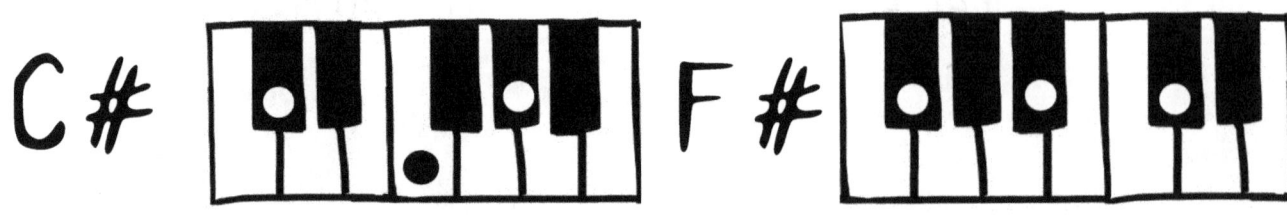

Improvising TOGETHER on White Keys

Now try it on **any white keys**.

Remember ideas for playing your melody:

step up or **step down**
repeat a note
jump from note to note
fast or **slow**
loud or **quiet**
long or **short**

The only rule is only white keys now. Otherwise, HAVE FUN!

Your teacher, grown up, or a friend can play these two sandwiches/triads under your improv if you like:

♡ 106

Improvising Both Hands Together

Now, let's improv with mixing sandwiches and melodies.

Put your left hand first on a C sandwich:

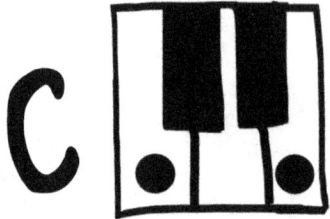

Play the C sandwiches counting to four for each time:

C 2 3 4   C 2 3 4   C 2 3 4

Keep going!

We can also write it like this:

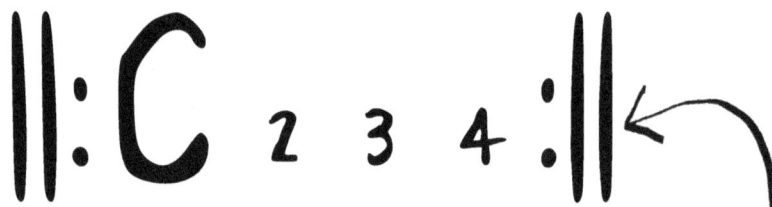

These lines mean to **REPEAT** whatever is inside of them as many times as you want!

After you get that going, add your RH melody on top!

Keep your RH fingers on these notes starting on the note C for now.
Imaginary glue them if you need.

Play ONE note at a time. Imagine it's a song or a melody.

Keep It Up!

Keep your RH in the same place for playing the melody:

But try it with your left hand on the F sandwich:

F 🎹

||: F 2 3 4 :||

Try it also with the LH on the G sandwich:

G 🎹

||: G 2 3 4 :||

♡ 108

Let's try some more with our RH on C:

From here on out, repeat these patterns of the sandwiches in the repeat signs with your LH to create different improvised songs.

Here are the sandwiches:

C [keyboard] F [keyboard] G [keyboard]

||: C 2 3 4   F 2 3 4 :||

||: F 2 3 4   C 2 3 4 :||

||: F 2 3 4   G 2 3 4 :||

||: G 2 3 4   C 2 3 4 :||

||: G 2 3 4   F 2 3 4 :||

Stay on C in your RH for now:

Here you can try four chord patterns in your LH. We won't write the numbers, but still COUNT TO FOUR.

||: C   F   G   G :||

||: F   F   C   C :||

||: C   G   F   F :||

Can you make some patterns and try too?

||:   :||

||:   :||

♡110

Now, try the patterns with your RH on G:

C [keyboard] F [keyboard] G [keyboard]

||: C F G G :||

||: F F C G :||

||: C G C C :||

||: C C F G :||

Your turn to make more patterns:

||:   :||

||:   :||

Here are some minor sandwiches we can use for improv.

(For more practice with minor sandwiches, go to page 281.)

Em [keyboard] Am [keyboard]

Try your RH on E and on A as melody options: [keyboard 1 2 3 4 5] [keyboard 1 2 3 4 5]

||: Am F C C :||

||: Am C Am F :||

||: Am Em C C :||

||: C Am C Em :||

Your turn. Make new patterns with these sandwiches:

||:   :||

||:   :||

♡ 112

Let's try a few more, adding the Dm sandwich:

Dm

Your RH could go on the note D too:

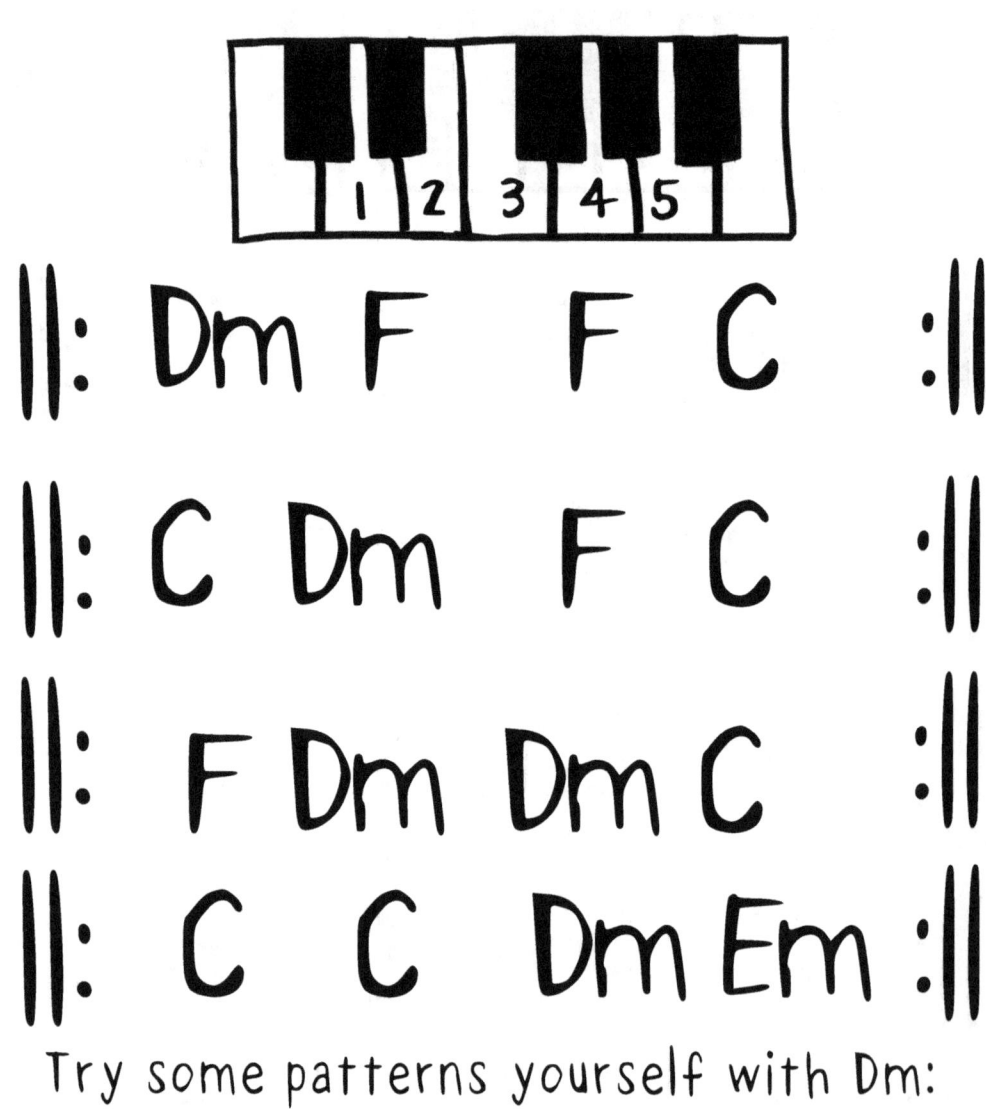

||: Dm F F C :||

||: C Dm F C :||

||: F Dm Dm C :||

||: C C Dm Em :||

Try some patterns yourself with Dm:

||:   :||

||:   :||

Here is a page for you to write some of your own improv patterns to play with!

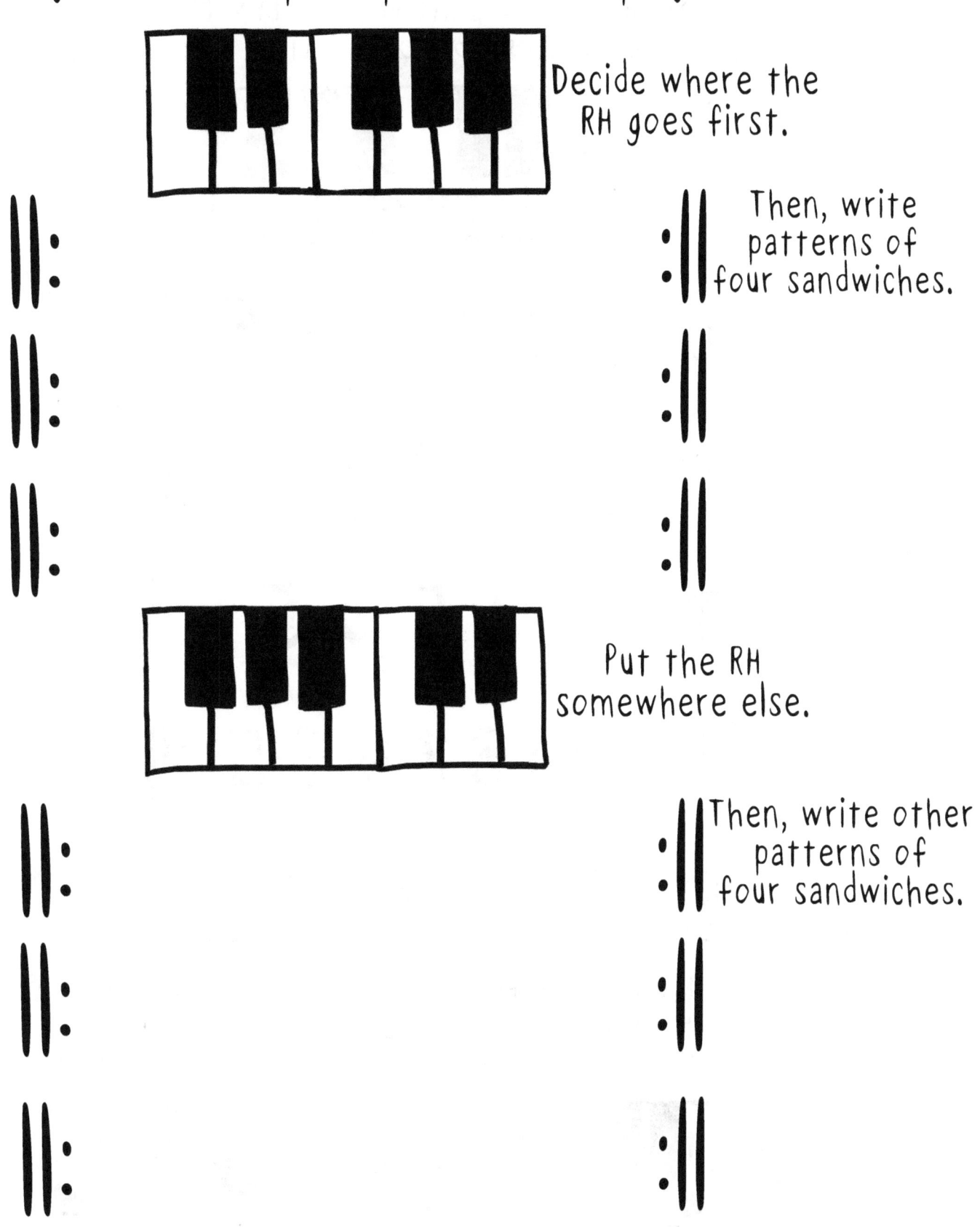

Decide where the RH goes first.

Then, write patterns of four sandwiches.

Put the RH somewhere else.

Then, write other patterns of four sandwiches.

Now, you can improv anytime you want to without even writing anything down.

♡ 114

Patterns in Improv

You can also try patterns with your RH while you improv different sandwiches. Try these RH patterns on C first before adding the chords.

① ‖: 1 2 3 4 5 :‖

② ‖: 1 3 2 _ :‖

③ ‖: 1 5 3 5 :‖

④ ‖: 1 3 2 4 3 5 :‖

⑤ ‖: 3 2 1 2 3 _ :‖

Now, play those patterns and change the sandwich each time you start the pattern again or repeat the same sandwich while you repeat the pattern.

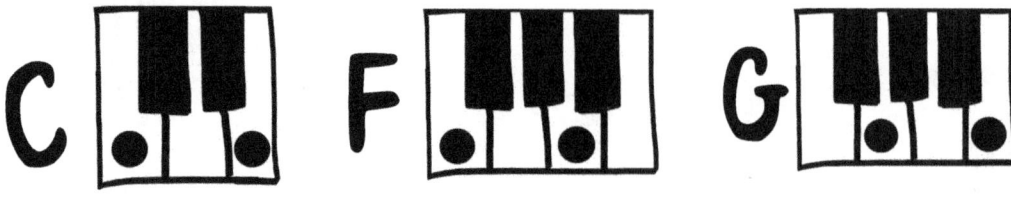

More Patterns in Improv

Now, play the sandwich and play the pattern under that sandwich to play these short melodies.

① C   C   F   F
   1 2 3   1 2 3   1 2 3   1 2 3

② C   C   F   F
   3 2 1   3 2 1   4 4 1   4 4 1

③ F   F   C   C
   1 3 2   1 3 2   1 2 3   1 3 2

④ F   F   C   C
   5 1 1   5 1 1   1 3 5   5 1 1

⑤ C   F   F   C
   1 1 2   1 1 3   1 1 4   1 1 2

Also, another idea is to choose which hand does chords and which hand does the melody and then switch.

Write Your OWN Patterns in Improv

Write in the rest of the sandwiches that you would like for these patterns:

① C [ ] [ ] [ ]
   1 2 3   1 2 3   1 2 3   1 2 3

② C [ ] [ ] [ ]
   3 2 1   3 2 1   4 4 1   4 4 1

③ F [ ] [ ] [ ]
   1 3 2   1 3 2   1 2 3   1 3 2

Write in your own finger number melody patterns:

④ F   F   C   C
   [ ] [ ] [ ] [ ]

⑤ C   F   F   C
   [ ] [ ] [ ] [ ]

If you like improvising and now you want some more interesting ways to play your sandwiches to make your own music, you can look at these pages:

Pages 282-283 to play with different rhythms.
Pages 284-285 to play different finger number orders.
Pages 286-289 and page 325 (warm ups 66 and 67) to play them as fifths.
Pages 290-291 to play them as triads (double decker sandwiches).
Pages 294-295 to play those triads in different finger number patterns.

Great Job Improvising with Sound!

Keep it up without written music.
You already know how to improvise!

Remember these doodle shapes and lines?

 single swirls

 circles

 raindrops/petals

Let's add a few NEW doodles so you can make something spontaneous and different!

 zigzag lines

 swirly lines

 hearts

 squares

Keep doodling and color this!

Our Songbook

Welcome to playing songs.
Welcome to singing songs.
Welcome to **singing and playing** at the same time!

Now that **we know how to play sandwiches** and **we know how to play melodies** with numbers, we can start playing all sorts of songs!

On the LEFT PAGE of our songbook, you will see which sandwiches to use

You can play those **sandwiches** and **sing the songs** while reading the lyrics (words). Just play the sandwich when you see the word it's above in the song.

On the RIGHT PAGE of our songbook, you will see where to put your RH **on the piano**

You'll see the finger numbers for **the melody** of the same song. Above those numbers are sandwiches, so you can play the melody in your right hand and the sandwiches in your left hand at the same time.

To know **the first note to sing** on the left side page, play the first note on the right page. That's the first note you will sing.

If you're ready, play the song with all the sandwiches with one hand. Then try both hands together. Or play one sandwich in one hand and one or two in the other. Or start by playing only C sandwiches, then F, then G, while someone else plays the others.

You can **try a duet**, where each person plays one of the pages.

Maybe, have someone listen to you play and **guess the song**!

Also, have fun **coloring doodles** on each page!

Making music is exciting and you're just starting your adventure.

♡ 120

Songs in This Category

Row Row Row Your Boat..............123
Mary Had a Little Lamb.................125
Ring Around the Rosie.................127
Rain, Rain Go Away......................129
London Bridge is Falling Down.....131
Skip to My Lou...............................133
Do Your Ears Hang Low?..............135
Are You Sleeping?........................137
There is Thunder......................... 139
Your Song......................................141

Songs with C and G Chords

C G

RH on C

Row, Row, Row Your Boat

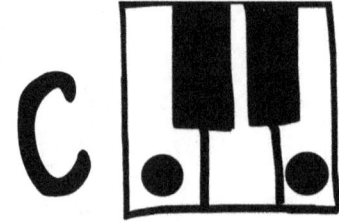

C   C
Row, row, row your boat

C   C
Gently down the stream.

C   C
Merrily, merrily, merrily, merrily

C   C
Life is but a dream.

Extra Verses or Extra Lyric Ideas

Drive, drive, drive your car quickly down the road.
Fly, fly, fly your plane, gently through the sky.
Chug, chug, chug your train quickly down the track.

Row Row Row Your Boat

C   C
1_1_ 1_2 3_
Row, row, row your boat

C   C
3_2 3_4 5_
Gent ly down the stream.

C
1 1 1   5 5 5
Merr i ly, merr i ly,

C
3 3 3   1 1 1
Merr i ly, merr i ly

C   C
5_4 3_ 2 1_
Life is but a dream.

♡124

Mary Had a Little Lamb

C　　C

Mary had a little lamb,

G　　C

Little lamb,　little lamb.

C　　C

Mary had a little lamb

G　　C

Whose fleece was white as snow.

> Extra Verses or Extra Lyric Ideas

Use different names and animals
Ex: James had a little cat.
Jodi had a little sloth.
Cara had a little monkey.
Matthew had a little fish.

Mary Had a Little Lamb

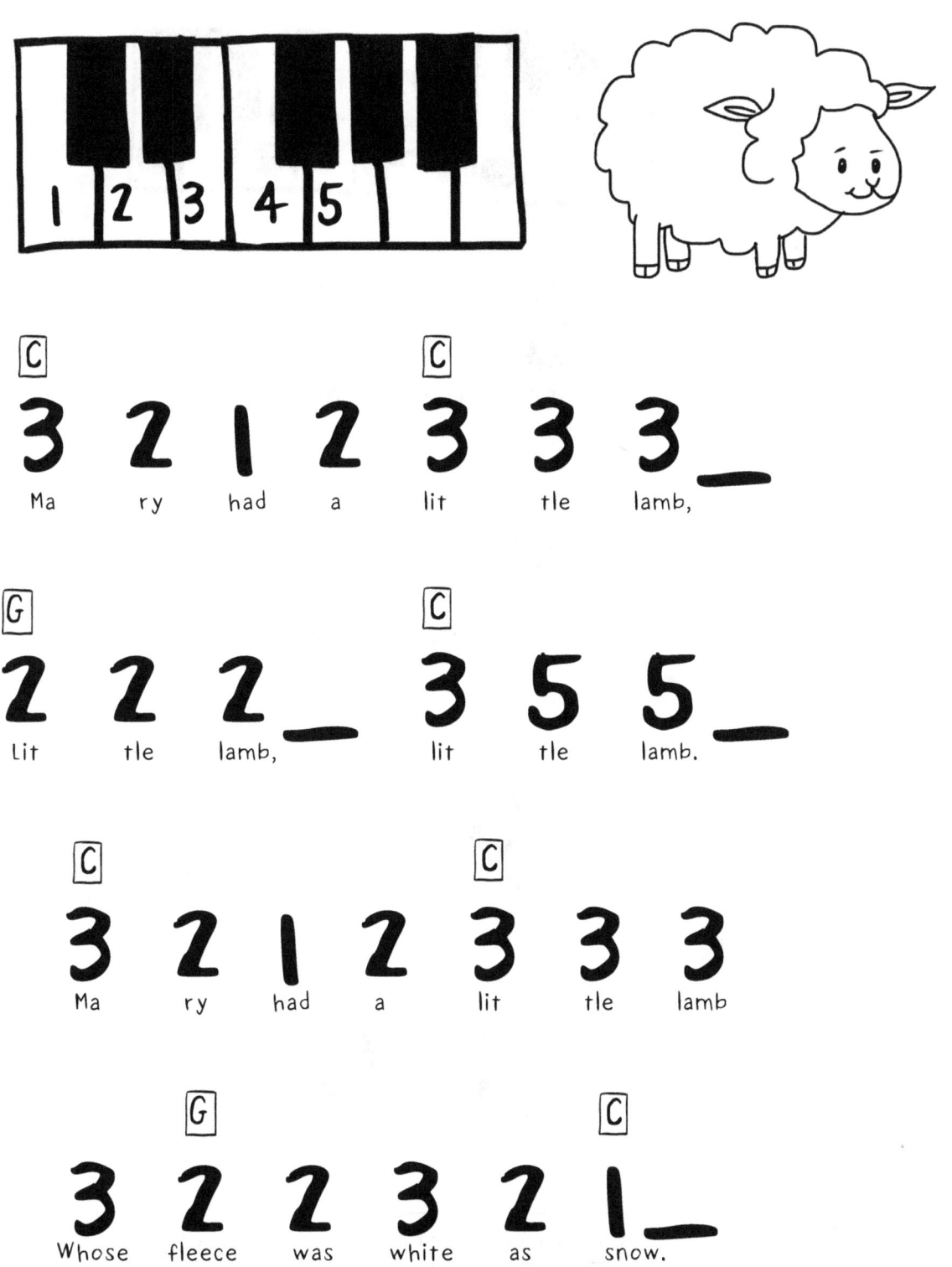

Ring Around the Rosie

C   C

Ring around the rosie,

C   C

Pocket full of posies,

C C

Ashes, Ashes,

G C

We all fall down.

> Extra Verses or Extra Lyric Ideas

Cows are in the meadow eating buttercups.
Ashes, ashes, we all stand up.

Feel the lovely sunshine, flowers all around.
Jump a little, jump a little, jump right off the ground.

Ring Around the Rosie

[C] 5 5 3 ⑤ [C] 5_ 3
Ring a round the ro sie,

[C] 5 5 3 ⑤ [C] 5_ 3
Poc ket full of po sies,

[C] 5_ 3 [C] 5_ 3
  A shes,   A shes,

3 [G] 5_ 5_ [C] 1_
We all   fall   down.

♡ 128

Rain, Rain Go Away

C

Rain, rain, go away,

C   C

Come again another day.

G   G

We want to go outside and play.

G   C

Rain, rain, go away.

> Extra Verses or Extra Lyric Ideas

Change the weather:
Thunder, go away.
Lightning, go away.
Fog clouds, go away.

Rain, Rain Go Away

C　　　　　　　C
5_ 3_　5 5 3_
Rain,　rain,　go a way,

C　　　　　　　　　C
5 5 3　⑤　5 5 3_
Come a gain　a　no ther day.

G　　　　　　　G
3 4 4 2 2　4 4 2_
We want to go out side and play.

G　　　　　　C
5 4 3 2 3 1 1
Ra in, ra in, go a way.

♡130

London Bridge is Falling Down

C   C
London Bridge is falling down,

G   C
Falling down, falling down.

C   C
London Bridge is falling down,

G C
My fair lady.

| Extra Verses or Extra Lyric Ideas |

Use other cities.
Use your city!

Seattle Bridge is falling down.
New York Bridge is falling down.

Skip to My Lou

C   **C**
Lou, Lou, skip to my Lou.

G   **G**
Lou, Lou, skip to my Lou.

C   **C**   **G**   **C**
Lou, Lou, skip to my Lou. Skip to my Lou, my darlin!

C   **C**
Lost my partner, what'll I do?

G   **G**
Lost my partner, what'll I do?

C   **C**   **G**   **C**
Lost my partner, what'll I do? Skip to my Lou, my darlin!

> **Extra Verses or Extra Lyric Ideas**
>
> Try with different actions
> Hop to my Lou.
> Run to my Lou.
> Twirl to my Lou.
> Jump to my Lou.
> Walk to my Lou.
> Tip toe to my Lou.

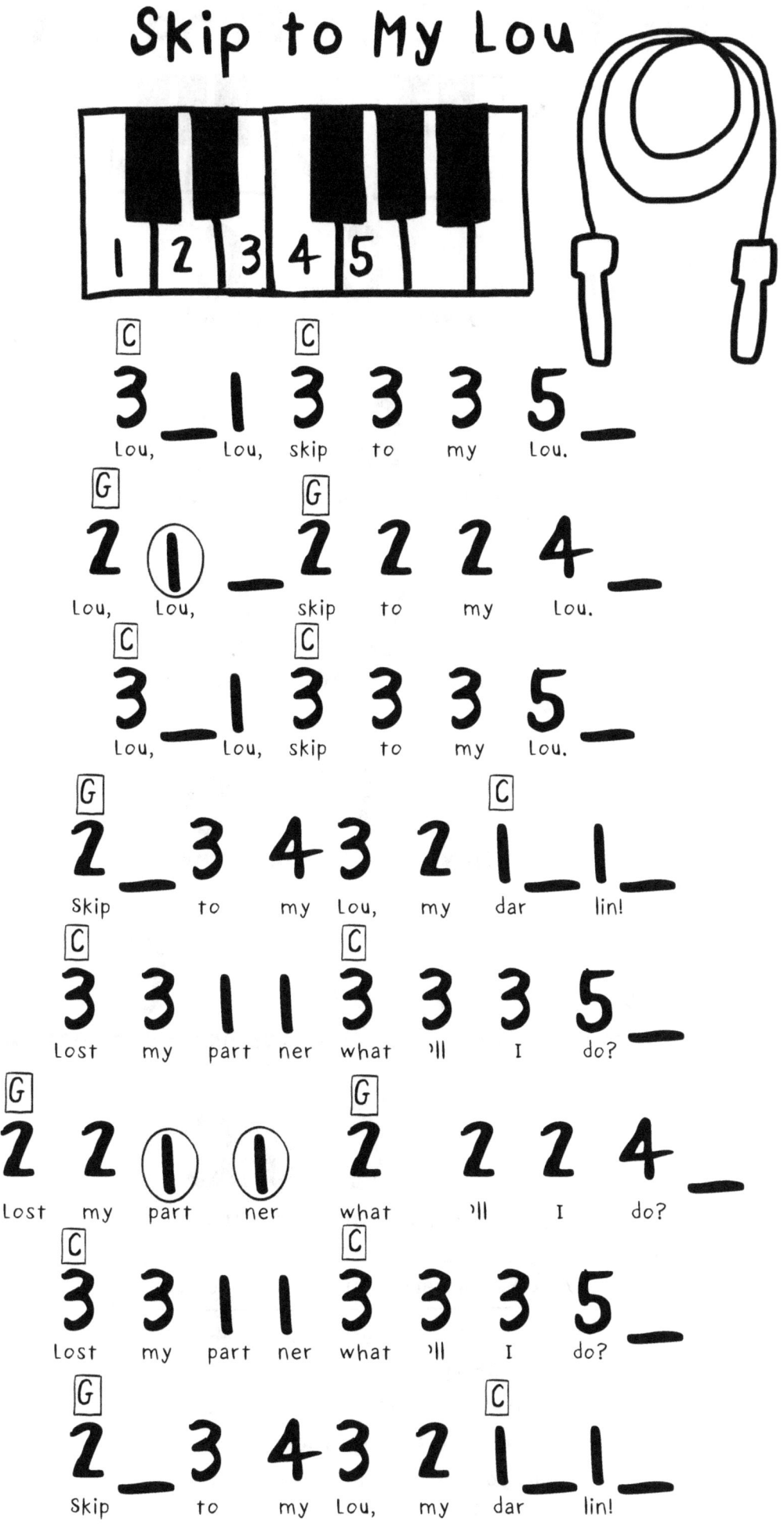

Do Your Ears Hang Low?

C [piano chord]   G [piano chord]

C   C
Do your ears hang low?

C   C
Do they wobble to and fro?

C   C
Can you tie 'em in a knot?

G   G
Can you tie 'em in a bow?

C   C   C   C
Can you throw 'em over your shoulder like a continental soldier

C G C
Do your ears hang low?

> Extra Verses or Extra Lyric Ideas

Do your ears hang high?
Do they reach up to the sky?
Are they curly when they're wet?
Are they shaggy when they're dry?
Can you throw them over your shoulder
like a continental soldier?
Do your ears hang high?

Do Your Ears Hang Low?

          [C]   [C]
3 2 1_ 1 1_
Do your ears hang low?

      [C]   [C]
3 4 5_ ⑤ 5_ 4 5_
Do they wob ble to and fro?

      [C]   [C]
1 2 3_ 3 3_3 3_
Can you tie 'em in a knot?

      [G]   [G]
1 3 3_ 2 2_ 2 2_
Can you tie 'em in a bow?

         [C]   [C]
3 2 1_ 1 1 1_ 2 1_5
Can you throw 'em o ver your shoul der

      [C]   [C]
3 4 5_ ⑤ 5 4 5_5
like a con tin en tal sol dier?

      [C] [G] [C]
1 2 3_ 2_ 1_
Do your ears hang low?

♡136

Are You Sleeping?

C 🎹 **G** 🎹

C   **C**

Are you sleeping? Are you sleeping?

C   **C**

Brother John, Brother John?

C   **C**

Morning bells are ringing.

C   **C**

Morning bells are ringing.

C G C   C G C

Ding, ding, dong. Ding, ding, dong.

> Extra Verses or Extra Lyric Ideas

Use your name: Are you sleeping? Are you sleeping? Miss Jodi?

Or, the song also has a version in French:
Frère Jacques, Frère Jacques.
Dormez-vous, dormez-vous?
Sonnez le matines, sonnez le matines.
Ding ding dong. Ding ding dong.

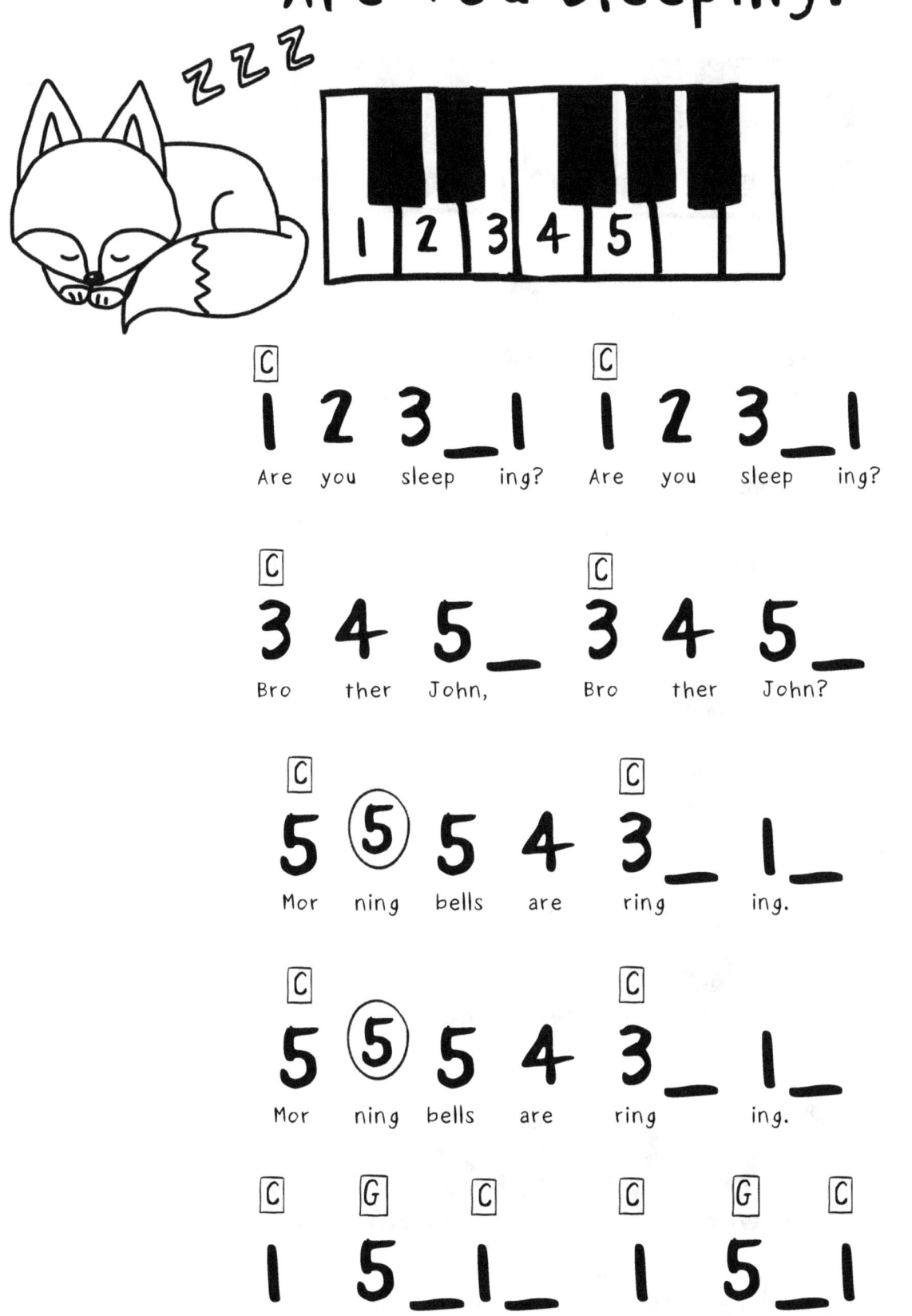

There Is Thunder

C   C
I hear thunder! I hear thunder!

C   C
Oh! don't you? Oh! don't you?

C
Pitter, patter raindrops,

C
Pitter, patter raindrops,

C G C   C G C
I'm wet through! I'm wet through!

> Extra Verses or Extra Lyric Ideas

Try different weather:
I see lightning!
I see rain clouds!
I see snowflakes!

There Is Thunder

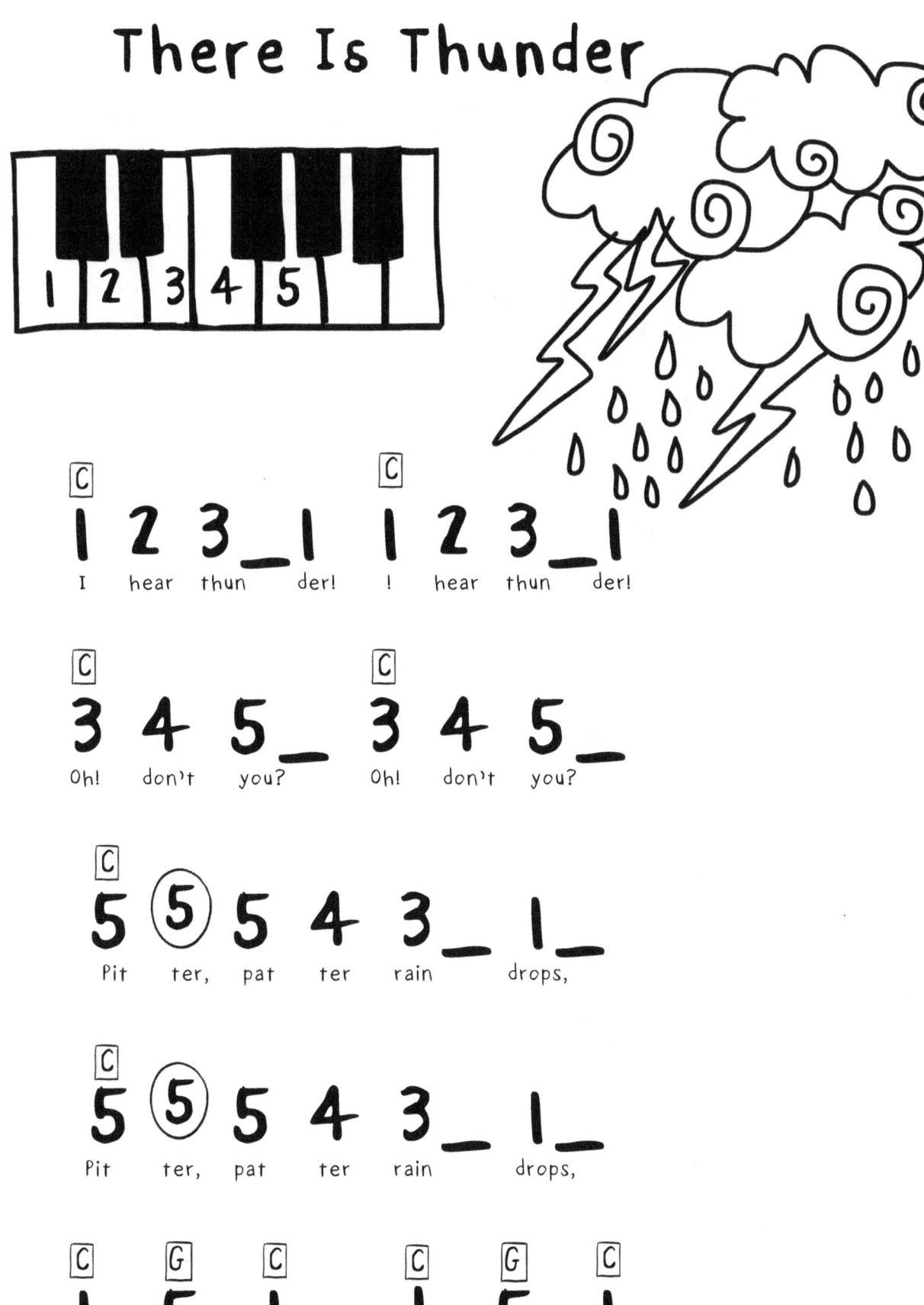

[C] 1 2 3_1 [C] 1 2 3_1
I hear thun der! I hear thun der!

[C] 3 4 5_ [C] 3 4 5_
Oh! don't you? Oh! don't you?

[C] 5 (5) 5 4 3_ 1_
Pit ter, pat ter rain drops,

[C] 5 (5) 5 4 3_ 1_
Pit ter, pat ter rain drops,

[C] 1 [G] 5_1_ [C] 1 [G] 5_1
I'm wet through! I'm wet through!

★ This is the same melody as Are You Sleeping, but with different words.

♡ 140

Name of YOUR Song _____

Write in your own words under the sandwiches.
Make sure to put the chord above the word
where you should play that chord.

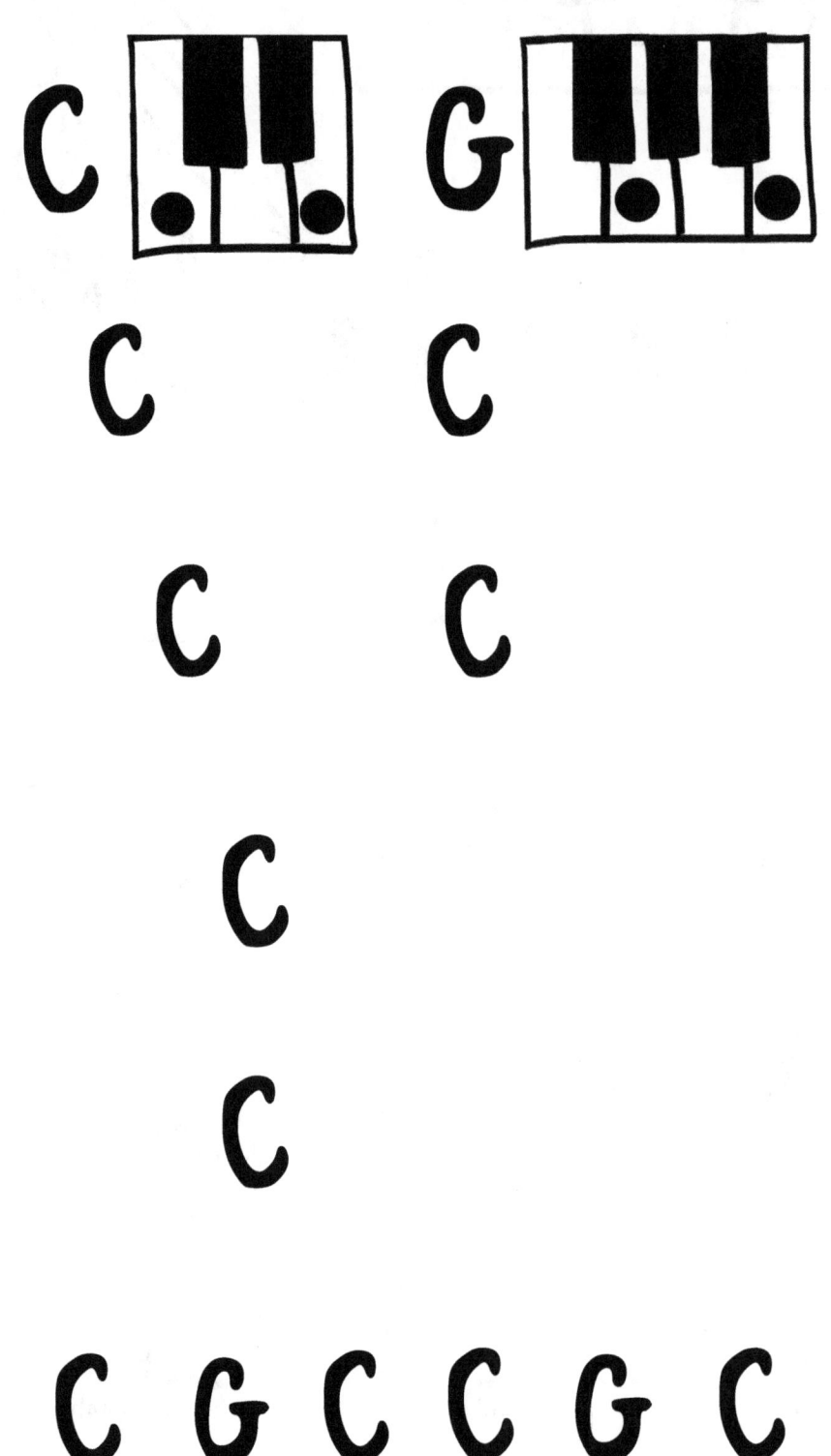

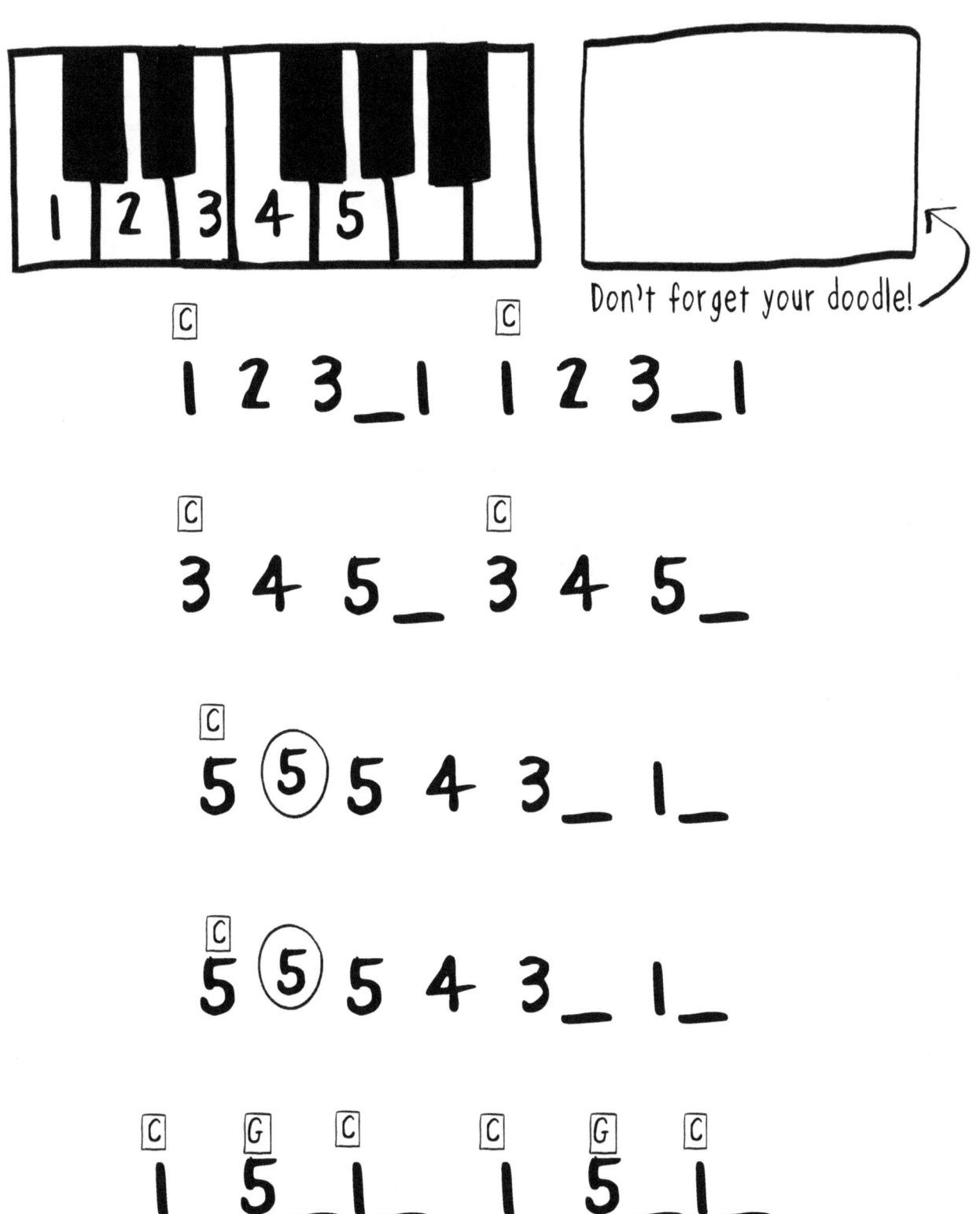

Song in This Category

The Farmer in the Dell……………………145

Songs with C and F Chords

C / **F**

RH on C

1 2 3 4 5

♡144

The Farmer in the Dell

F   F
The farmer in the dell,

F   F
The farmer in the dell,

F   F
Hi-ho, the derry-o,

C   F
The farmer in the dell.

> Extra Verses or Extra Lyric Ideas

The farmer takes a wife.
The wife takes a child.
The child takes a nurse.
The nurse takes a cow.
The cow takes a dog.
The dog takes a cat.
The cat takes a rat.
The rat takes the cheese.
The cheese stands alone.

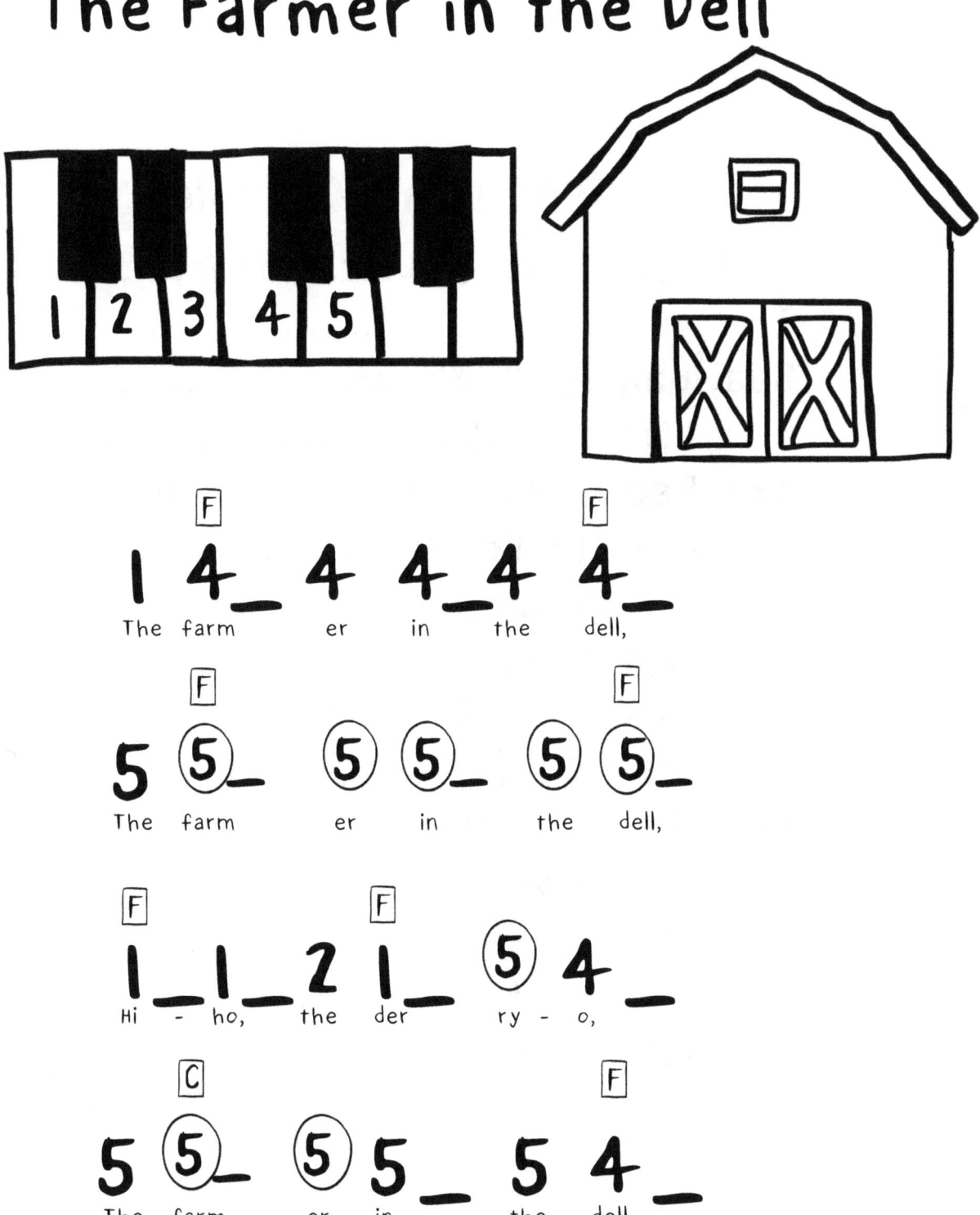

Songs in This Category

Twinkle, Twinkle Little Star............149
The ABC's...........................151
Baa, Baa Black Sheep...................153
Five Little Ducks......................155
The Bear Went Over the Mountain..157
I'm a Little Teapot....................159
Hickory Dickory Dock...................161
This Old Man...........................163
He's Got the Whole World...............165
Alice the Camel........................167
Peas Porridge Hot......................169
On Top of Spaghetti....................171
Humpty Dumpty..........................173
Lavender's Blue........................175
For He's a Jolly Good Fellow...........177

Songs with C F and G Chords

C | F | G

RH on C

1 2 3 4 5

Twinkle, Twinkle Little Star

C C F C
Twinkle, twinkle little star,

F C G C
How I wonder what you are.

C F C G
Up above the world so high.

C F C G
Like a diamond in the sky.

C C F C
Twinkle, twinkle little star,

F C G C
How I wonder what you are.

Twinkle, Twinkle Little Star

[C] 1 1 [C] 5 5 [F] ⑤ ⑤ [C] 5 —
Twin kle, twin kle lit tle star,

[F] 4 4 [C] 3 3 [G] 2 2 [C] 1 —
How I won der what you are.

[C] 5 5 [F] 4 4 [C] 3 3 [G] 2 —
Up a bove the world so high.

[C] 5 5 [F] 4 4 [C] 3 3 [G] 2 —
Like a dia mond in the sky.

[C] 1 1 [C] 5 5 [F] ⑤ ⑤ [C] 5 —
Twin kle, twin kle lit tle star,

[F] 4 4 [C] 3 3 [G] 2 2 [C] 1 —
How I won der what you are.

*So, I want you to see how the next three songs are actually the same melody!

♡ 150

The ABC's - The Alphabet

C   F   G
(piano chord diagrams)

C   C   F   C
A B C D E F G

F   C   G   C
H I J K L M N O P

C   F C   G
Q   R S T U V

C F C   G
W X Y and Z

C   C   F C
Now I know my A B C's.

F   C   G   C
Next time won't you sing with me?

151 ☆

The ABC's - The Alphabet

C	C	F	C
1 1	5 5	⑤ ⑤	5_
A B	C D	E F	G

F	C	G	C
4 4	3 3	2 2 2 2	1_
H I	J K	L M N O	P

C	F	C	G
5 5	4_	3 3	2_
Q R	S	T U	V

C	F	C	G
5 5 5_	4_	3 3	2_
Dou ble u	X	Y and	z.

C	C	F	C
1 1	5 5	⑤ ⑤	5_
Now I	know my	A B	C's.

F	C	G	C
4 4	3 3	2 2	1_
Next time	won't you	sing with	me?

★ This is the same melody as Twinkle Twinkle Little Star but with different words and rhythm.

♡ 152

Baa, Baa Black Sheep

C C F C

Baa, baa, black sheep, have you any wool?

F C G C

Yes sir, yes sir, three bags full.

C F C G

One for the master. One for the dame.

C F C G

One for the little boy who lives down the lane.

C C F C

Baa, baa, black sheep, have you any wool?

F C G C

Yes sir, yes sir, three bags full.

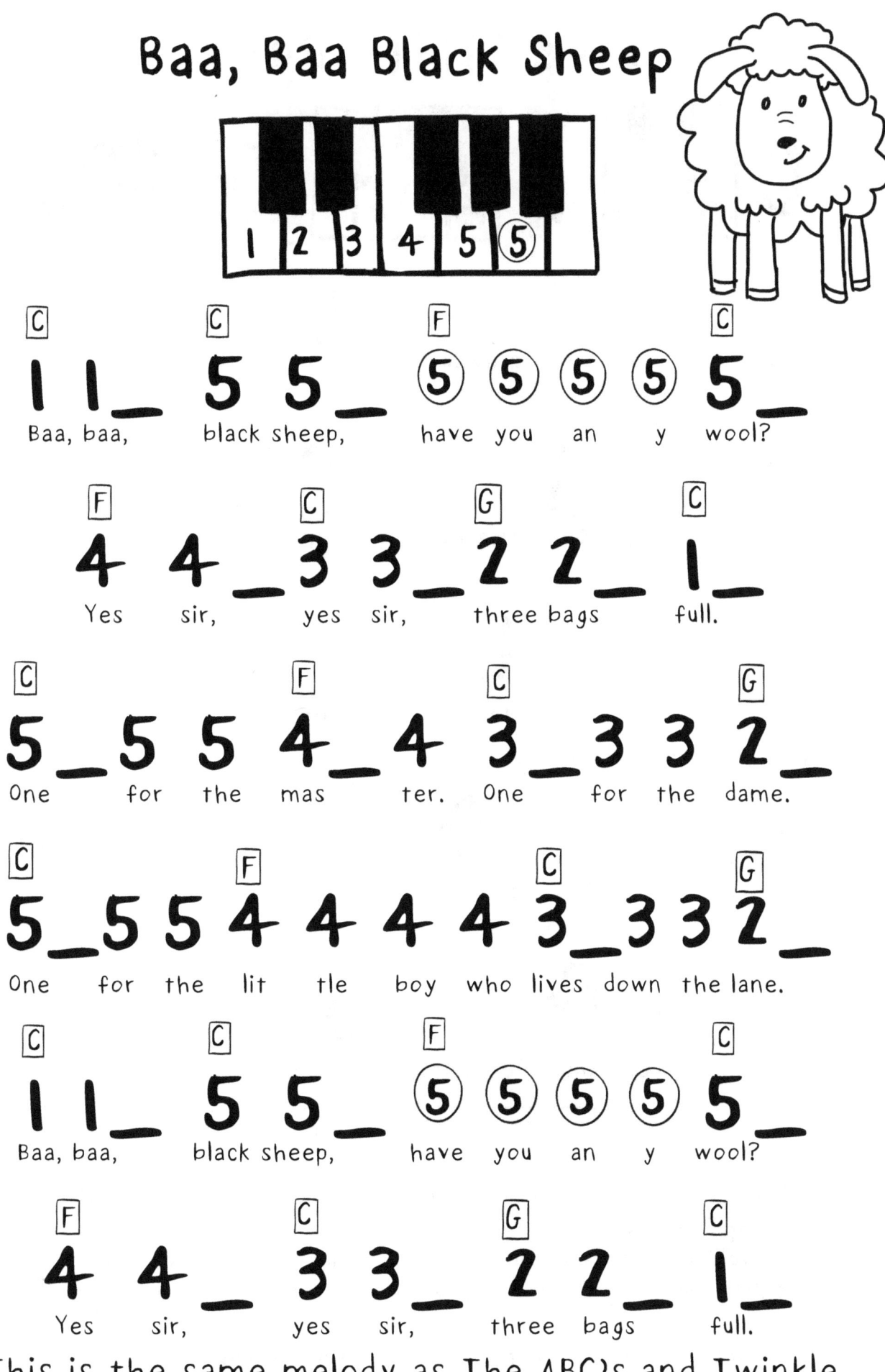

Five Little Ducks

C   **F**   **G**

      C   G
Five little ducks went out one day,

     G   C
Over the hills and far away.

       C
Mother duck said,

       G
"Quack, quack, quack, quack,"

    G   G   C
But only four little ducks came back.

> Extra Verses or Extra Lyric Ideas

Four little ducks went out one day, but only three little ducks came back.
Three little ducks went out one day, but only two little ducks came back.
Two little ducks went out one day, but only one little duck came back.
One little duck went out one day, but none of the five little ducks came back.

Sad mother duck went out one day, over the hills and far away.
Mother duck called "quack quack quack QUACK" and all of the five little ducks came back.

Five Little Ducks

[C] 3_ 5 5 5_3 [G] 3_ 2 2_
Five   lit tle ducks went out   one day,

[G] 2 5 5 5 2 [C] 2_ 1 1_
O ver the hills and far   a way.

[C] 3 3 5 5 3 [G] 3 2 4_
Mo ther duck said, "Quack, quack, quack, quack"

4 [G] 5_ 5 5_
But   on   ly   four

4 4 [G] 3_ 2 [C] 1_
Lit tle ducks came back.

♡ 156

The Bear Went Over the Mountain

C   F

The bear went over the mountain.

G   C

The bear went over the mountain.

C   F   G   C

The bear went over the mountain, to see what he could see.

G   C G   C

To see what he could see, to see what he could see.

C   F

The other side of the mountain,

G   C

The other side of the mountain,

C   F   G   C

The other side of the mountain was all that he could see.

> Extra Verses or Extra Lyric Ideas

Use other animals to go over the mountain:
The elephant went over the mountain.
The giraffe went over the mountain.
The deer went over the mountain.
The squirrel went over the mountain.

157 ☆

The Bear Went Over the Mountain

[C] 1 3_3 3 2 3   [F] 4_3
☆ The bear went o ver the   moun tain.
  The o ther side of the   moun tain.

[G] 3 2_2 2 1 2   [C] 3_1
   The bear went o ver the   moun tain.
   The o ther side of the   moun tain.

[C] 2 3_3 3 2 3   [F] 4_⑤_
   The bear went o ver the   moun tain,
   The o ther side of the   moun tain,

⑤ [G] 5_5 4 [C] 2 1_
   To see what he could see.
   was all that he could see. ♡ → 2nd time **end here** ♡

3 [G] 5_5 ⑤_⑤ [C] 5_
   To see what he could see.
                                → 1st time **repeat to** ☆

*This is actually the same melody the song
For He's a Jolly Good Fellow on page 177.

♡ 158

I'm a Little Teapot

C   C F C

I'm a little teapot short and stout.

F C G C

Here is my handle. Here is my spout.

C   C

When I get all steamed up,

F C

Hear me shout,

C C G C

Just tip me over and pour me out!

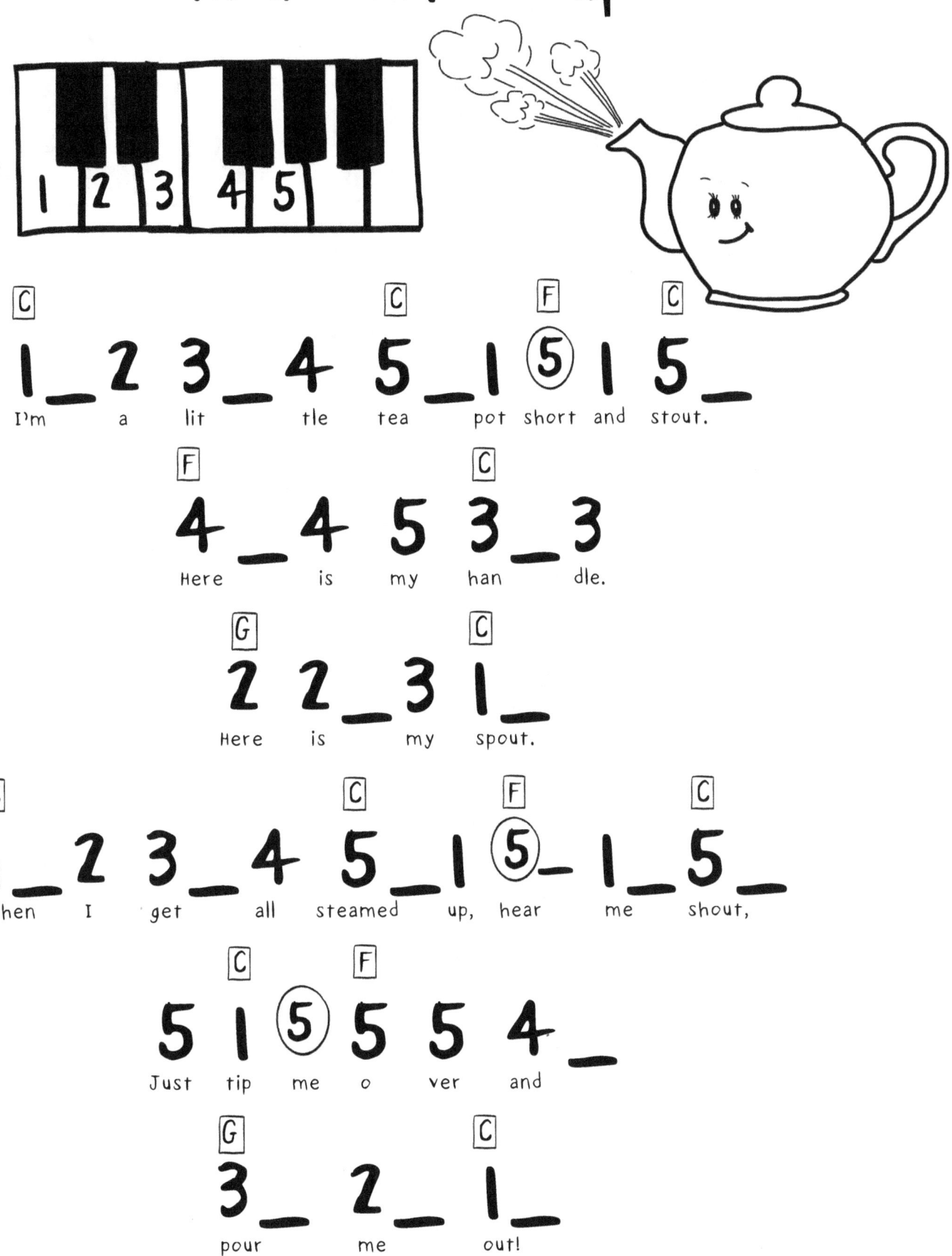

Hickory Dickory Dock

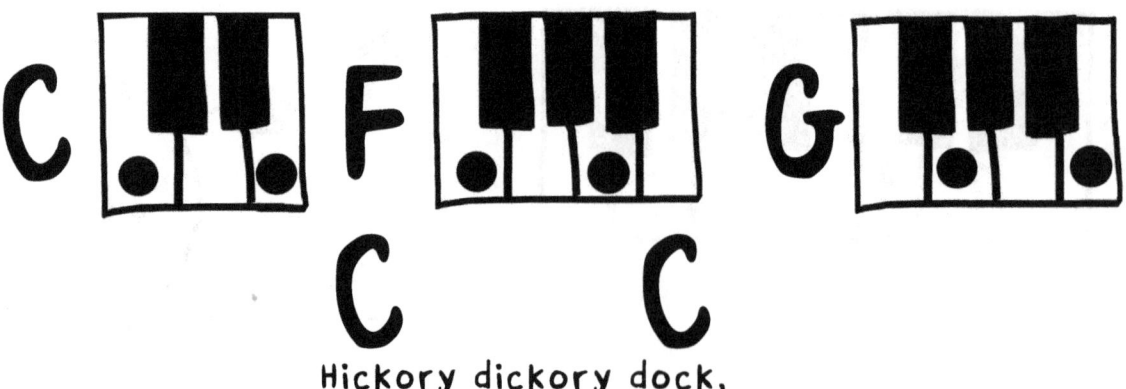

C   **C**

Hickory dickory dock,

C   **C**

The mouse ran up the clock.

C

The clock struck one. Ding!

F

The mouse ran down.

G   **C**

Hickory dickory dock.

> Extra Verses or Extra Lyric Ideas

Make the clock have different hours and make the bell ring that number of times!
The clock struck two... ding, ding.
The clock stuck three... ding, ding, ding.

Hickory Dickory Dock

[C]   [C]
3   4   5   4   3   2   3_
Hick or y dick or y dock,

[C]   [C]
3   3_ 5   4_ 2   3_
The mouse ran up the clock.

          [C]
3   3_ 3   5_
The clock struck one.   Ding!

     [F]
5   4_   4   ⑤_
The mouse ran down.

[G]   [C]
5   ⑤   5   4   3   2   1_
Hick o ry dick o ry dock

♡ 162

This Old Man

C **F** **G**

C   C

This old man, he plays one.

F   G

He plays knick knack on my thumb

C

With a knick knack paddy wack

C

Give a dog a bone.

G   C

This old man comes rolling home.

> Extra Verses or Extra Lyric Ideas

He plays two. He plays knick knack on my shoe.
He plays three. He plays knick knack on my knee.
He plays four. He plays knick knack on my door.
He plays five. He plays knick knack on my hive.
He plays six. He plays knick knack on my sticks.
He plays seven. He plays knick knack up to heaven.
He plays eight. He plays knick knack on my plate.
He plays nine. He plays knick knack on my spine.
He plays ten. He plays knick knack now and then.

This Old Man

[C]   [C]

5_ 3 5_   5_ 3 5_
This old man, he plays one.

[F]   [G]

(5) 5 4 3   2 3 4_
He plays knick knack on my thumb.

         [C]

3 4 5_ 1_   1 1 1_
With a knick knack pad dy wack

[C]

1 2 3 4 5_
Give a dog a bone.

[G]   [C]

5_ 2 2_ 4   3 2 1_
This old man came rol ling home.

♡ 164

He's Got the Whole World

C C C C
He's got the whole world in his hands.

G G G G
He's got the whole world in his hands.

C C C C
He's got the whole world in his hands.

G G C
He's got the whole world in his hands.

> Extra Verses or Extra Lyric Ideas

Choose other people and things he's got in his hands.
He's got you and me in his hands.
He's got all the little babies.
He's got the sisters and the brothers.
He's got everyone's house in his hands.

He's Got the Whole World

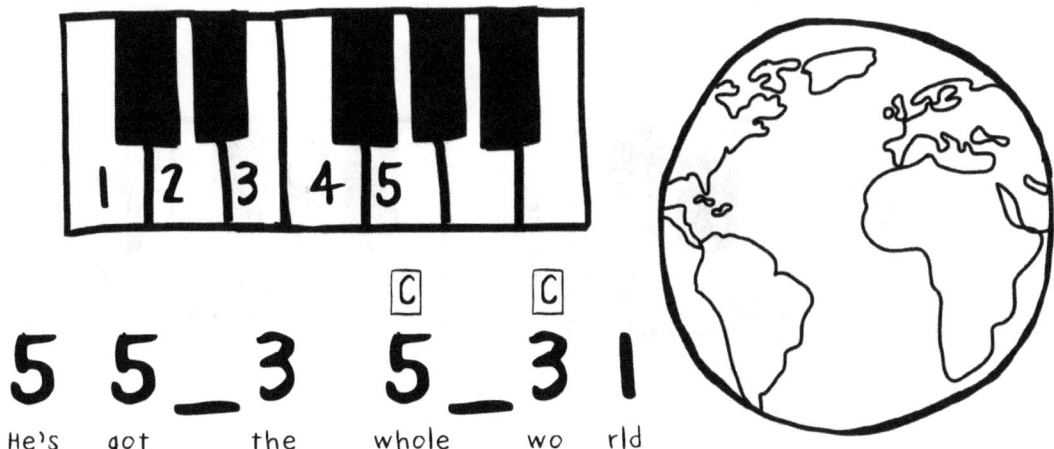

5　5_3　[C]5_3　[C]1
He's　got　the　whole　wo　rld

[C]5　(5)_5_　5　5_3
In　his　hands.　He's　got　the

[G]4_　[G]2　[G](1)　5　[G](5)_5
Whole　wor　ld　in　his　hands.

5　5　3　[C]5_3　[C]1
He's　got　the　whole　wo　rld

[C]5　(5)_5_　5　5　3
In　his　hands.　He's　got　the

[G]5　5_　[G]4　2_[C]1_
whole world　in　his　hands.

♡ 166

Alice the Camel

C   C
Alice the camel has two humps.

G   C
Alice the camel has two humps.

C   C
Alice the camel has two humps.

   G   C
So go, Alice, go.

| Extra Verses or Extra Lyric Ideas |

Change the number if you like:
Alice the camel has three humps.
Alice the camel has four humps.

Alice the Camel

[C]

| | | _ | | | | _
Al ice   the ca mel has

[C]

3 _ 1 _
Two   humps.

[G]

2 2 _ 2 2 2 2 _
Al ice the ca mel has

This sandwich is before the words because it should be played before you sing the words. → [C]

3 _ 1 _
Two   humps.

[C]

| | _ | | | | _
Al ice   the ca mel has

[C]

3 _ 1 _
Two   humps.

[G]   [C]

1 3 _ 2 2 _ 1 _
So go, Al ice, go.

♡ 168

Peas Porridge Hot

C　　　F　　　C

Peas porridge hot, peas porridge cold,

F　　C　　G　　C

Peas porridge in the pot, nine days old.

C　　　F　　　C

Some like it hot. Some like it cold,

F　　C　　G　　C

Some like it in the pot, nine days old.

Peas Porridge Hot

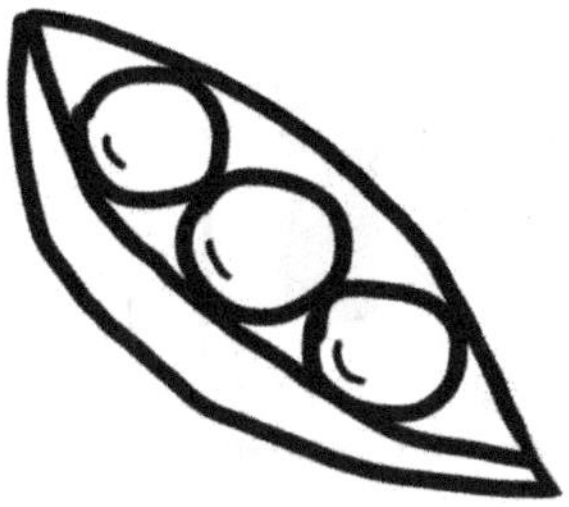

[C]
1_ 1 1 5_
Peas porr idge hot,

[F]   [C]
(5)_ (5) (5) 5_
Peas porr idge cold,

[F]   [C]
4_ 4 4 3 3 3_
Peas porr idge in the pot,

[G]   [C]
2 2 1_
Nine days old.

[C]
1_ 1 1 5_
Some like it hot.

[F]   [C]
(5)_ (5) (5) 5_
Some like it cold.

[F]   [C]
4_ 4 4 3 3 3_
Some like it in the pot,

[G]   [C]
2 2 1_
Nine days old.

♡ 170

On Top of Spaghetti

          F   **C**
On top of spaghetti, all covered with cheese,

          G
I lost my poor meatball,

          C
When somebody sneezed.

         F   **C**
It rolled off the table and onto the floor,

        G   **C**
And then my poor meatball rolled right out the door.

> Extra Verses or Extra Lyric Ideas

It rolled in the garden and under a bush,
And then my poor meatball was nothing but mush.

The mush was as tasty as tasty could be,
And early next summer it grew into a tree.

The tree was all covered with beautiful moss.
It grew great big meatballs and tomato sauce.

So if you eat spaghetti all covered with cheese,
Hold on to your meatball and don't ever sneeze.

On Top of Spaghetti

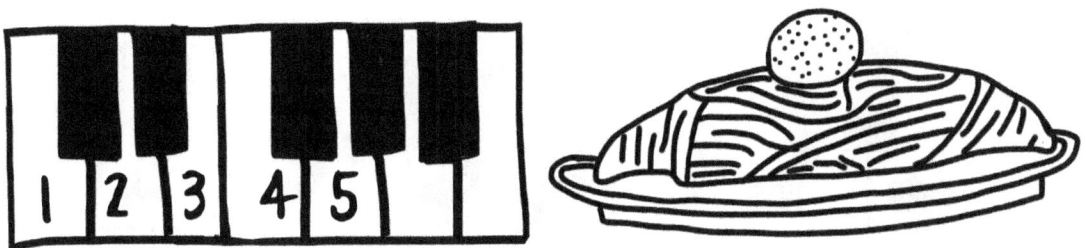

1 1 3 5 [F]1_ ⑤_
On top of spa ghet ti,

⑤ 4 5 ⑤ [C]5_
All cov ered with cheese,

1 1 3 5 [G]5_ 2_
I lost my poor meat ball,

3 4 3 2 [C]1_
When some bo dy sneezed.

1 1 3 5_ [F]1_ ⑤_ ⑤ 4 5 ⑤ [C]5_
It rolled off the ta ble and on to the floor,

1 1 3 5 [G]5_ 2_
And then my poor meat ball

3 4 3 2 [C]1_
Rolled right out the door.

♡172

Humpty Dumpty

C   G   C
Humpty Dumpty sat on a wall.

C   G   C
Humpty Dumpty had a great fall.

F   C
All the king's horses,

G   C
And all the king's men,

F   C
Couldn't put Humpty

G   C
Together again.

Humpty Dumpty

[C] 1_1 [G] 3_3 2 3 [C] 2 1_
Hump ty Dump ty sat on a wall.

[C] 3_3 [G] 5_5 4 5 [C] 4 3_
Hump ty Dump ty had a great fall.

[F] (5) (5) (5) [C] 5 5 5
All the king's hor ses, and

[G] 4 4 4 [C] 3_
All the king's men,

[F] 4 4 4 [C] 3 3
Could n't put Hump ty

[G] 3 2 3 [C] 2 1_
to ge ther a gain.

♡ 174

Lavender's Blue

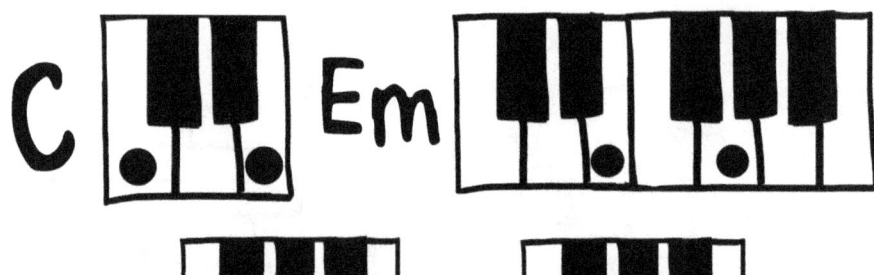

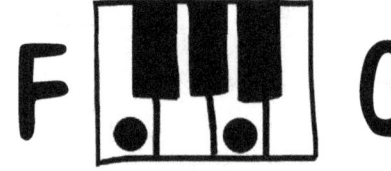 

C   Em
Lavender's blue, dilly dilly,

F   F
Lavender's green.

C   C
When you are king, dilly dilly,

F G C
I shall be queen.

> Extra Verses or Extra Lyric Ideas

Lavender's green, dilly dilly,
Lavender's blue.
If you love me, dilly dilly,
I will love you.

Let the birds sing, dilly dilly,
Let the lambs play.
We shall be safe, dilly dilly,
Out of harms way.

I love to dance, dilly dilly,
I love to sing.
When I am queen, dilly dilly,
You'll be my king.

Lavender's Blue

[C] [Em]
1 5 5 5_
La ven der's blue,

4 3 2 1
Dil ly dil ly,

[F] [F]
1_ (5) (5) (5)_
La ven der's green.

[C] [Em]
1 5 5 5_
When you are king,

4 3 2 1
Dil ly dil ly,

[F] [G] [C]
4_ 3_ 2_ 1_
I shall be queen.

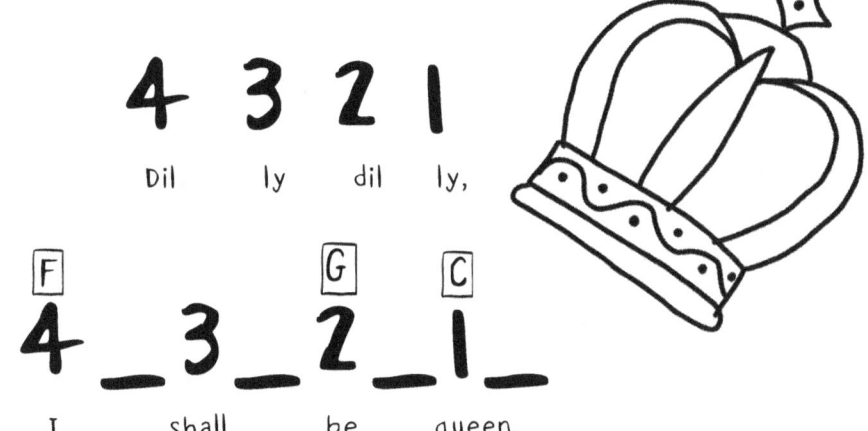

♡176

For He's a Jolly Good Fellow

C	F	G	C

For he's a jolly good fellow, for he's a jolly good fellow,

C	F	G	C

For he's a jolly good fellow, which nobody can deny.

C	C	C	C

Which nobody can deny, which nobody can deny,

C	F	G	C

For he's a jolly good fellow, for he's a jolly good fellow,

C	F	G	C

For he's a jolly good fellow, which nobody can deny!

For He's a Jolly Good Fellow

☆ 1 [C]3_3 3 2 3 [F]4_3
For he's a jol ly good fel low,

3 [G]2_2 2 1 2 [C]3_1_
For he's a jol ly good fel low,

2 [C]3_3 3 2 3 [F]4_⑤_
For he's a jol ly good fel low,

⑤ [G]5 5 5 4_ 2 [C]1_
Which no bo dy can de ny. ♡ 2nd time
→ end here ♡

[C]3 5 5 5 ⑤_ ⑤ [C]5_
Which no bo dy can de ny,

[C]3 5 5 5 ⑤_ ⑤ [C]5_
Which no bo dy can de ny! → 1st time
repeat to ☆

★This is actually the same melody as
The Bear Went Over the Mountain on page 157.

♡178

Songs in This Category

Old MacDonald Had a Farm............181
I'm Bringing Home a Baby Bumblebee..183
Do You Know the Muffin Man?...185
Six Little Ducks..........................187
Three Little Kittens....................189

Songs with RH on G

Old MacDonald Had a Farm

C   F C G C

Old MacDonald had a farm,   E-I-E-I-O

C   F C G C

And on his farm he had a cow,   E-I-E-I-O

C   C

With a moo moo here, and a moo moo there.

C C C C

Here a moo, there a moo, everywhere a moo moo.

C   F C G C

Old MacDonald had a farm,   E-I-E-I-O

> Extra Verses or Extra Lyric Ideas

And on the farm he had a pig. With an oink oink here.
And on that farm he had a cat. With a meow meow here.
And on that farm he had a dog. With a woof woof here.
And on that farm, he had a chicken. With a bawk bawk here.
And on that farm he had a rooster. With a cockadoodle here.

I'm Bringing Home a Baby Bumblebee

C   F C C
I'm bringing home a baby bumblebee.

G   G G   G
Won't my mommy be so proud of me?

C   F C C
I'm bringing home a baby bumblebee.

Ouch! It stung me!

> Extra Verses or Extra Lyric Ideas

I'm squishing up a baby bumblebee.
Yuck, it's all over.

I'm wiping off a baby bumblebee.
Now, I'm all clean.

I'm Bringing Home a Baby Bumblebee

G **C**
1 4 _ ⑤ 5 4
I'm bring ing home a

F **C** **C**
2 2 1 1 4 _
Ba by bum ble bee.

G **G**
5 5 ⑤ ⑤
Won't my mom my

G **G**
5 ⑤ 5 _ 4 2 _
Be so proud of me?

G **C**
1 4 ⑤ 5 4
I'm bring ing home a

F **C** **C**
2 2 1 1 4 _
Ba by bum ble bee.

Ouch! It stung me!

♡ 184

Do You Know the Muffin Man?

C   C

Oh, do you know the muffin man,

F   G

The muffin man, the muffin man?

C   C   F G C

Do you know the muffin man, that lives on Drury Lane?

C   C

Oh, yes, I know the muffin man,

F   G

The muffin man, the muffin man.

C   C   F G C

Oh, yes, I know the muffin man, that lives on Drury Lane.

Six Little Ducks

C   **G**

Six little ducks that I once knew,

G   **C**

Fast ones, skinny ones, fair ones too.

C   **G**

But the one little duck with the feather on his back,

G   **C**

He led the others with his quack, quack, quack.

G   **C**

Quack, quack, quack-quack, quack, quack.

G   **C**

He led the others with his quack, quack, quack.

> Extra Verses or Extra Lyric Ideas

Down to the river they would go,
Wibble wobble, wibble wobble to and fro.
But the one little duck with the feather on his back,
He led the others with a quack, quack, quack.

Home from the river they would come,
Wibble wobble, wibble wobble ho-hum-hum.

Six Little Ducks

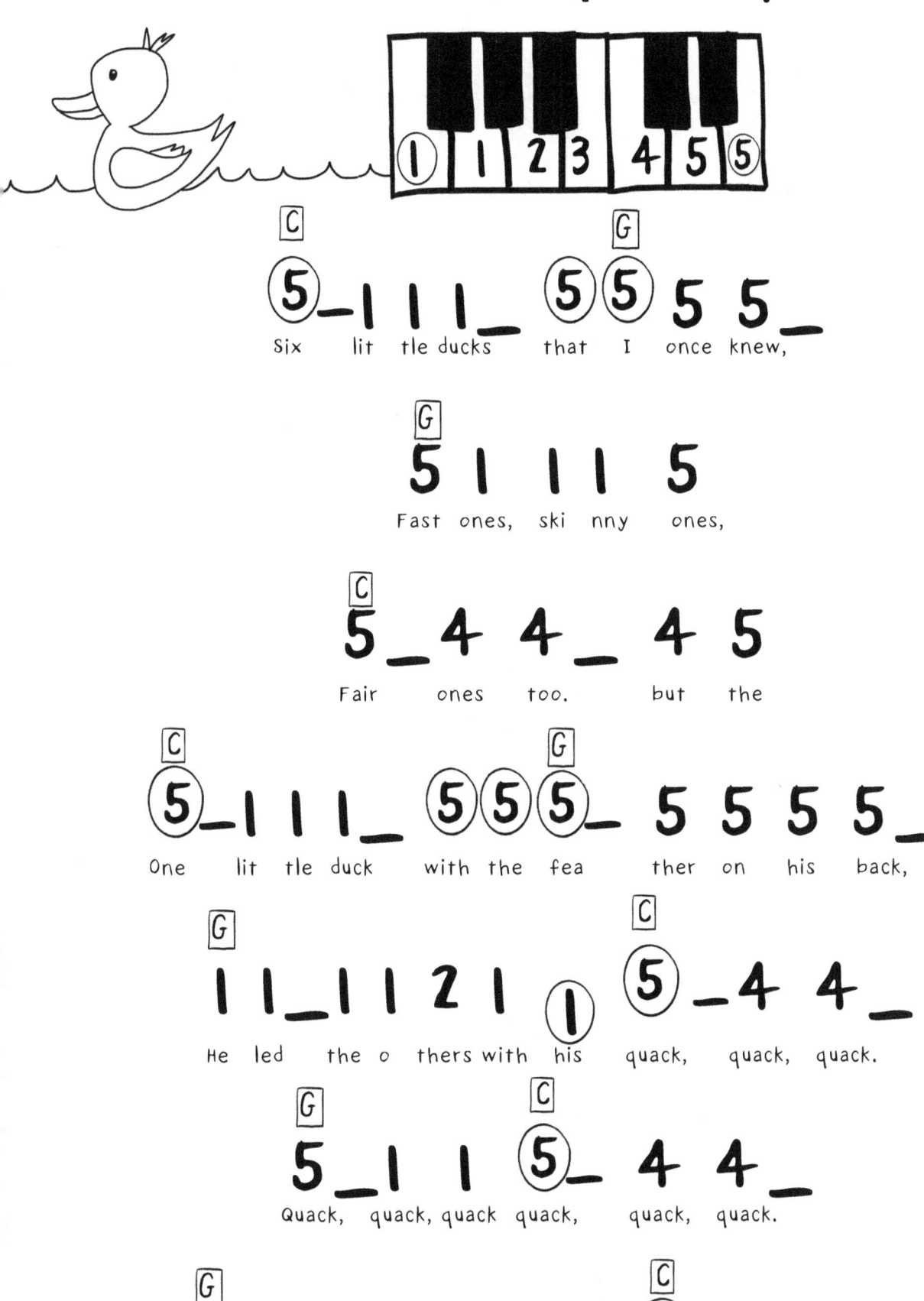

Three Little Kittens

C
Three little kittens

C
They lost their mittens

F G C
And they began to cry,

C   C
Meow, meow, meow, meow,

F G C
Meow, meow, meow.

> Extra Verses or Extra Lyric Ideas

What other animals lost their mittens?

Three little dogs lost their mittens and they began to cry, woof woof woof.
Three little ducks have lost their mittens and they began to cry, quack quack, quack.

Three Little Kittens

[C]
4 4 4 1 1 1
Three lit tle kit tens they

[C]
⑤_⑤ 4 4 4
Lost their mit tens and

[F]   [G]   [C]
5_5 3_3 4_
They be gan to cry,

[C]   [C]
4_1_ ⑤_4_
Meow, meow, meow meow.

[F] [G] [C]
5_ 3_ 4_
Meow, meow, meow.

♡190

Songs in This Category

If You're Happy and You Know It....... 193
Apples and Bananas...................... 195

Songs with RH on A

RH on B

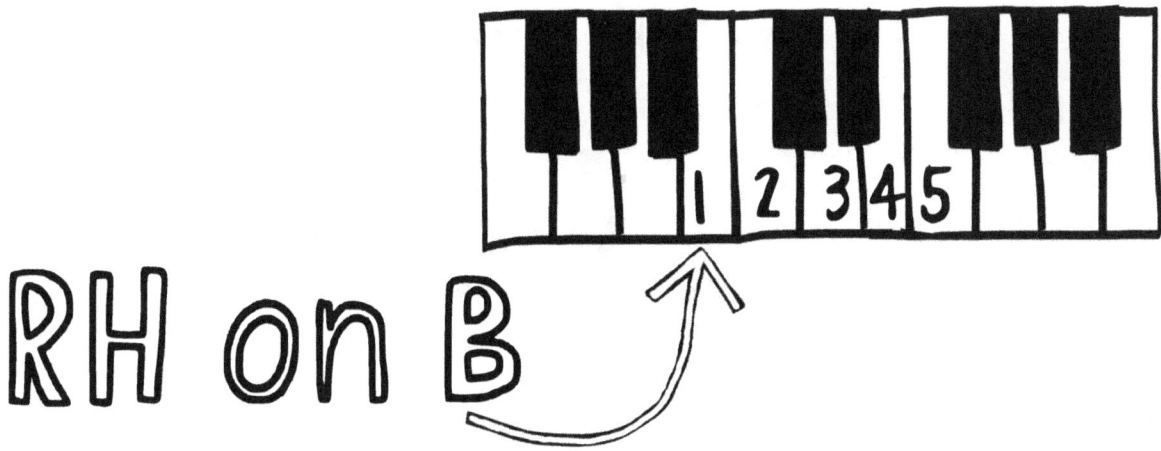

If You're Happy and You Know It

   G   C   C   G G

If you're happy and you know it, clap your hands.

    G   G   C C

If you're happy and you know it, clap your hands.

       F   F

If you're happy and you know it,

      C   C

Then your face will surely show it.

    G   G   C

If you're happy and you know it, clap your hands.

> **Extra Verses or Extra Lyric Ideas**

Try other emotions:

If you're sad and you know it, say boo hoo!
If you're angry and you know it, stomp your feet.
If you're excited and you know it, shout hooray!

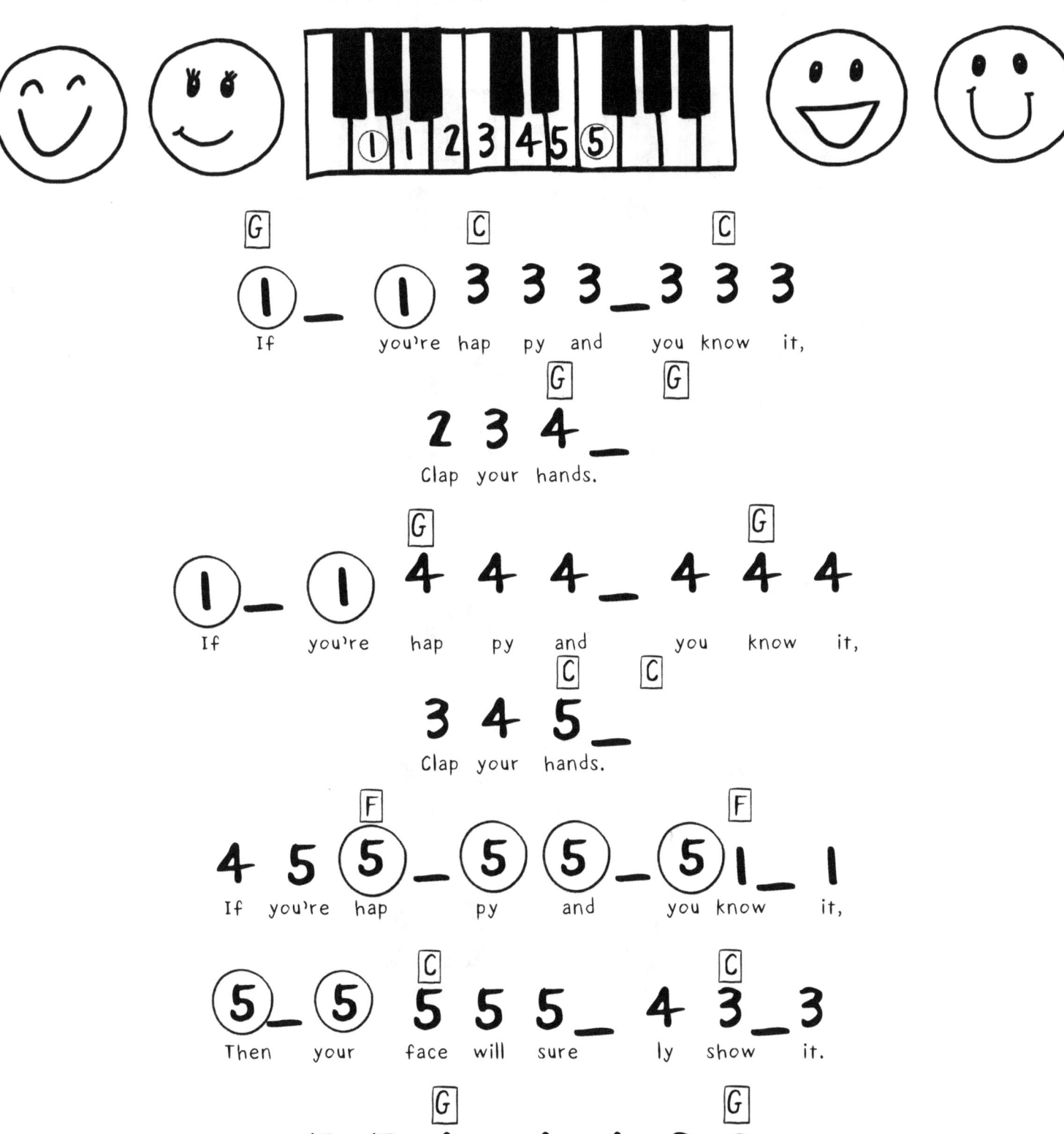

Apples and Bananas

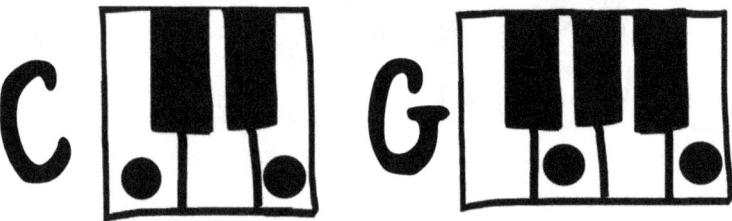

This chord is before the song starts so play it before you start singing.

G   **C C C**
         I like to eat, eat, eat,

C   **G**
       apples and bananas.

G   **G G G**
         I like to eat, eat, eat,

G   **C C**
       apples and bananas.

> Extra Verses or Extra Lyric Ideas

Take the words eat, apples and bananas and use different vowel sounds to make the words sound silly.

Apples and Bananas

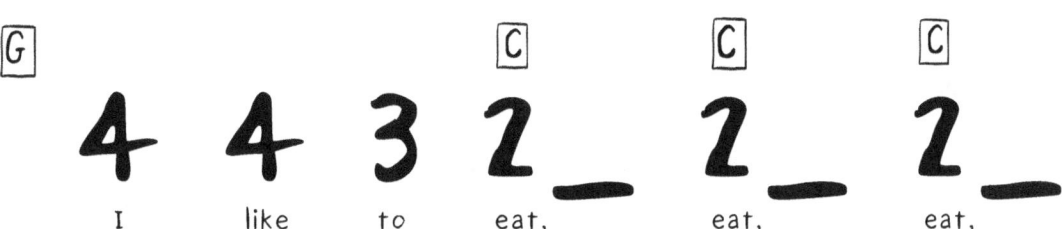

♡196

Songs in This Category

A Switcheroo Song.....................199
The More We Get Together.......200
Bingo..203
Hey Diddle Diddle........................205
Yankee Doodle.............................207
Rockabye Baby............................209
The Ants Go Marching................212
Skidamarink...................................216
Happy Birthday............................219

Songs That SWITCH RH Positions

Make sure to LOOK at any new right hand positions and move your hand to play them. Try this on the next page before the songs.

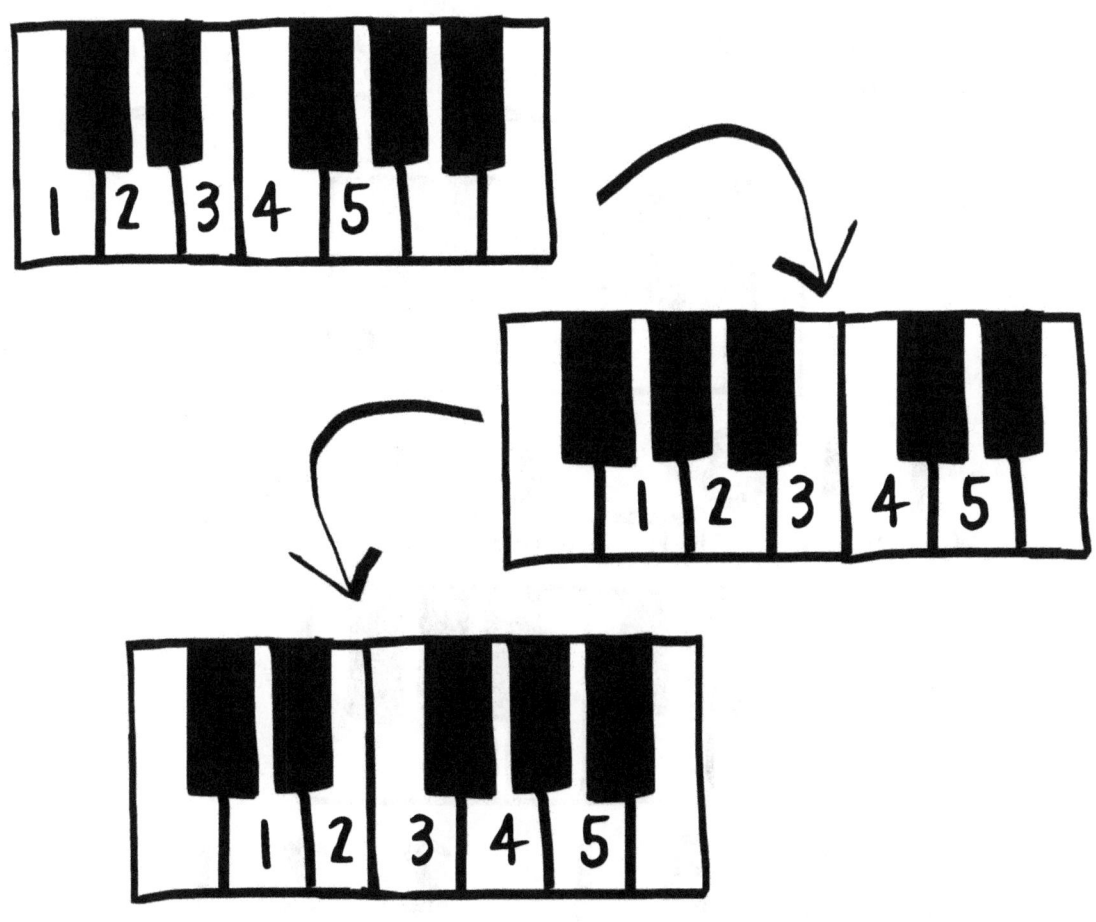

A Switcheroo Song

1 2 3 1_ 3 2 1_
I like to switch, switch er oo.

1 2 3 1_ 2 3_
Can you switch too? Woo hoo!

1 1 3_ 2 2 4_
Watch me switch. Here I go.

5 5 3 1 2 2 1_
It is fun to switch er oo.

The More We Get Together

C   C   G   C
The more we get together, together, together.

C   C   G   C
The more we get together, the happier we'll be.

G   C   G   C
'Cause your friends are my friends and my friends are your friends.

C   C   G   C
The more we get together, the happier we'll be.

[Extra Verses or Extra Lyric Ideas]

Try other things we can do together:

The more we read together. 'Cause your books are my books.
The more we sing together. 'Cause your songs are my songs.
The more we dance together. 'Cause your dance is my dance.
The more we cook together. 'Cause your food is my food.

♡ 200

The More We Get Together

[C]
3 5_ ⑤ 5 4 [C] 3_ 1
The more we get to ge ther,

[G]
1 2_ 5 5 [C] 3 1
To ge ther, to ge ther.

[C]
3 5_ ⑤ 5 4 [C] 3_ 1
The more we get to ge ther,

[G]
1 2 2 5 [C] 5 1_
The hap pi er we'll be.

201 ☆

The More We Get Together

[G] [C]
4 5_1 1 ⑤_4 4
'Cause your friends are my friends and

[G] [C]
5_1 1 ⑤ 4
My friends are your friends.

[C] [C]
3 5_ ⑤ 5 4 3_ 1
The more we get to ge ther,

[G] [C]
1 2 2 5 5 1_
The hap pi er we'll be.

♡202

Bingo

C   C
There was a farmer who had a dog and

C G C
Bingo was his name-o.

C F   G C   C F
B-I-N-G-O,   B-I-N-G-O,   B-I-N-G-O,

G   C
And Bingo was his name-o.

> Extra Verses or Extra Lyric Ideas

Spell your name instead of Bingo!

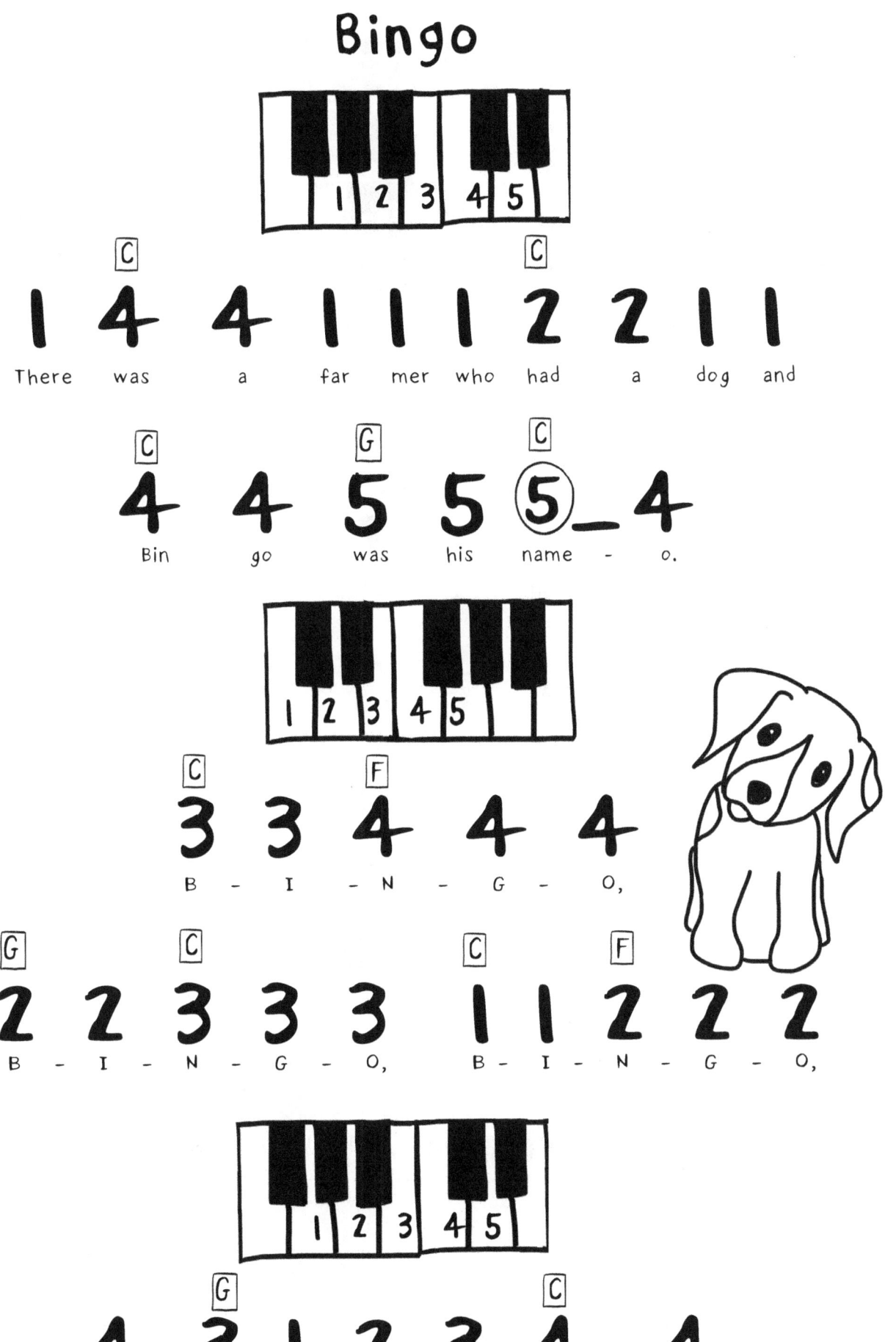

Hey Diddle Diddle

C   G

Hey Diddle diddle the cat and the fiddle,

C   G

The cow jumped over the moon.

F   C

The little dog laughed to see such a sight and

G   C

The dish ran away with the spoon.

Hey Diddle Diddle

[C]
3 3 3 3 4 5
Hey Did dle did dle the

[G]
2 2 2 2 1 2
Cat and the fid dle, the

[C]   [G]
3_ 3 3 4 5 2_
Cow jumped o ver the moon.

[F]
3 4 4 4 4 5 (5)
The lit tle dog laugh ed to

[C]
5 3 1 2 3 5
See such a sight and the

[G]   [C]
1 1 1 1 2 3 4_
Dish ran a way with the spoon.

♡206

Yankee Doodle

C   C   C   G

Yankee Doodle went to town riding on a pony.

C   F   G   C

Stuck a feather in his hat and called it macaroni.

F   F

Yankee Doodle, keep it up,

C   C

Yankee Doodle dandy.

F   F

Mind the music and the step

G   C

And with the girls be handy.

Yankee Doodle

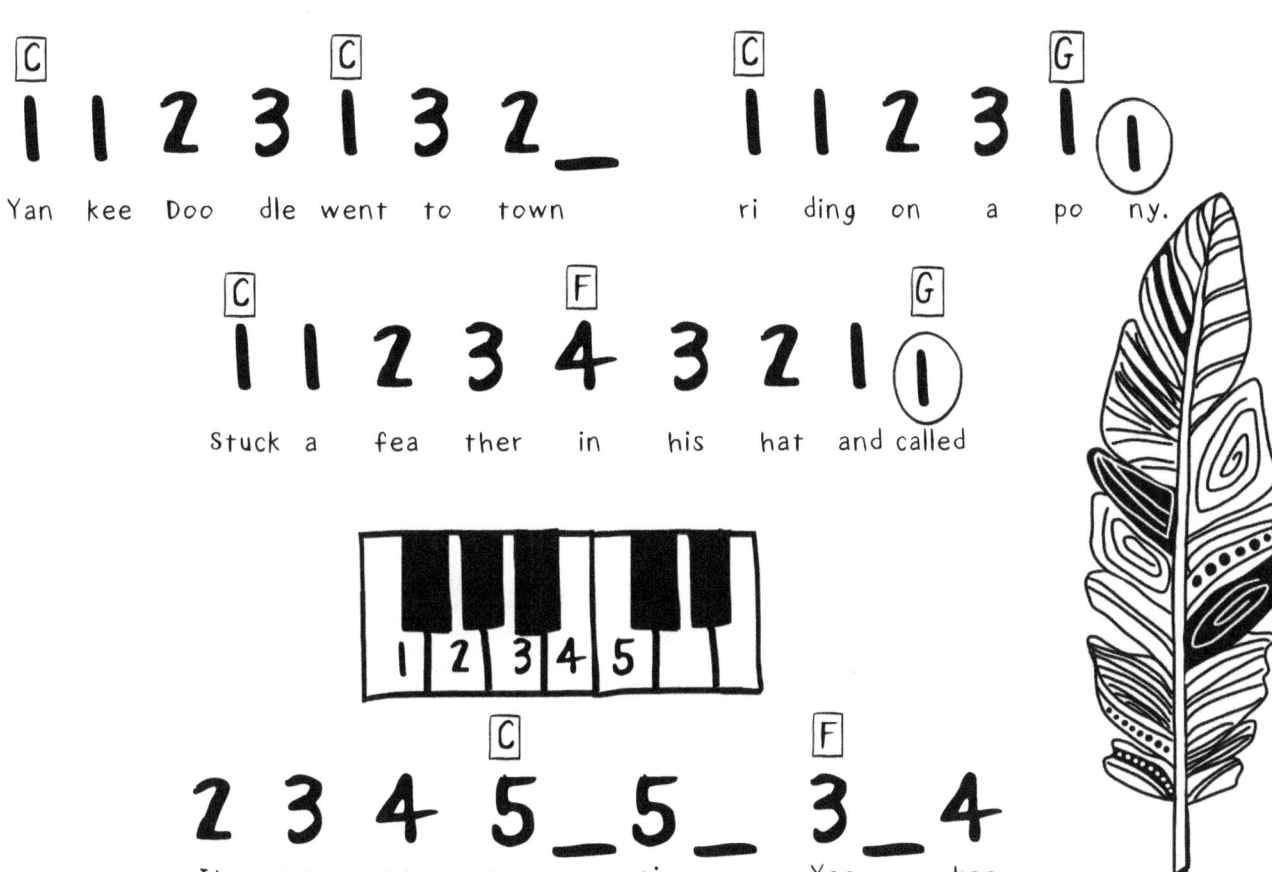

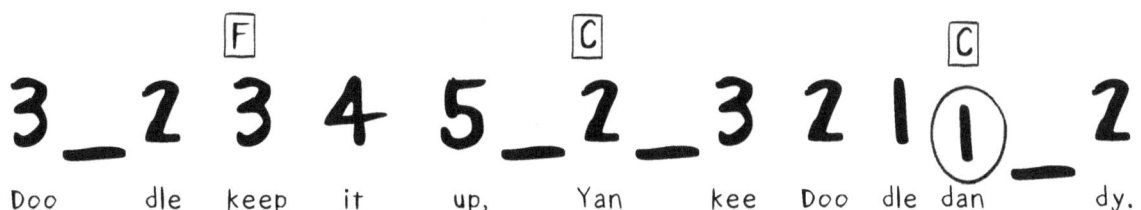

♡ 208

Rockabye Baby

C   C C   G
Rockabye baby, in the treetop.

F   G   G   C
When the wind blows, the cradle will rock.

C   C   C   G
When the bough breaks, the cradle will fall.

F   G F G C
And down will come baby, cradle and all.

Rockabye Baby

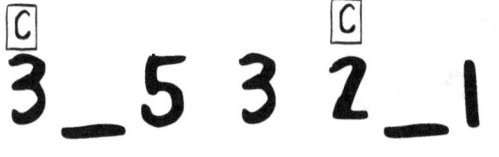
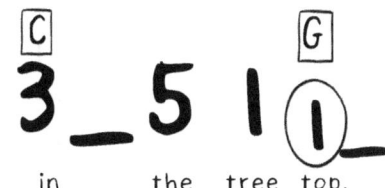

[C] 3_5 3 [C] 2_1 [C] 3_5 1 [G] (1)_
Rock a bye ba by, in the tree top.

[F] 4_5 4 [G] 3_
When the wind blows,

2 2 1 [G] (5) [C] 5_
The cra dle will rock.

[C] 3_5 3 [C] 2_1 [C] 3_5 1 [G] (1)_
When the bough breaks, the cra dle will fall

(5) [F] 5_1 4 [G] 3 1_ [F] 2
And down will come ba by, cra -

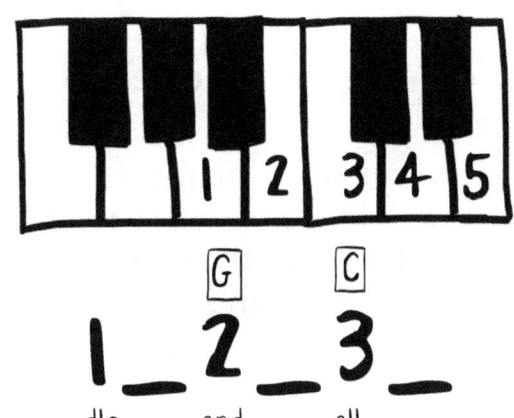

[G] 1_ [C] 2_ 3_
dle and all.

♡210

Listening Practice

The next song is THE ANTS GO MARCHING.
So, I would like to give you some listening practice
that sounds like marching and also
ones inspired by other bugs, such as bees.

MUSIC PIECE NUMBER ① March in D Major by Johann Sebastian Bach

Let's march. The ants go marching along and we can listen to this march by the composer Bach and march along with the music. One, two three, four. Move along, two, three, four.

MUSIC PIECE NUMBER ② Surprise Symphony No. 94 in G Major by Joseph Haydn

Surprise! The ants have taken over your picnic. Listen for the "surprise" in this song when there is a loud part after the quiet part.

MUSIC PIECE NUMBER ③ Flight of the Bumblebee by Rimsky Korsakov

Another bug that can interrupt a picnic and show up in the summer are bumblebees. This song is like a group of bumblebees buzzing about. Can you make a buzzing bee with your finger and buzz and fly with the music? Or pretend to be a bee yourself?

The Ants Go Marching

Notice that this E sandwich doesn't have an m. It's a major sandwich and not the same as the Em (Page 280 for more info).

Am   **Am**   **C**   **C**
The ants go marching one by one, hurrah, hurrah.

Am   **Am**   **C**   **C**
The ants go marching one by one, hurrah, hurrah.

C   **G**
The ants go marching one by one.

Am   **G**
The little one stops to suck his thumb,

AmE   **Am E**   **AmE**   **AmE**
And they all   go   march ing   down to the ground,

AmE   **Am**   **E**
To get out of the rain, BOOM! BOOM! BOOM!

> Extra Verses or Extra Lyric Ideas

The ants go marching one by one. The little one stops to suck his thumb.
The ants go marching two by two. The little one stops to tie his shoe.
The ants go marching three by three. The little one stops to climb a tree.
The ants go marching four by four. The little one stops to shut the door.
The ants go marching five by five. The little one stops to take a dive.
The ants go marching six by six. The little one stops to pick up sticks.
The ants go marching seven by seven. The little one stops to pray to heaven.
The ants go marching eight by eight. The little one stops to roller skate.
The ants go marching nine by nine. The little one stops to check the time.
The ants go marching ten by ten. The little one stops to shout, the end!

The Ants Go Marching

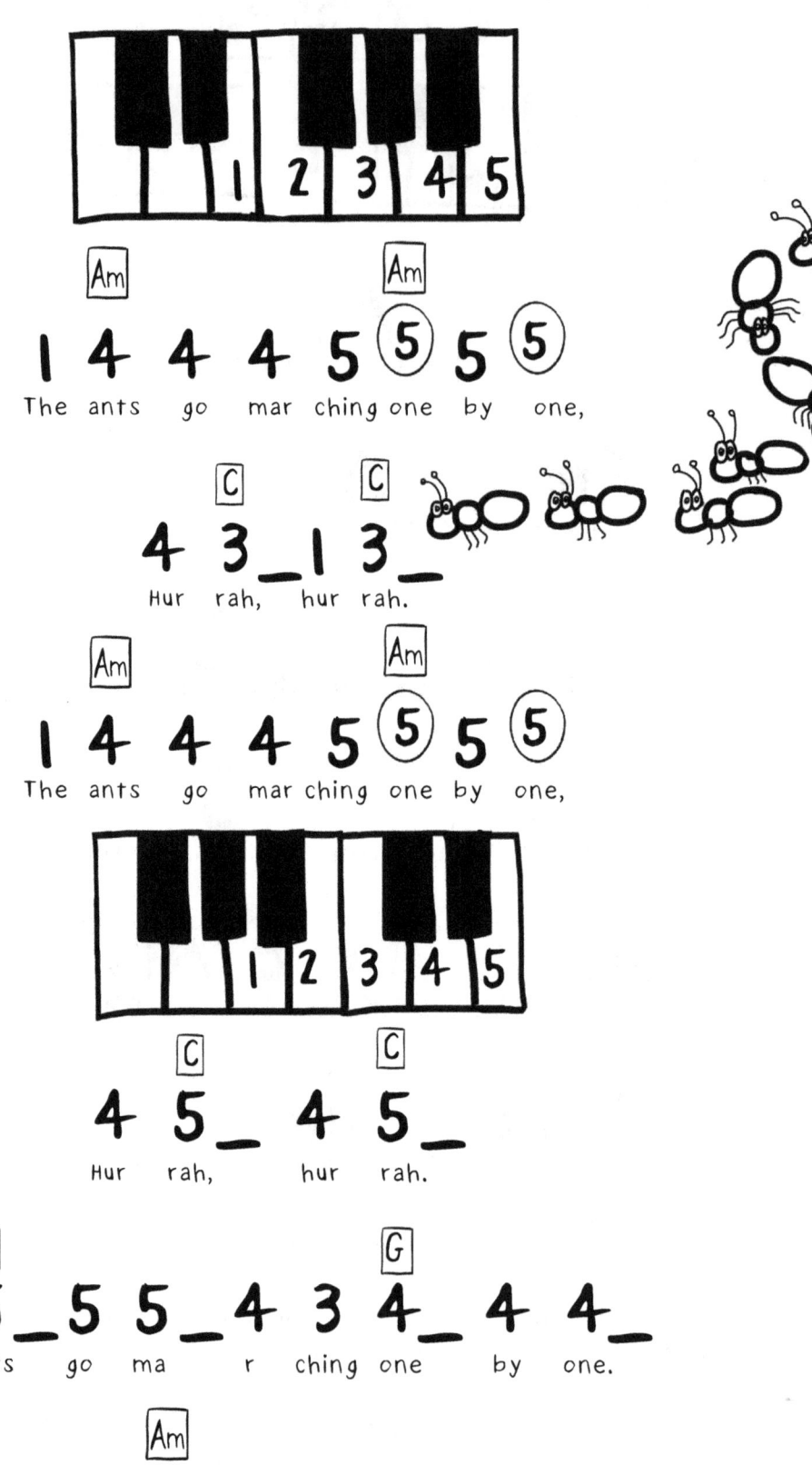

[Am] [Am]
1 4 4 4 5 ⑤ 5 ⑤
The ants go mar ching one by one,

[C] [C]
4 3_1 3_
Hur rah, hur rah.

[Am] [Am]
1 4 4 4 5 ⑤ 5 ⑤
The ants go mar ching one by one,

[C] [C]
4 5_ 4 5_
Hur rah, hur rah.

[C] [G]
3 5_5 5_4 3 4_ 4 4_
The ants go ma r ching one by one.

[Am]
2 3 3 3 3 2 1
The lit tle one sto ps to

213 ☆

The Ants Go Marching

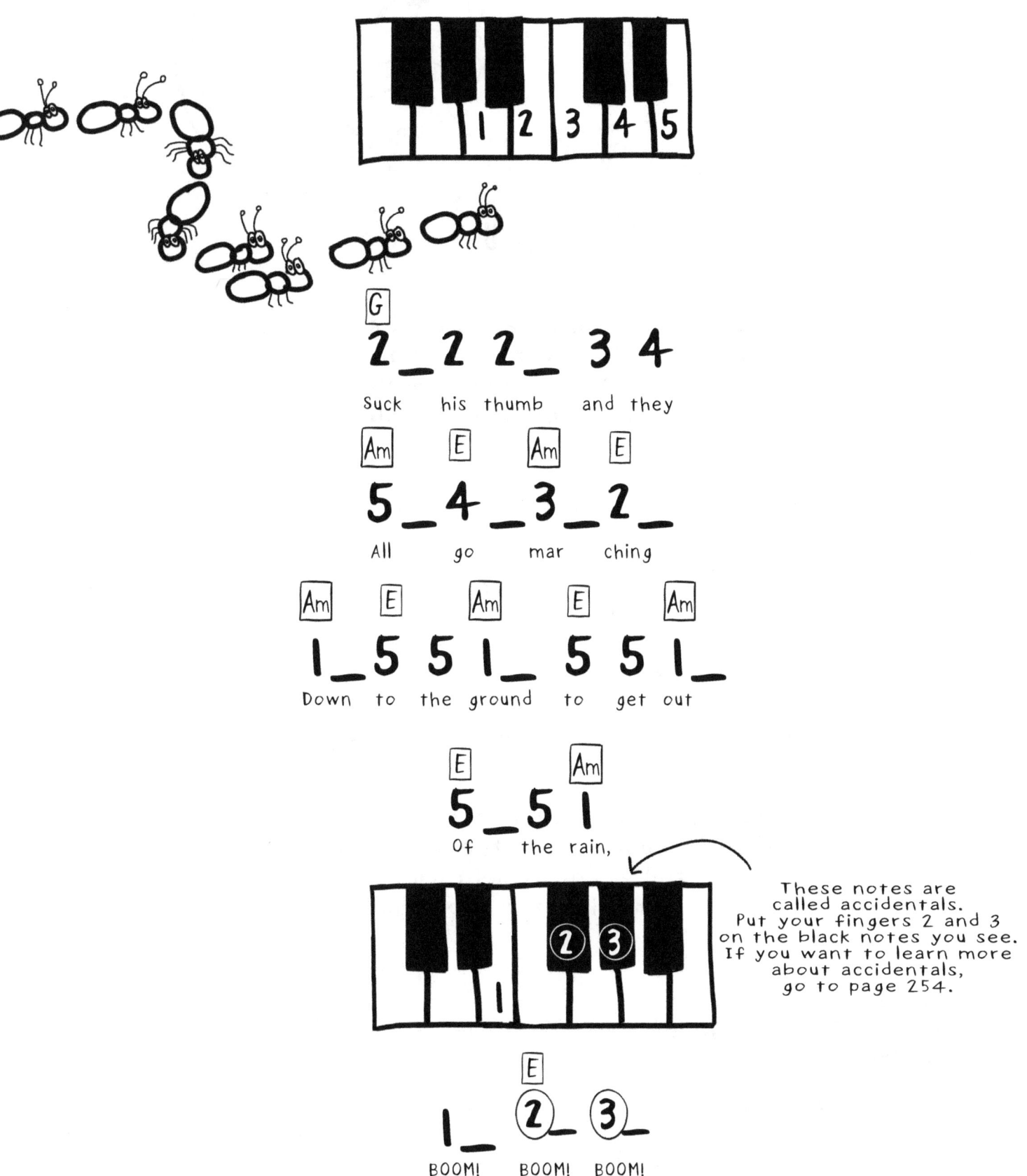

Listening Practice

The next song is called SKIDAMARINK.
So, I would like to give you some
listening that is from some possible
classical pieces about LOVE.

MUSIC PIECE NUMBER ① Fur Elise by Ludwig van Beethoven

Quite possibly one of the most famous piano
pieces of all time, this piece is "For Elise."
Who would you write a song for if you wanted
to show them how much you love them with music?

MUSIC PIECE NUMBER ② Clair de Lune by Claudde Debussy

This famous piece is about the moonlight.
Can you imagine a night under the stars and the moonlight
with your family and friends celebrating the beauty of life?
You can picture birds, fireflies, and shooting stars while you listen.

MUSIC PIECE NUMBER ③ Wiegenlied Brahm's Lullaby by Johannes Brahms

When you listen to this lullaby, you will possibly recognize it too.
My mom used to sing it to me when I was a child.
It's a sweet lullaby. Lullaby and goodnight.

Skidamarink

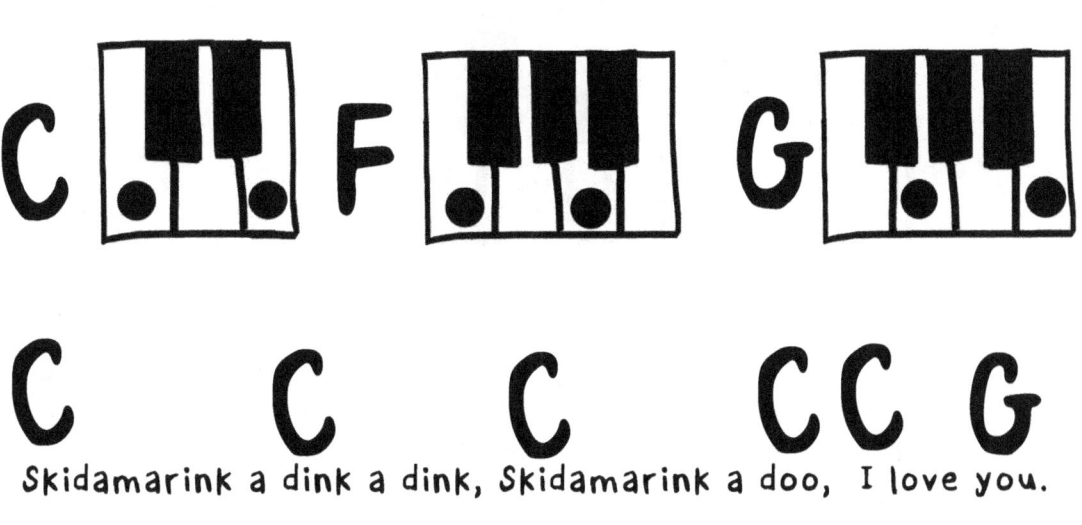

C   C   C   C C G

Skidamarink a dink a dink, Skidamarink a doo, I love you.

G   G   G   G G C

Skidamarink a dink a dink, Skidamarink a doo, I love you.

C   C   F   F

I love you in the morning and in the afternoon.

G   G   G   G

I love you in the evening and underneath the moon.

C   C   C   C

Oh, Skidamarink a dink a dink, Skidamarink a doo.

C G C

I love you!

♡ 216

Skidamarink

[C] 3 3 3 3_ [C] 1 4_ 4 4_
Ski da ma rink_ a dink_ a dink,_

[C] 3 3 3 3_ [C] 1 4_
Ski da ma rink_ a doo,_

[C] 3_ 4_ [G] 5_
I_ love_ you._

[G] 4 4 4 4_ 4 [G] 5_ 5 5_
Ski da ma rink_ a dink_ a dink,_

[G] 4 4 4 4_ 4 [G] 5_
Ski da ma rink_ a doo,_

[G] 4_ 5_ [C] 3_
I_ love_ you!

Skidamarink

[C]
1 4_ 4 4_ 4 4_1_
I love you in the mor ning

[F]
1 2_ 2 2 2 2_
And in the af ter noon.

[G]
2 5_5 5 5 5_2_
I love you in the ev ning

[G]
2 3_3 3_3 3_ 2_
And un der neath the moon, oh!

[C]   [C]   [C]
3 3 3 3_ 1 4_ 4 4_
Ski da ma rink a dink a dink,

[C]
3 3 3 3_ 1 4_
Ski da ma rink a doo,

[C] [G] [C]
3_ 1_ ⑤_
I love you.

Happy Birthday

G C   G

Happy Birthday to you.

G   C

Happy Birthday to you.

C   F

Happy Birthday dear friend.

C   GC

Happy Birthday to you.

Happy Birthday

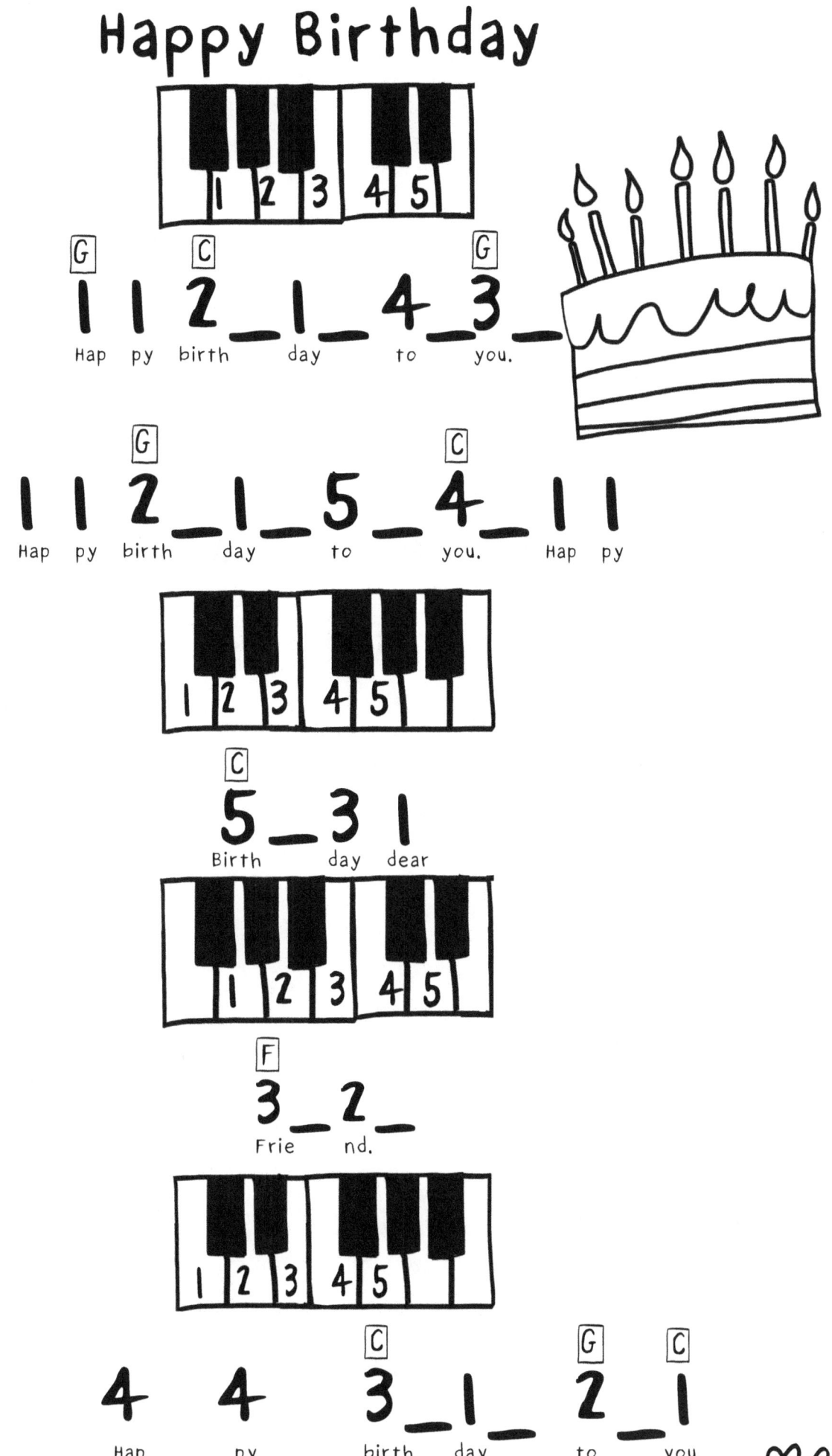

[G]
1 1 [C]2_1_4_[G]3_
Hap py birth day to you.

[G]
1 1 2_1_[C]5_4_1 1
Hap py birth day to you. Hap py

[C]
5_3 1
Birth day dear

[F]
3_2_
Frie nd.

4 4 [C]3_1_ [G]2_[C]1
Hap py birth day to you.

♡220

Songs in This Category

The Wheels on the Bus...............223
Shoo Fly.................................225
Hush Little Baby.......................227
You Are My Sunshine..................229

Songs That SWITCH to the Note G

Sometimes, you only need to switch your hand position to play one note. In these next songs, you just need to move to play the note G when the music says Ⓖ. You can try it first by moving your RH to Ⓖ.

The first position starts here.

Then to here.

Just make sure to put it back right after.

Or if you are only playing the melody, you can keep your left hand on Ⓖ and play that note with LH finger number 1 when you see Ⓖ.

♡222

The Wheels on the Bus

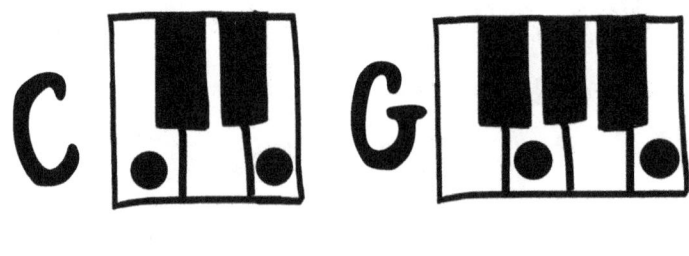

G C   C

The wheels on the bus go round and round,

G   C

Round and round, round and round.

G C   C

The wheels on the bus go round and round,

G   C

All through the town.

> Extra Verses or Extra Lyric Ideas

The wipers on the bus go, swish, swish, swish.
The doors on the bus open and shut.
The babies on the bus go, wah, wah, wah.
The horn on the bus goes, beep, beep, beep.
The lights on the bus go on and off.
The children on the bus go up and down.
The driver on the bus says, bye, bye, bye.

The Wheels on the Bus

[G] [C]
(G) 1_ 1 1 1_ 3
The wheels on the bus go

[C] [G]
5 3 1_ 2 (1) (G)_
Round and round, round and round,

[C]
5 3 1_
Round and round.

[G] [C]
(G) 1_ 1 1 1_ 3
The wheels on the bus go

[C]
5 3 1_
Round and round,

[G] [C]
2_ (G)_ (G) 1_
All through the town.

♡224

Shoo Fly

C   **G**

Shoo, fly, don't bother me.

G   **C**

Shoo, fly, don't bother me.

C   **G**

Shoo, fly, don't bother me,

G   **G C**

For I belong to somebody.

C   **C**   **C**   **G**

I feel, I feel, I feel like a morning star.

G   **G**   **G**   **C**

I feel, I feel, I feel like a morning star.

> Extra Verses or Extra Lyric Ideas

What other insects or bugs could you shoo away?

Shoo bee, don't bother me.
Shoo spider, don't bother me.
Shoo beetle, don't bother me.

Shoo Fly

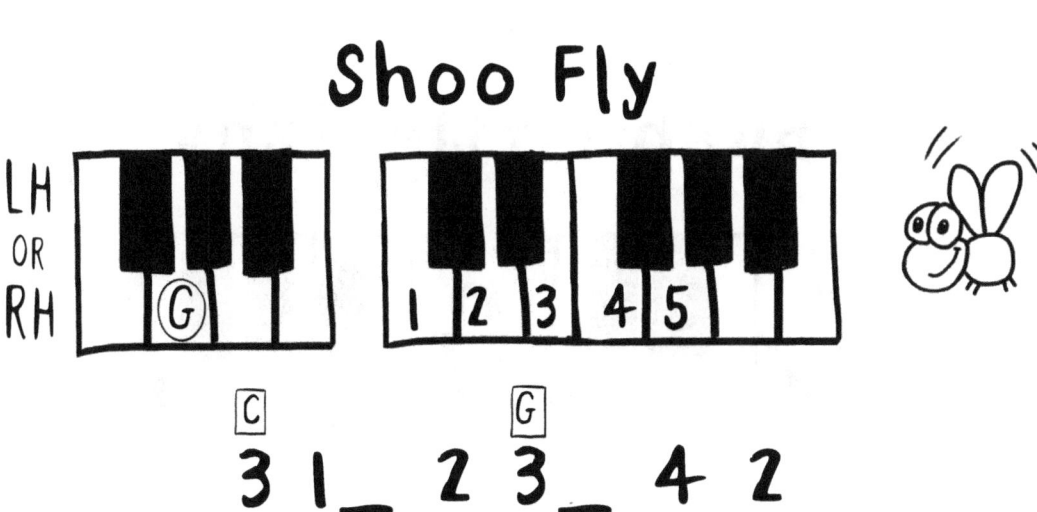

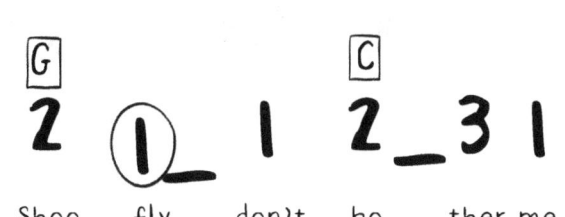

Shoo, fly, don't bother me.

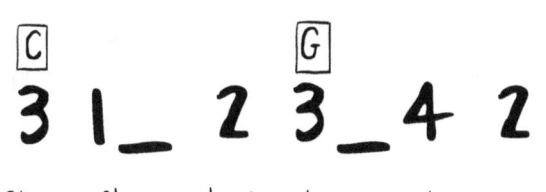

Shoo, fly, don't bother me.

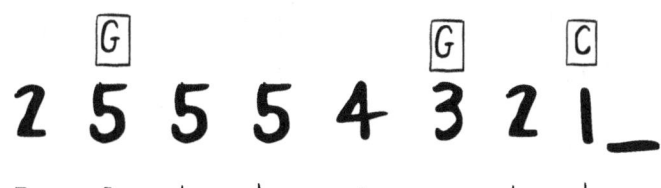

Shoo, fly, don't bother me,

For I belong to somebody.

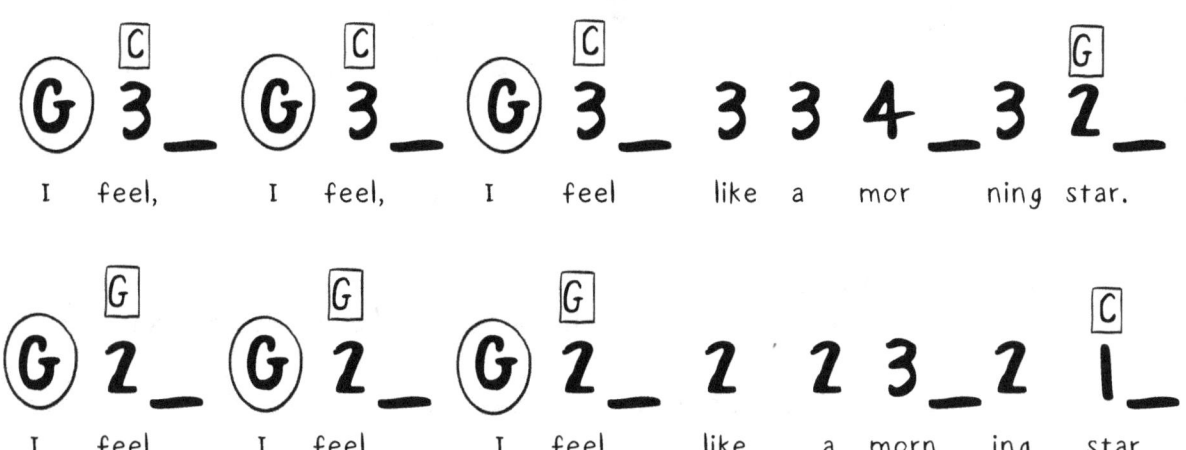

I feel, I feel, I feel like a morning star.

I feel, I feel, I feel like a morning star.

Hush Little Baby

C C G G

Hush, little baby, don't say a word.

G G C C

Mama's going to buy you a mockingbird.

C C G G

And if that mockingbird don't sing,

G G C C

Mama's going to buy you a diamond ring.

> Extra Verses or Extra Lyric Ideas

Try to say if something breaks or doesn't work,
Mama will buy something else (whether it rhymes or not). For example:

And if that diamond rings gets broke, Mama's gonna buy you a new toy boat.
And if that toy boat doesn't float, Mama's gonna buy you a toy train.
If that toy train doesn't go, Mama's gonna buy you a new baseball.
End it with:
And if that thing doesn't work, you'll still be the sweetest little baby in town.

Hush Little Baby

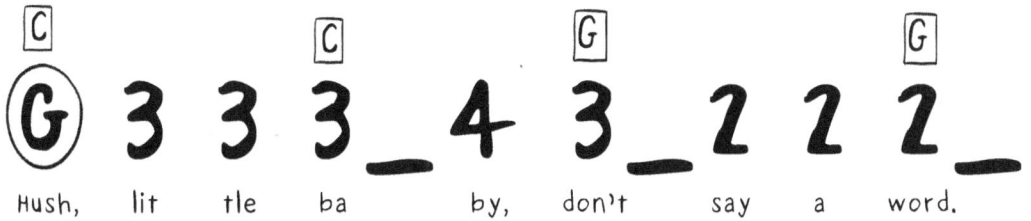

Hush, little baby, don't say a word.

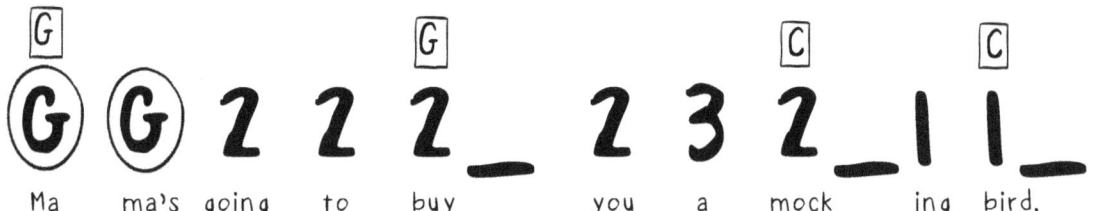

Mama's going to buy you a mocking bird.

If that mocking bird don't sing,

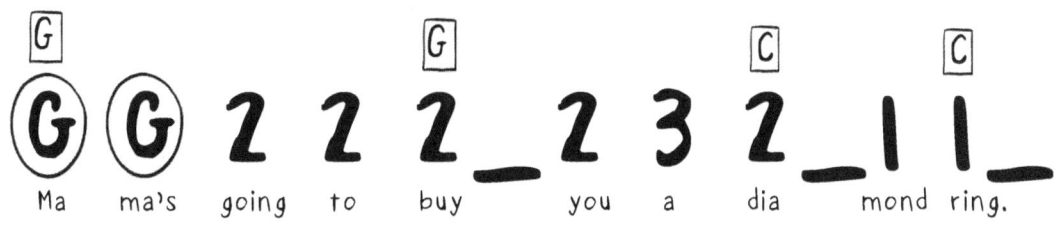

Mama's going to buy you a diamond ring.

♡228

You Are My Sunshine

C   C

You are my sunshine, my only sunshine.

F   C

You make me happy when skies are gray.

F   C

You'll never know dear how much I love you.

C G C

Please don't take my sunshine away.

229☆

You Are My Sunshine

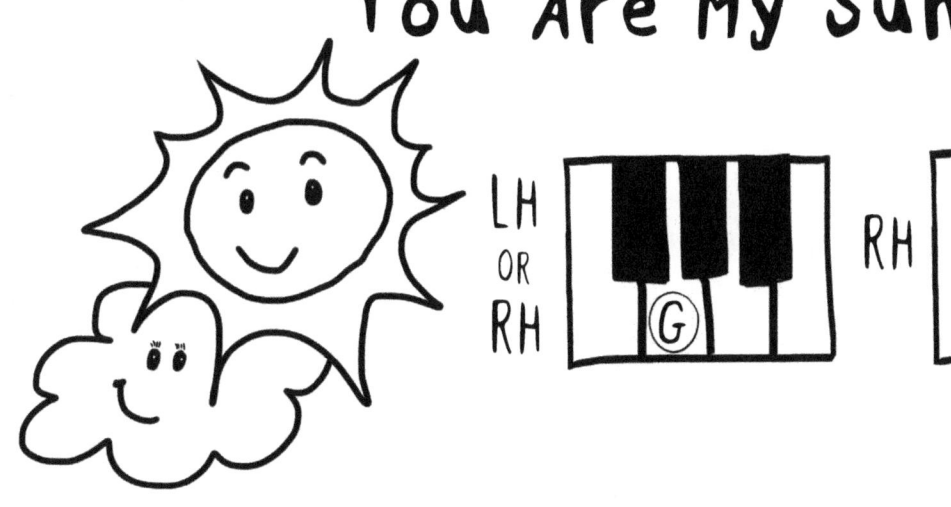

                 [C]   [C]

(G) 1 2 3_ 3_ 3 2 3 1_ 1_
You are my sun shine, my on ly sun shine.

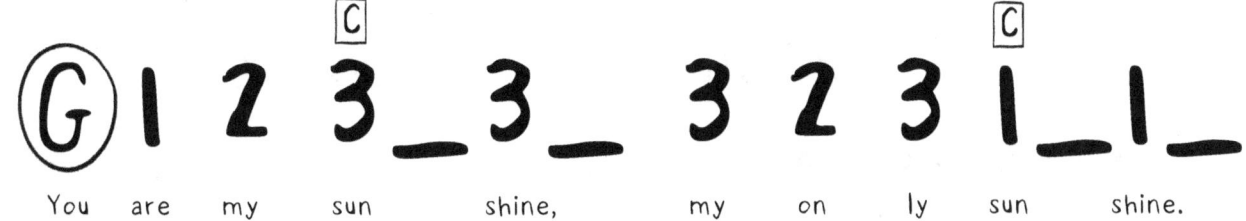
You make me hap py when skies are grey.

You'll ne ver know dear how much I love you.

Please don't take my sun shine a way.

♡230

Songs in This Category

Pop Goes the Weasel......................233
The Itsy Bitsy Spider......................235
Down By the Station......................237
Where Is Thumbkin?......................239
My Bonnie Lies Over the Ocean............241
If All of the Raindrops......................243
Here We Go Looby Loo......................245
She'll Be Coming Round the Mountain...247
I've Been Working on the Railroad........250

Songs That Go Over the Mountain

Sometimes, you want to play a note just below a position.
In this case, I call it **going over the mountain**.
Refer back to page 75 if you want to practice first.
You can go over one or two mountains!

♡232

Pop Goes the Weasel

C G C
All around the mulberry bush

C G C
The monkey chased the weasel.

C G C
The monkey thought was all in fun.

F G C
Pop! Goes the weasel.

| Extra Verses or Extra Lyric Ideas |

Use other animals:

The dog chased the cat.
The cat chased the rat.
The eagle chased the squirrel.

The Itsy Bitsy Spider

C   C   G   C

The itsy bitsy spider went up the water spout.

C   C   G   C

Down came the rain and washed the spider out.

C   C   G   C

Out came the sun and dried up all the rain and

C   C   G   C

The itsy bitsy spider went up the spout again.

> Extra Verses or Extra Lyric Ideas

The itsy bitsy spider went up the kitchen wall.
On went the fan and made the spider fall.
Off went the fan, no more did it blow.
So the itsy bitsy spider back up the wall did go.

The Itsy Bitsy Spider

[C] 5 1_1 1 2 **[C]** 3_3
The it sy bit sy spi der

[G] 3 2 1 2 3 **[C]** 1_
Went up the wa ter spout.

[C] 3_3 4 **[C]** 5_5
Down came the rain and

[G] 4 3 4 5 **[C]** 3_
Washed the spi der out.

[C] 1_1 2 **[C]** 3_3_ **[G]** 2 1 2
Out came the sun and dried up all

[C] 3 1 (2) (2) **[C]** 1 1 2 **[C]** 3_3
The rain and the it sy bit sy spi der

[G] 3 2 1 2_3 **[C]** 1_
Went up the spout a gain.

♡ 236

Down by the Station

```
C        C G    C
```
Down by the station early in the morning

```
C        C   G  C
```
See the little pufferbellies all in a row.

```
C       C G     C
```
See the engine driver pull the little handle,

```
  C    C
```
Puff, puff Toot, toot,

```
  G C
```
Off we go!

237 ☆

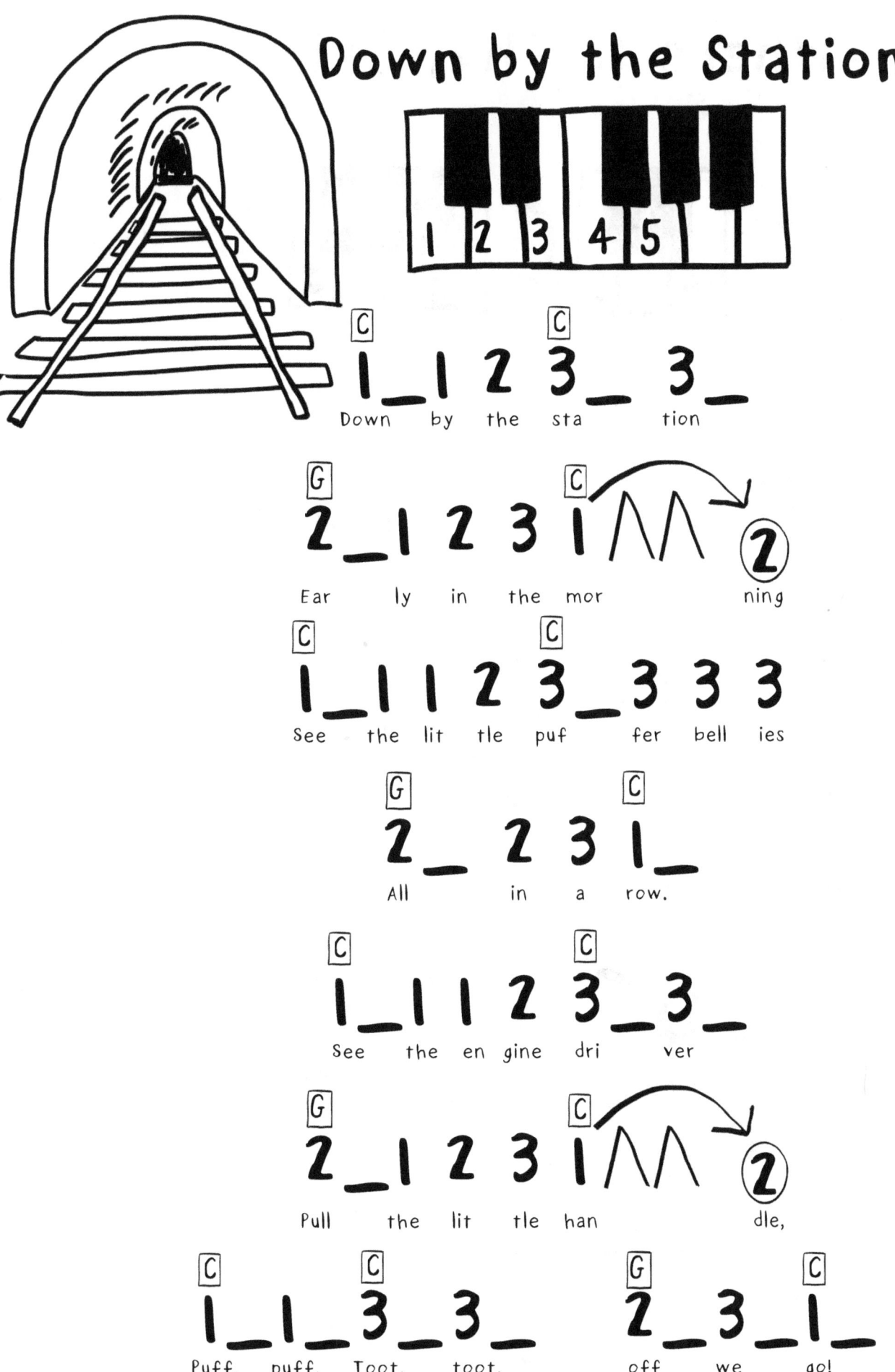

Where Is Thumbkin?

C   **C**
Where is thumbkin? Where is thumbkin?

C   **C**
Here I am, here I am.

C   **C**
How are you today, sir? Very well, I thank you.

C G C   C G C
Run a way.   Run a way.

| Extra Verses or Extra Lyric Ideas |

Try it with:

Where is baby? Where is baby?
Where's the whole family? Where's the whole family?

239 ☆

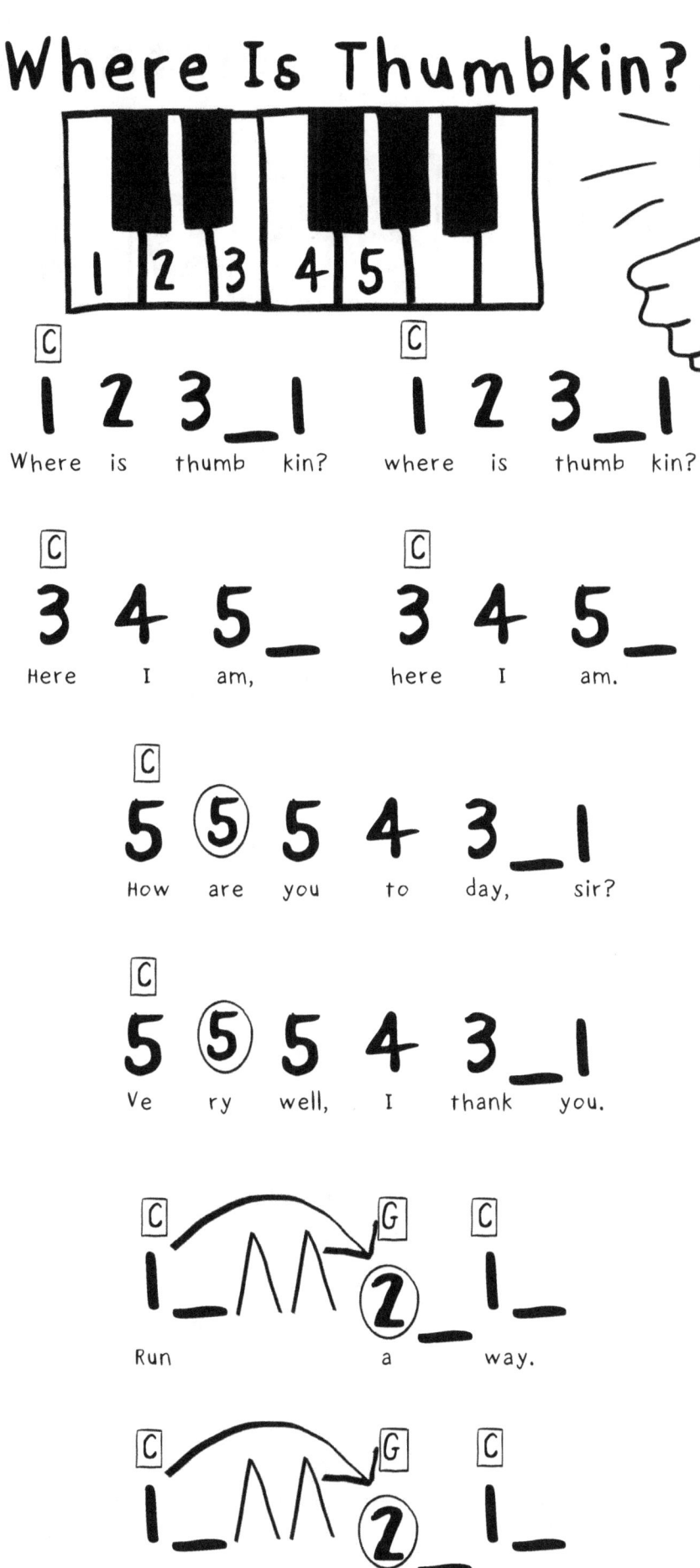

My Bonnie Lies Over the Ocean

G C   F   C
My bonnie lies over the ocean.

G C   F   G
My Bonnie lies over the sea.

G C   F   C C F   G   C
My Bonnie lies over the ocean. Oh bring back my Bonnie to me.

C   F
Bring back, bring back,

G   C
Oh bring back my Bonnie to me, to me.

C   F   G   C
Bring back, bring back, oh bring back my Bonnie to me.

241

If All of the Raindrops

C   **F**   **G**

G C   C   G   C
If all of the raindrops were lemon drops and gum drops,

C   F G   C
Oh what a rain that would be.

C   F   C   G
I'd stand outside with my mouth opened wide,

C   F   C   G
Ah ah ah ah ah ah ah ah ah ah.

G C   C   G   C
If all of the raindrops were lemon drops and gum drops,

C   F   C
Oh what a rain that would be.

> Extra Verses or Extra Lyric Ideas

Think of other candies or sweets that could be falling from the sky:

If all of the raindrops were donuts and cupcakes.
If all of the raindrops were cookies and chocolate bars.

If All of the Raindrops

[G] [C]   [C]   [G]   [C]
 5   1_1 2 3_   3 3 2_1 2 3 1 → 2
 If all of the rain drops were le mon drops and gum   drops,

        [C]   [F]   [C]
         1_1 3 2_1 ① 1_
         Oh what a rain that would be,

[C]   [F]   [C]   [G]
 5_5 3 4_4 2 3_ 3 1 2_
 I'd stand out side with my mouth open ed wide,

[C]   [F]   [C]   [G]
 5_5 3 4_4 2 3_ 3_ 1 2_
 Ah ah ah ah ah ah ah ah ah ah.

[G] [C]   [C]   [G]   [C]
 5   1_1 2 3_   3 3 2_1 2 3 1 → 2
 If all of the rain drops were le mon drops and gum   drops,

        [C]   [F]   [C]
         1_1 3 2_1 ① 1_
         Oh what a rain that would be.

♡244

Here We Go Looby Loo

C   **C**
Oh here we go looby loo.

C   **G**
Here we go looby light.

C   **C**
Here we go looby loo,

G   **C**
All on a Saturday night.

C   **C**
You put your right hand in.

C   **C**
You take your right hand out.

C   **C**   **C G C**
You give your right hand a shake, shake, shake and turn yourself about.

{ Extra Verses or Extra Lyric Ideas }

You put your left hand in, you take your left hand out.
You put your right foot in, you take your right hand out.
You put our left foot in, you take your left foot out.
You put your head in, you take your head out.

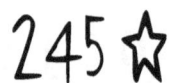

Here We Go Looby Loo

[C]　　　　　　　　　[C]
5_ 1 1 3_ 1 5_
Oh　here we go loo　by loo.

[C]　　　　　　　[G]
1 1 3_ 1 2_
Here we go loo　by light.

[C]　　　　　　　[C]
1 1 3_ 1 5_
Here we go loo　by loo,

[G]　　　　　　　　　　[C]　　　[C]　　　　　　　　　[C]
5 ⑤ 5 4 3 2 1 ② 1 1_1 1 1_
All on a Sa tur day night.　You put your right hand in.

　　[C]　　　　　　[C]
2 3_ 3 3_ 3 3_
You take your right hand out.

　　[C]　　　　　　　　[C]
4 5_5 5 5 5_5 5 5_
You give your right hand a shake, shake, shake,

　　[C]　　　[G]　[C]
4 3_3 2_2 1_
And turn your self a bout.

♡246

She'll Be Coming Round the Mountain

   G   C   C   C   C
She'll be comin' round the mountain when she comes.

        C   C   G G
She'll be comin' round the mountain when she comes.

        C   C
She'll be comin' round the mountain.

        F   F
She'll be comin' round the mountain.

       G   G   C
She'll be comin' round the mountain when she comes.

She'll Be Coming Round the Mountain

[G] 1 2 [C] 4 4_4
She'll be co min' round

[C] 4 2 1 ② 1 [C] 4_ [C]
The moun tain   when she comes.

[C] 1 2 3 3_ 3_ 3 [C] 5 3 2 1 [G] 2_ [G]
She'll be co min' round the moun tain when she comes.

5 4 [C] 3 3_ 3_ 3 2 1 [C]
She'll be com in' round the moun tain.

4 4 [F] 2 2_2_ 2 5 4 3 2 [F]
She'll be co min' round the moun tain. She'll be

[G] 1 1_1_1 ⑤ [G] 5 2 3 [C] 4_
Co min' round the moun tain when she comes.

♡ 248

Listening Practice

The next song is I'VE BEEN WORKING ON THE RAILROAD.
So, I would like to give you some listening practice
that sounds like trains, inspired by trains,
or might be something you would see on a train.

MUSIC PIECE NUMBER ① Eisenbahn-Lust-Walzer, Op. 89 by Johann Strauss

This piece of music celebrated the opening of a public railway.
It has railroad sounds incorporated into it.
Can you imagine yourself on a train ride while you listen to it?
Where are you traveling to?

MUSIC PIECE NUMBER ② Piano Concerto No. 1 by Peter Tchaicovsky

This piano piece takes you on a journey. A train takes you
on a journey too. Picture yourself where you are now, and
as you listen to it, imagine all the places you see as
you look out your imaginary train window.

MUSIC PIECE NUMBER ③ River Flows in You by Yiruma

Not all classical pieces were written many, many years ago.
This piece was written in the year 2001.
Picture a train traveling across hills, past mountains, and over
bridges with many rivers, flowing below as you travel
on a musical listening journey.

I've Been Working on the Railroad

C   F   G

    C   C F   C
I've been working on the railroad all the live long day.

 C   C   G   G
I've been working on the railroad just to pass the time away.

G   C F   C
Can't you hear the whistle blowing? Rise up so early in the morn.

F   C G   C
Can't you hear the captain shouting? "Dinah, blow your horn?"

C   F   G   C
Dinah won't you blow, Dinah won't you blow, Dinah won't you blow your horn?

C   F   G   C
Dinah won't you blow, Dinah won't you blow, Dinah won't you blow your horn?

C   C C   G
Someone's in the kitchen with Dinah. Someone's in the kitchen I know.

C   F G   C
Someone's in the kitchen with Dinah, strumming on the old banjo and singing,

C C   C   G
"Fee fi fiddley ay oh! Fee fi fiddley ay oh!

C F   G   C
Fee fi fiddley ay oh!" Strumming on the old banjo.

♡ 250

I've Been Working on the Railroad

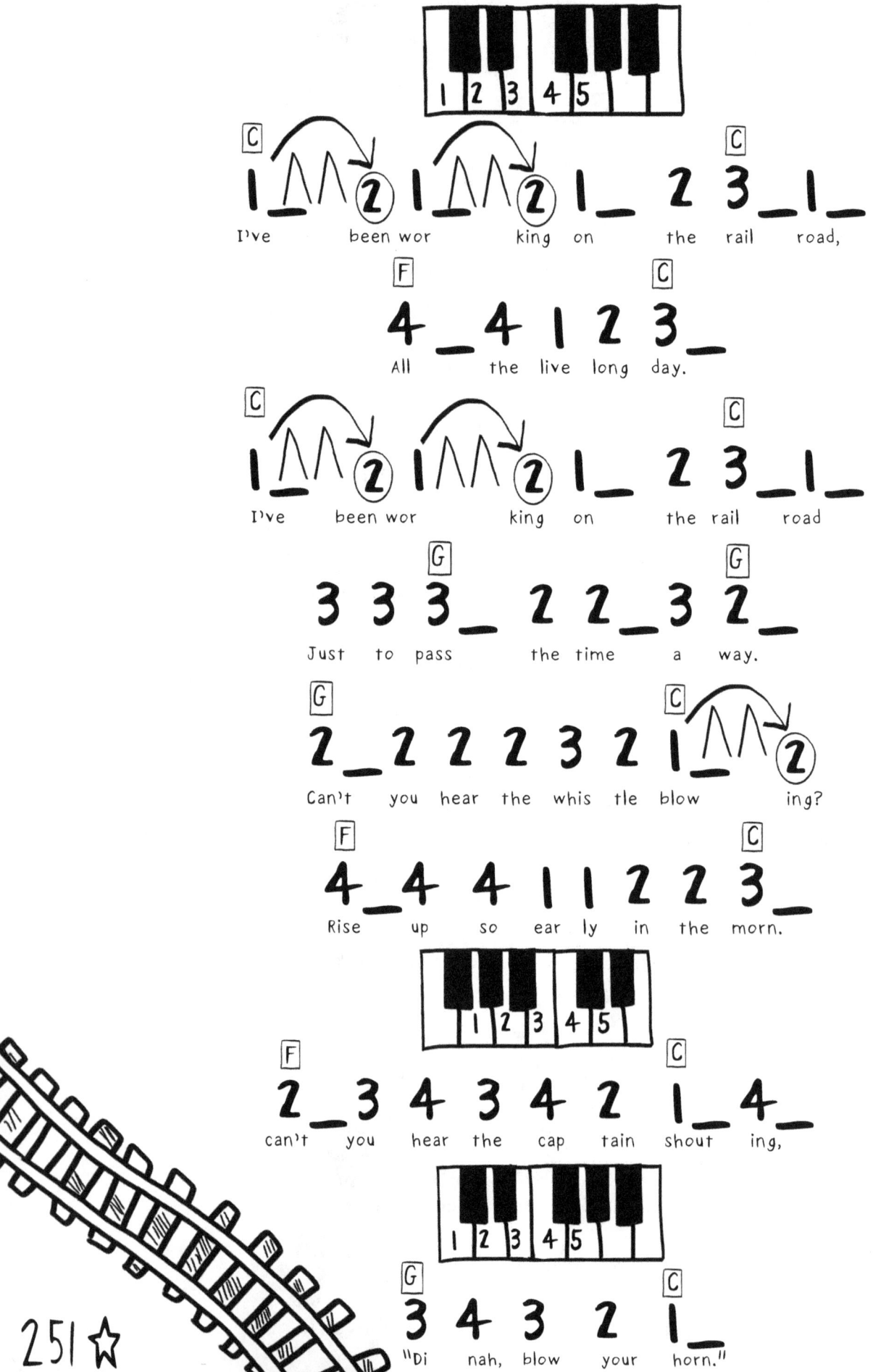

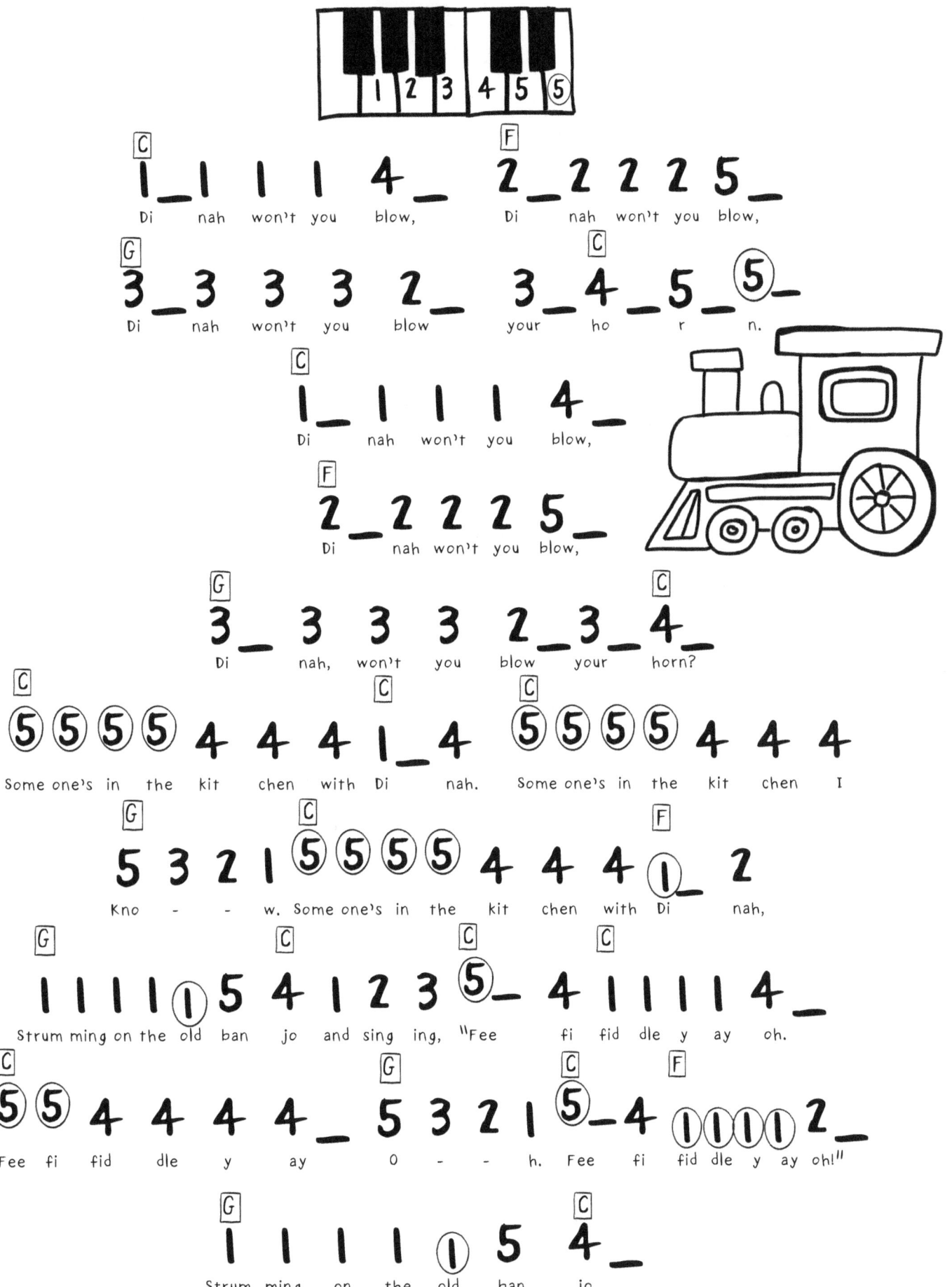

Songs in This Category

Head, Shoulders, Knees and Toes.......270
Down by the Bay................................272
The Hokey Pokey.................................274
Your Last Song....................................276

Songs That Use Accidentals

What are **accidentals**?
Turn the page and find out!

♡254

What Are ACCIDENTALS?

Accidentals are the notes on either side of a note ABOVE or BELOW them. They are the names for all the black notes, but not all accidentals are on the black keys. The note below is called **flat** and uses this symbol **b**. The note above is called **sharp** and uses this symbol **#**.

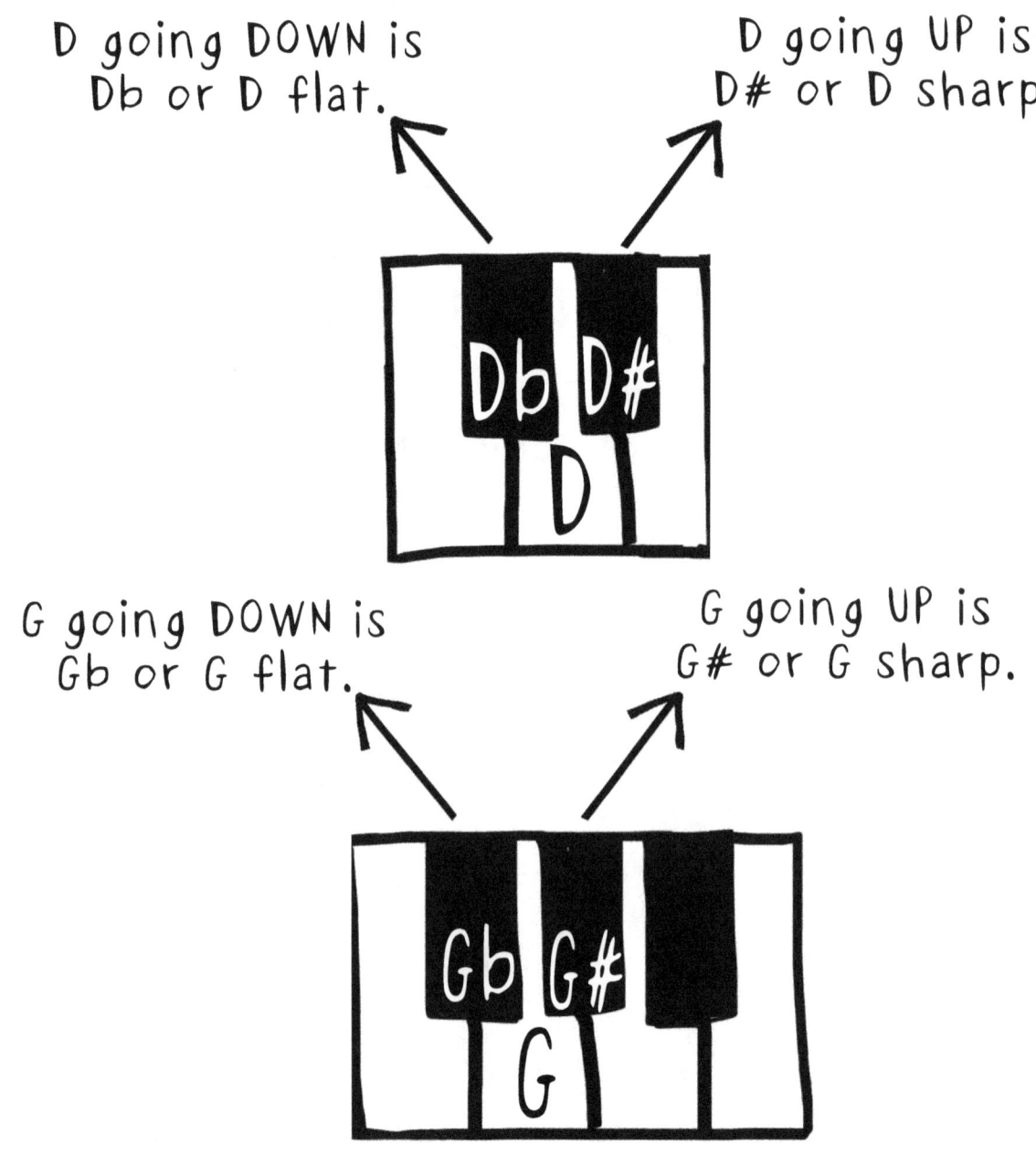

The CHROMATIC Scale
(All 12 notes on the piano)

Here are ALL the notes when going up with sharp (#) notes.

*Notice that between E and F as well as B and C there is only one step. (So F is technically also considered E# and C is considered B#).

Here are ALL the notes when going down with flat (b) notes.

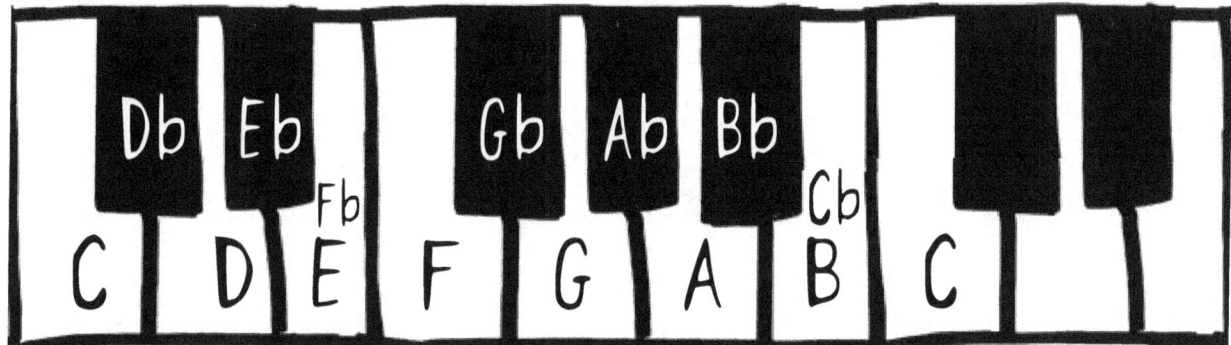

*Between E and F as well as B and C is still only one step. (So E is technically also considered Fb and B is considered Cb).

And, here are ALL the notes (both up and down) only focusing on the black note accidentals.

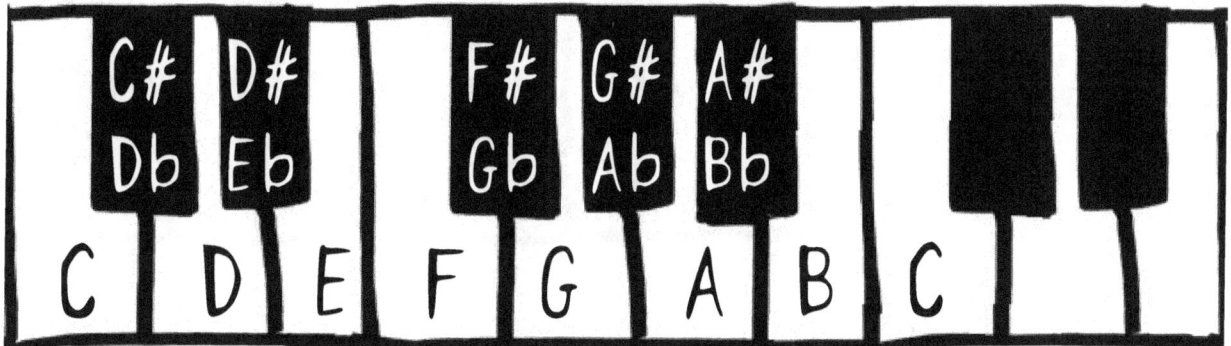

♡ 256

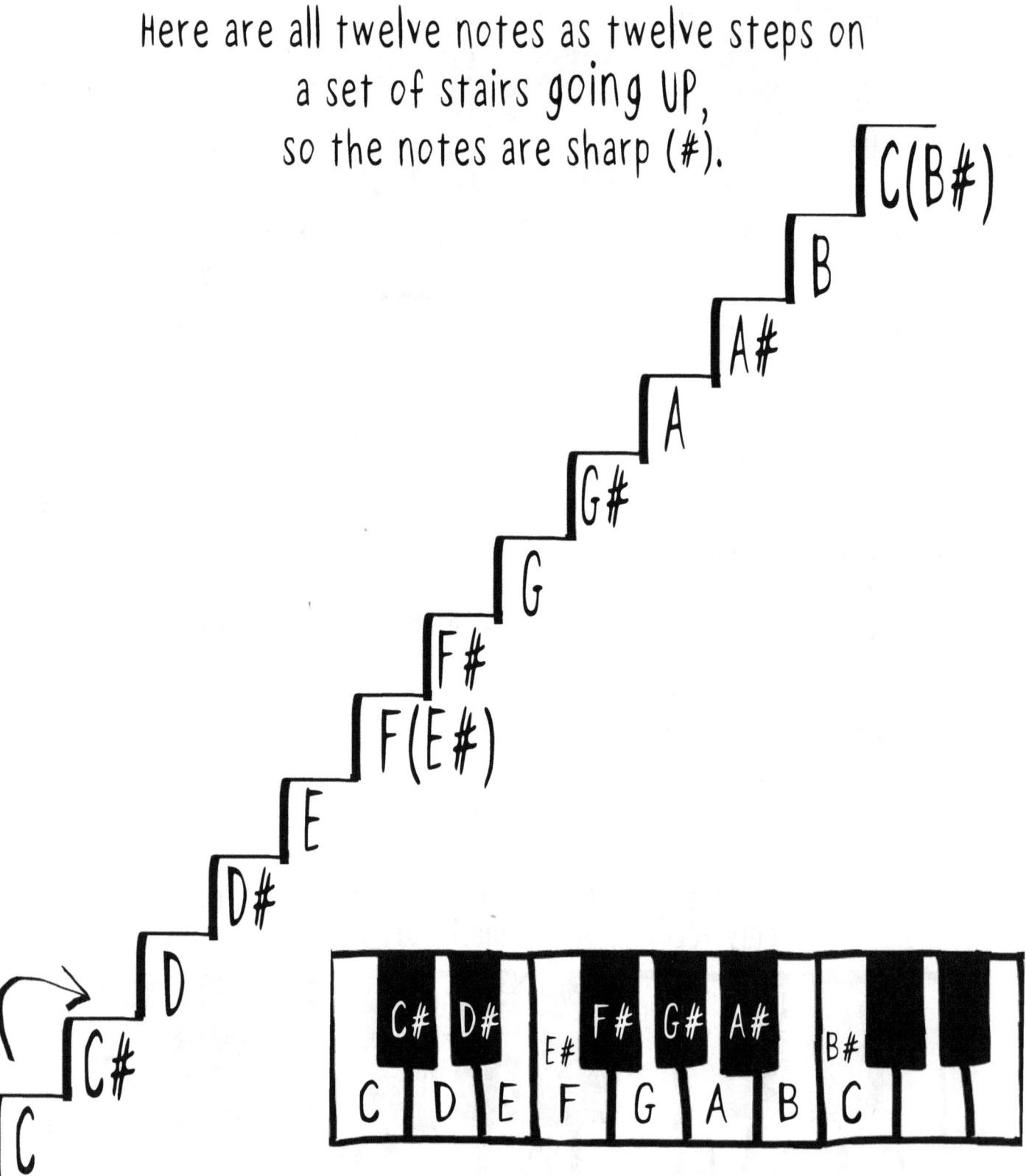

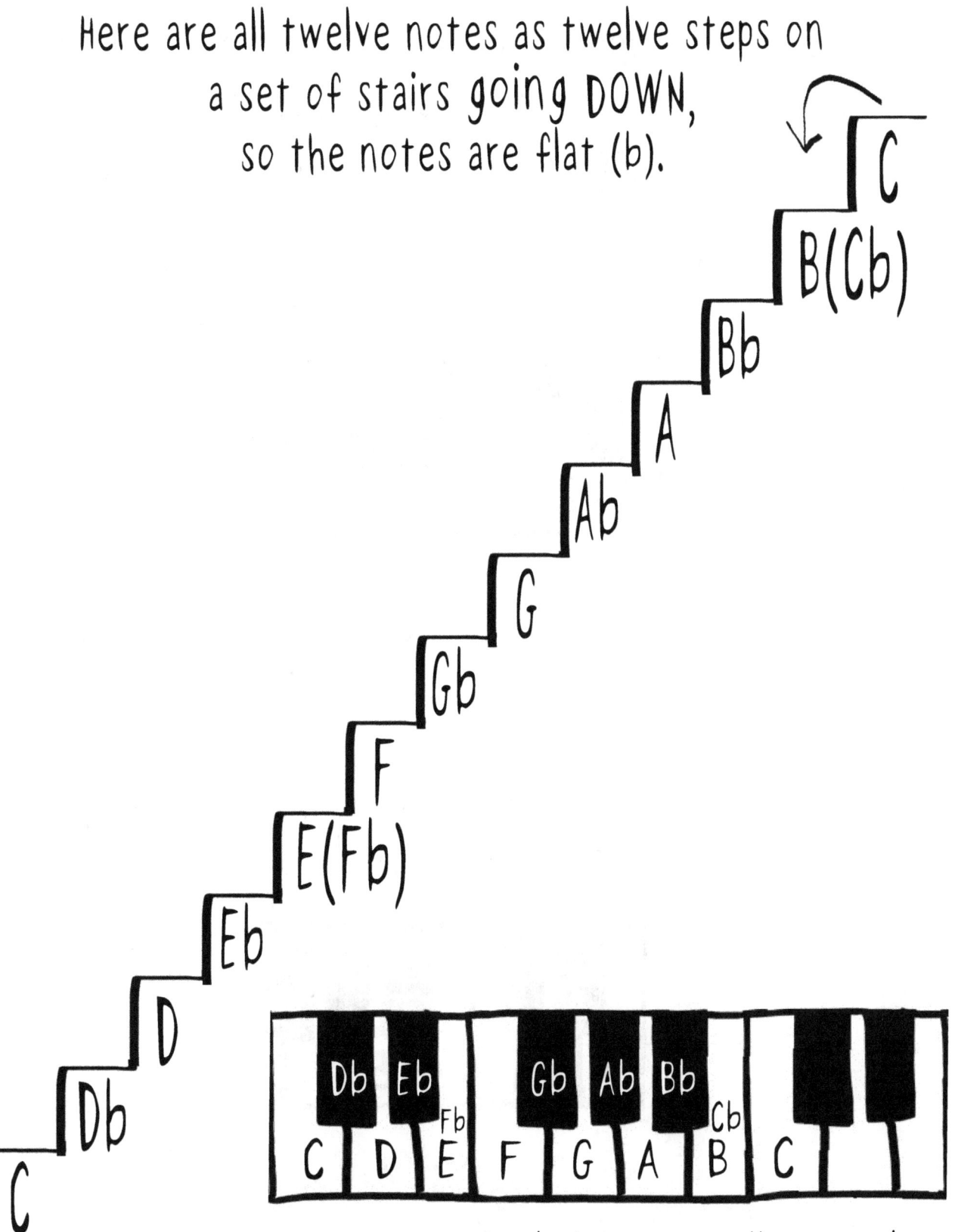

Writing Accidentals with Numbers

Accidentals are good to know for understanding music, but in this book, we only need to know which finger will play the accidental note.

You'll know because it will have a circle around it like this:

This one goes up!

And then, PAY ATTENTION to which direction the finger number with the circle goes:

This one goes down!

The Accidentals in This Book

These are the accidentals you'll need in the following songs:

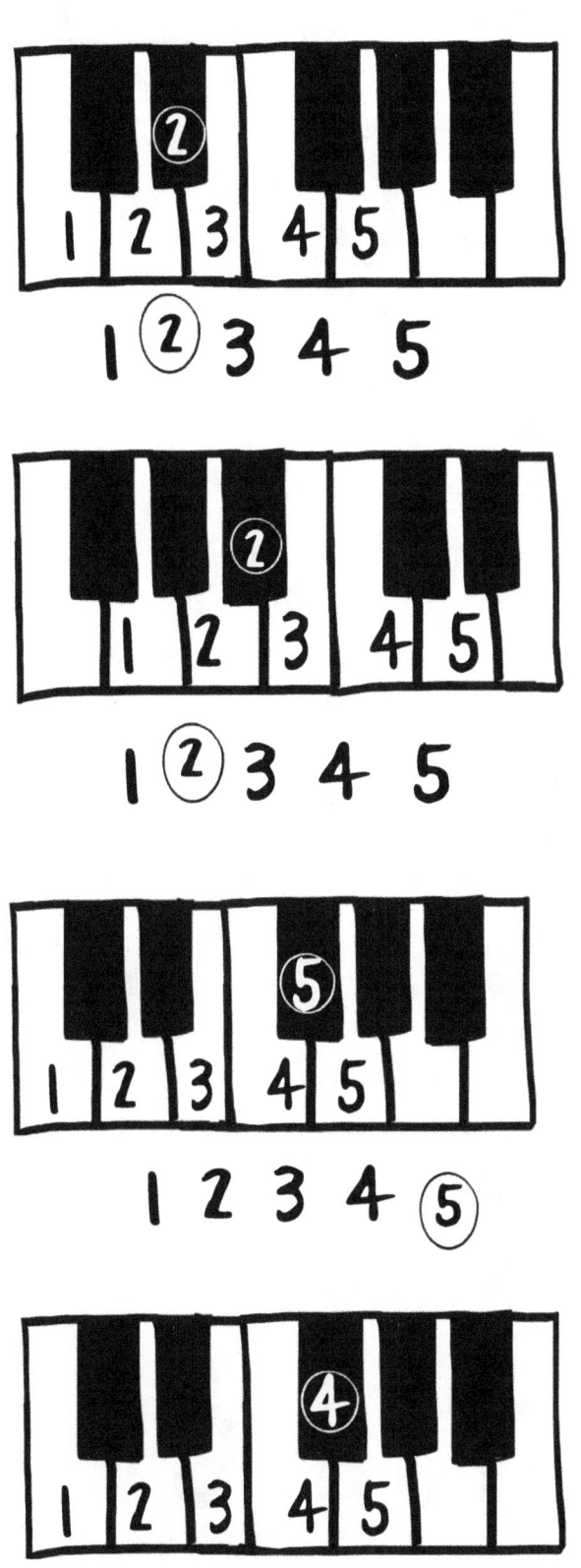
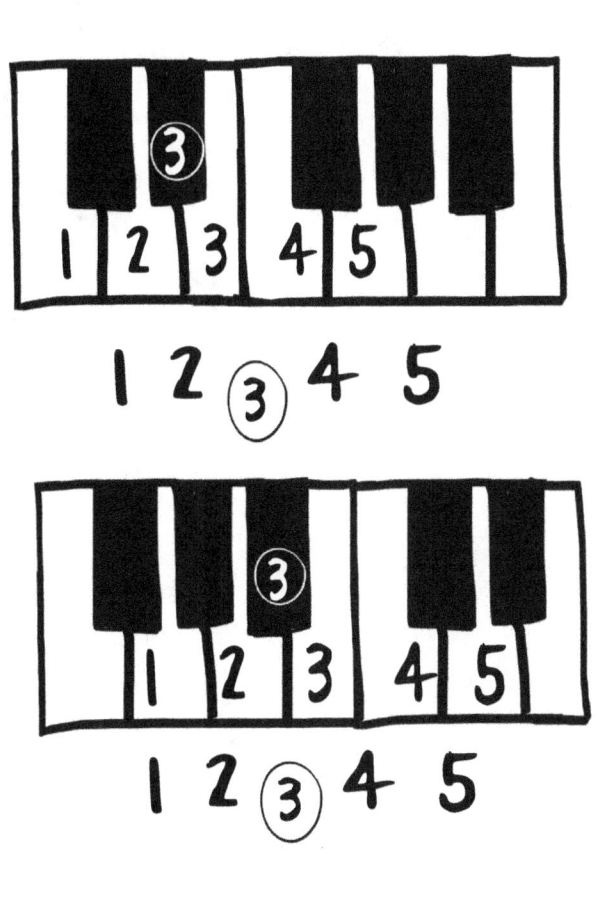

Try playing each of these five finger patterns, and then move on to the next pages to play songs!

Head, Shoulders, Knees, and Toes

C   C   C
Head, shoulders, knees and toes,

C
Knees and toes.

C   C   G
Head, shoulders, knees and toes,

G
Knees and toes,

C   C   F   F
And eyes and ears and mouth and nose.

G   G   C   C
Head, shoulders, knees and toes, knees and toes

Head, Shoulders, Knees and Toes

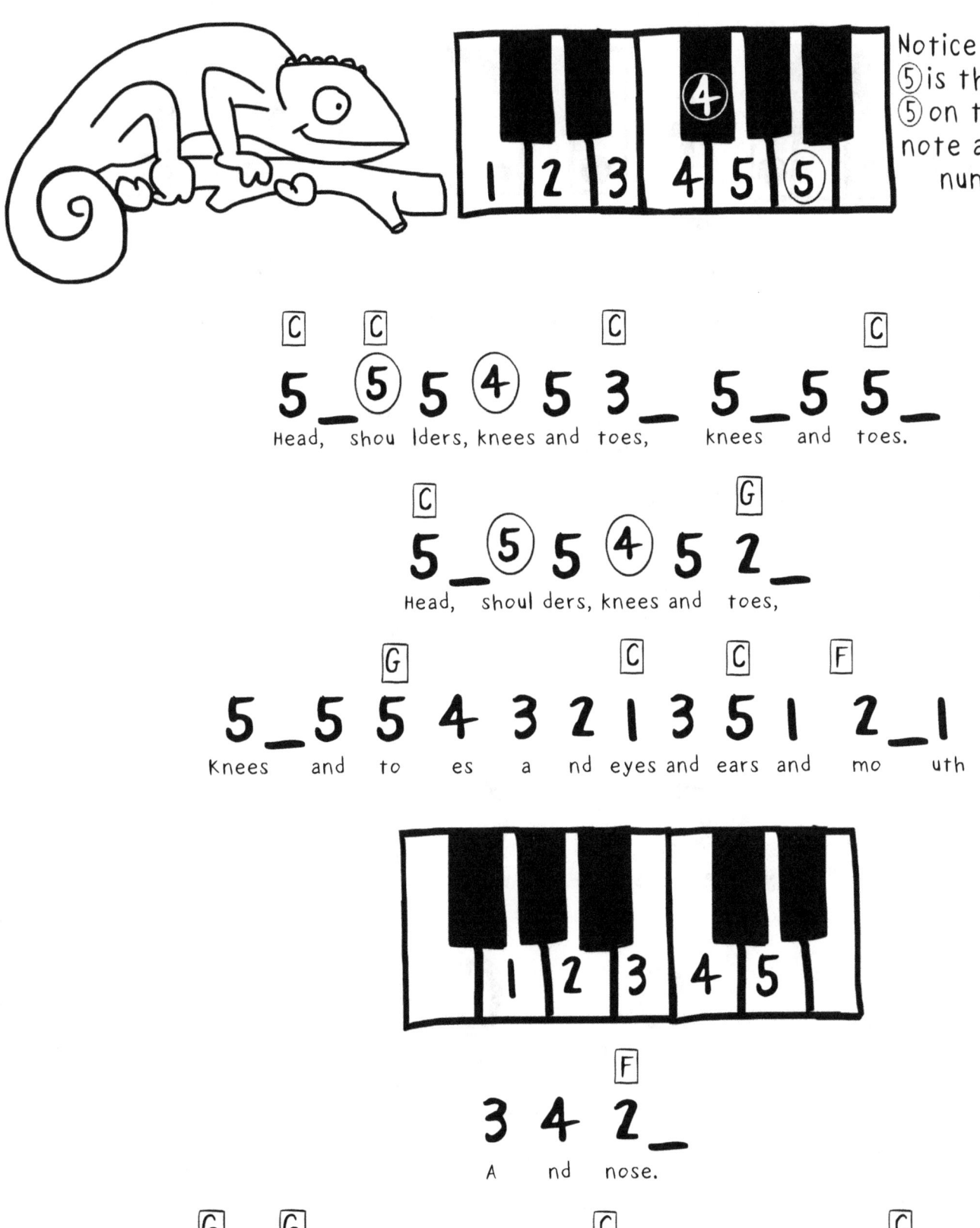

Down by the Bay

        C   G

Down by the bay, where the watermelons grow.

     G   C

Back to my home, I dare not go.

     F   C

For if I do, my mother will say,

     C   C

"Did you ever see a fly wearing a tie?"

     G   C

Down by the bay.

> Extra Verses or Extra Lyric Ideas

Here's where you can get creative with ideas and rhymes like:

Did you ever see a whale with a polka dot tail?
Did you ever see a frog walking his dog?
Did you ever see a mouse painting his house?
Did you ever seen a bear combing his hair?

272☆

Down by the Bay

            [C]
1   2   1   4 _
Down by the bay,

                     [G]
1   1   2   2   1   1   3 _
Where the wa ter me lons grow,

          [G]   [C]
1   2   1   3 _   1   2   3   4 _
Back to my home,   I dare not go.

     [F]   [C]
4   3   ③   2 _   4   3   3   2   1 _
For if I do,   my mo ther will say,

    [C]
1   2   3   2   3   2   3 _
"Did you e ver see a fly

[C]   [G]   [C]
3   3 _ 2   3 _   4   3 _ 2   1
Wear ing a tie?"   Down by the bay.

♡273

The Hokey Pokey

C G

G　　C　　C　G　　C　　C
You put your right foot in. You put your right foot out.

G　　C　　C　　G　　G
You put your right foot in and you shake it all about.

G　　　　G
You do the hokey pokey

G　　　　G
And you turn yourself around.

G　　　　GC
That's what it's all about.

| Extra Verses or Extra Lyric Ideas |

You put your left foot in.
You put your right hand in.
You put your left hand in.
You put your whole body in.

274 ☆

The Hokey Pokey

[G] [C] [C]
1 2 1 4 4_ 4
You put your right foot in.

[G] [C] [C]
1 2 1 4 4_ 4
You put your right foot out.

[G] [C] [C]
1 2 1 4 4_ 4_ 2 1
You put your right foot in and you

[G] [G]
3 ② 3 ② 3_
Shake it all a bout.

[G] [G]
② 3 ② 3 ② 3 1 2 1
You do the ho key po key and you

[G] [G]
3 ② 3 ② 3_
Turn your self a round.

[G] [G] [C]
1 1_ 1 2 3_ 4
That's what it's all a bout.

♡ 275

Name of Your Last Song _____

You have all the tools you need to make your own song!
Write it about anything! Follow the steps below:

Write in which sandwiches you want to use.

What doodle could you make here?

Then put the chords where you want them in the song.

Here you can write the words of your song.

276 ★

Name of Your Last Song _____

Choose where your RH will start for your melody.
Then write your song with the numbers and the words below them.

Write finger numbers 1-5 here on one of these.

Write sandwiches here.

Write the numbers for your melody here.

Transfer your words here under the numbers.

You can write as many songs as you like now that you know how!

♡277

Resources and Practice

There are still so many things to learn about music and this next section will give you some resources and practice, that will help you to continue to learn more.

Here's What You Can Learn and Practice Here

All Major Thirds	323
All Minor Thirds	324
Changing Sandwiches with Rhythm	325
Changing Thirds with Finger Number Patterns	327
Bigger Sandwiches (Intervals)	329
Double Decker Sandwiches (Triads)	334
Diatonic Triads	336
Changing Triads with Finger Number Patterns	338
All Major Triads	340
All Minor Triads	341
How Can You Learn More Songs?	342
Introduction to the Musical Staff	343
Warm Ups	357

Let's Make More Sandwiches

Let's first remember simple sandwiches, called thirds, with just TWO pieces of bread and ONE thing inside.

On the next two pages, we can practice ALL the white key major thirds (the simple sandwich that **sounds happy**).

Then we can practice ALL the white key minor thirds (the simple sandwich that **sounds sad**).

All Major Thirds (Simple Sandwiches)

Here are all the MAJOR THIRDS on the white keys

Notice they all have FOUR steps in-between the two notes.

A
B
C
D
E
F
G

Check here in these boxes when you've learned it.

All Minor Thirds (Simple Sandwiches)
Here are all the MINOR THIRDS on the white keys

Notice they all have THREE steps in-between the two notes.

Am

Bm

Cm

Dm

Em

Fm

Gm

Check here in these boxes when you've learned it.

♡ 281

Different Ways to Play Sandwiches

You can play the sandwiches once when you see them over the word they are above, but you can also play them with **a different RHYTHM.**

Let's just use C as an example:

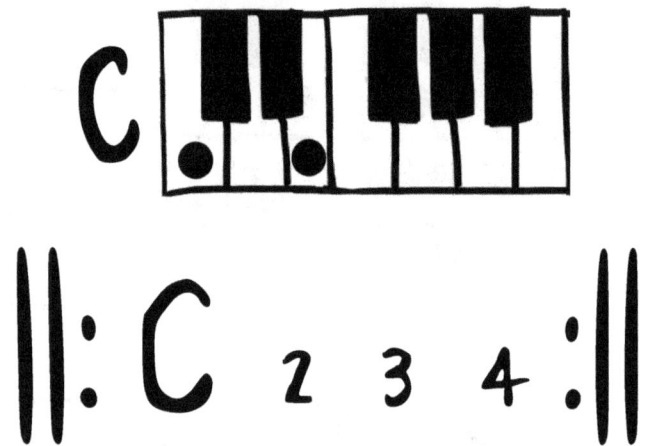

Using the chord C with four beats, let's try these rhythm patterns:

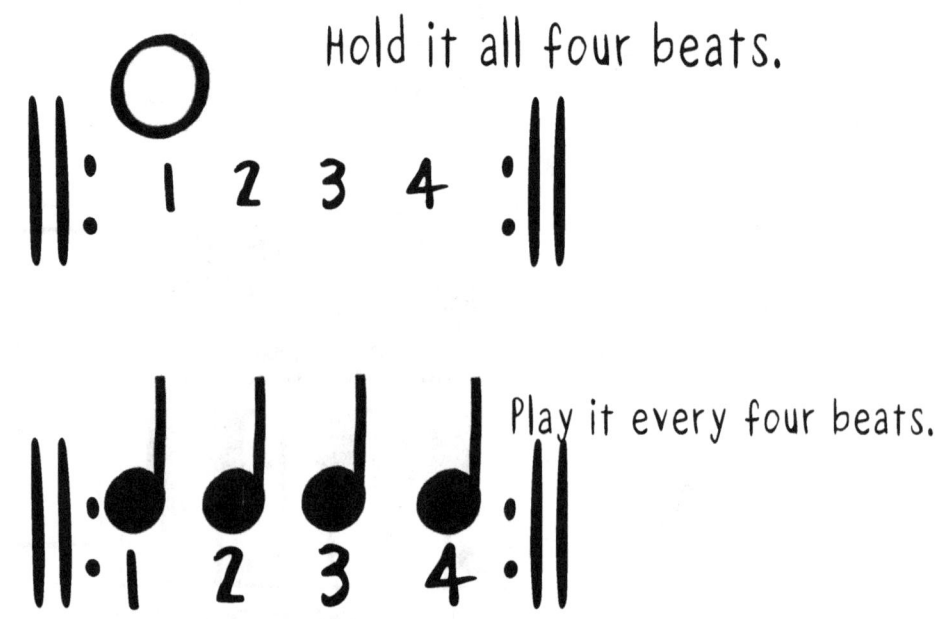

You can refer back to page 47 to practice some of these notes and rhythms.

Keep Changing it Up

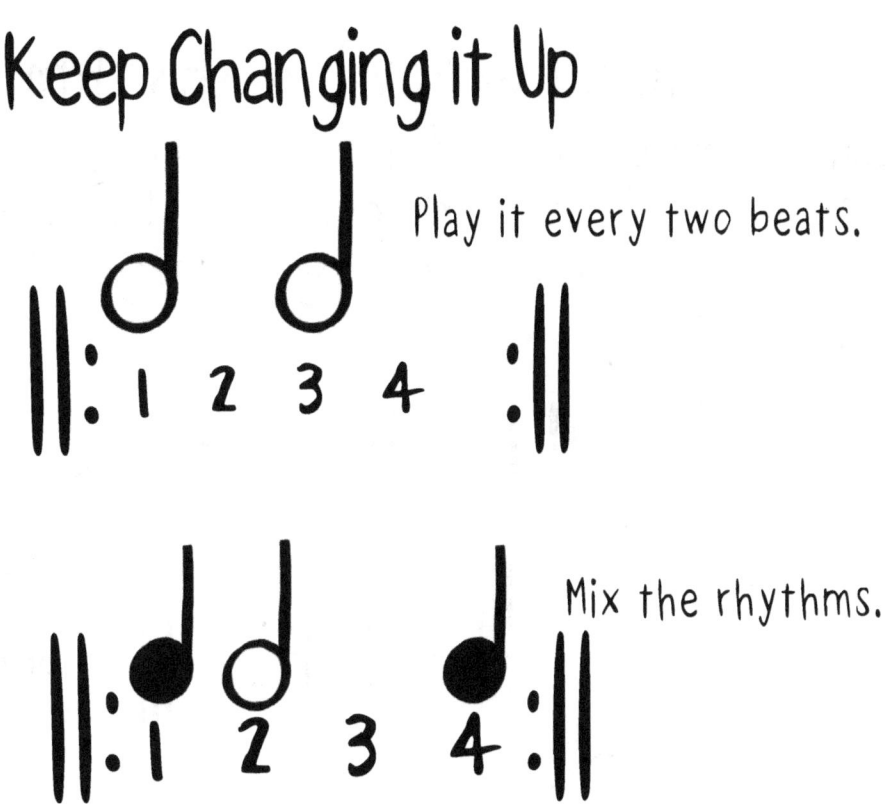

Play it every two beats.

Mix the rhythms.

Here are two options with a faster sounding rhythm using eighth notes.

Now, since you have more ways to play simple chords, go back and try songs from our songbook or improvise with these rhythms!

♡283

Left Hand Sandwich Rhythm Patterns

You can also make your sandwiches sound different by using different combinations of finger number patterns. Play any sandwich you want, but play it using these number combinations:

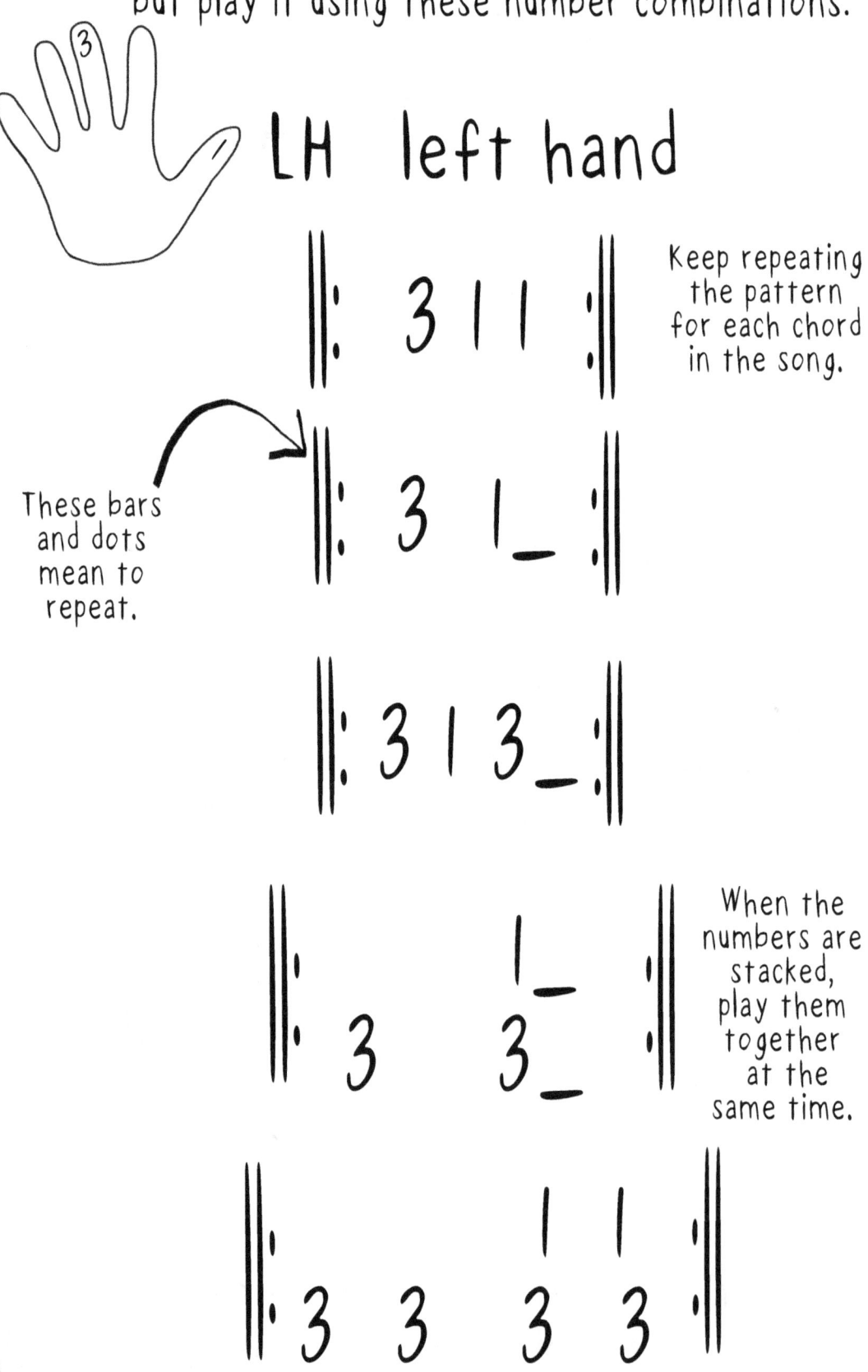

LH left hand

‖: 3 1 1 :‖   Keep repeating the pattern for each chord in the song.

‖: 3 1 1_ :‖   ← These bars and dots mean to repeat.

‖: 3 1 3_ :‖

‖: 3   1_/3_ :‖   When the numbers are stacked, play them together at the same time.

‖: 3 3 1/3 1/3 :‖

Right Hand Sandwich Rhythm Patterns

These are the same patterns, but how you would play them using your right hand?

RH right hand

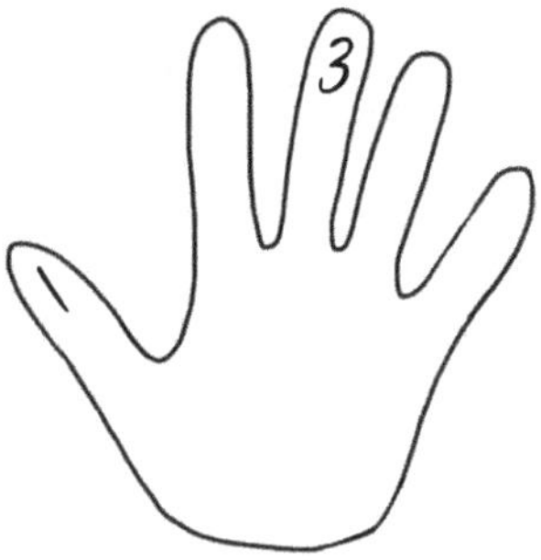

$\|: 1 \ 3 \ 3 :\|$

$\|: 1 \quad 3\_ :\|$

$\|: 1 \ 3 \ 1\_ :\|$

$\|: \ 1 \ \ \begin{matrix}3\_\\1\_\end{matrix} :\|$

$\|: 1 \ 1 \ \begin{matrix}3\ 3\\1\ 1\end{matrix} :\|$

♡285

Can We Add More to the Inside of our Sandwiches?

Before, we only had one thing in our sandwiches:

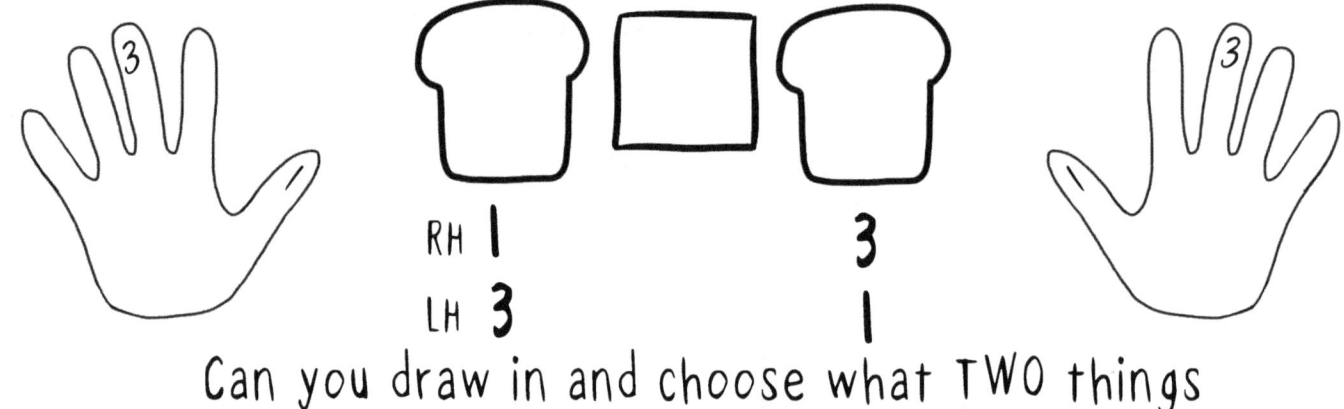

Can you draw in and choose what TWO things to put in these two bigger sandwiches?

Try a few sandwiches with these finger numbers.

Can you draw in and choose what THREE things to put in these two even bigger sandwiches?

Try some more sandwiches with these finger numbers.

NOW LET'S PLAY BIGGER SANDWICHES

You can keep your fingers in the same place.

one slice of bread

In musical terms, this is called a NOTE.

1

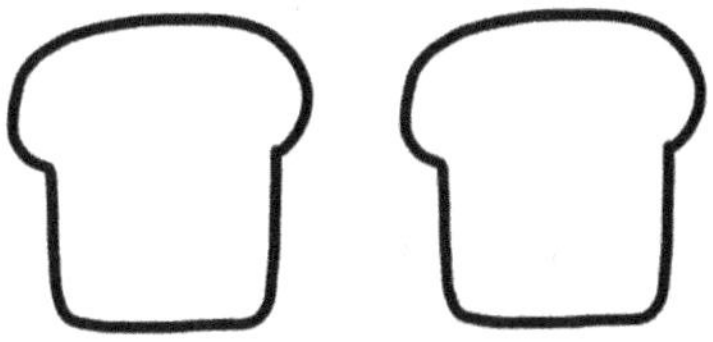

two slices of bread

In musical terms, this is called a second or a 2nd interval.

1 2

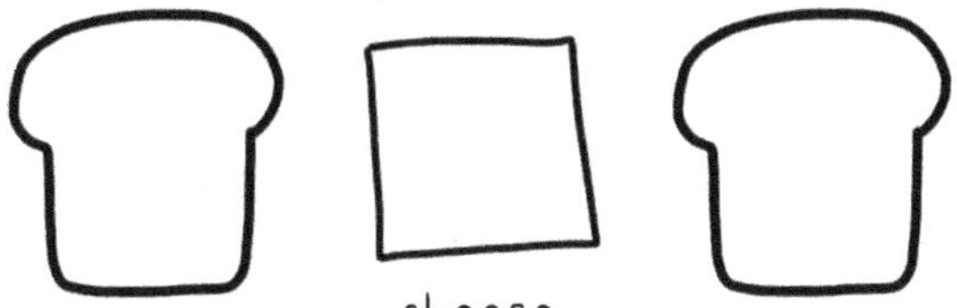

cheese

In musical terms, this is called a third or a 3rd interval.

1 3

add lettuce

In musical terms, this is called a fourth or a 4th interval.

1 4

add tomato

In musical terms, this is called a fifth or a 5th interval.

1 5

♡287

Another Way to Write BIGGER SANDWICHES

If we stack the finger numbers on top of each other like this, then you can play those two finger numbers together to make the different sandwiches, or musical intervals as we call them.

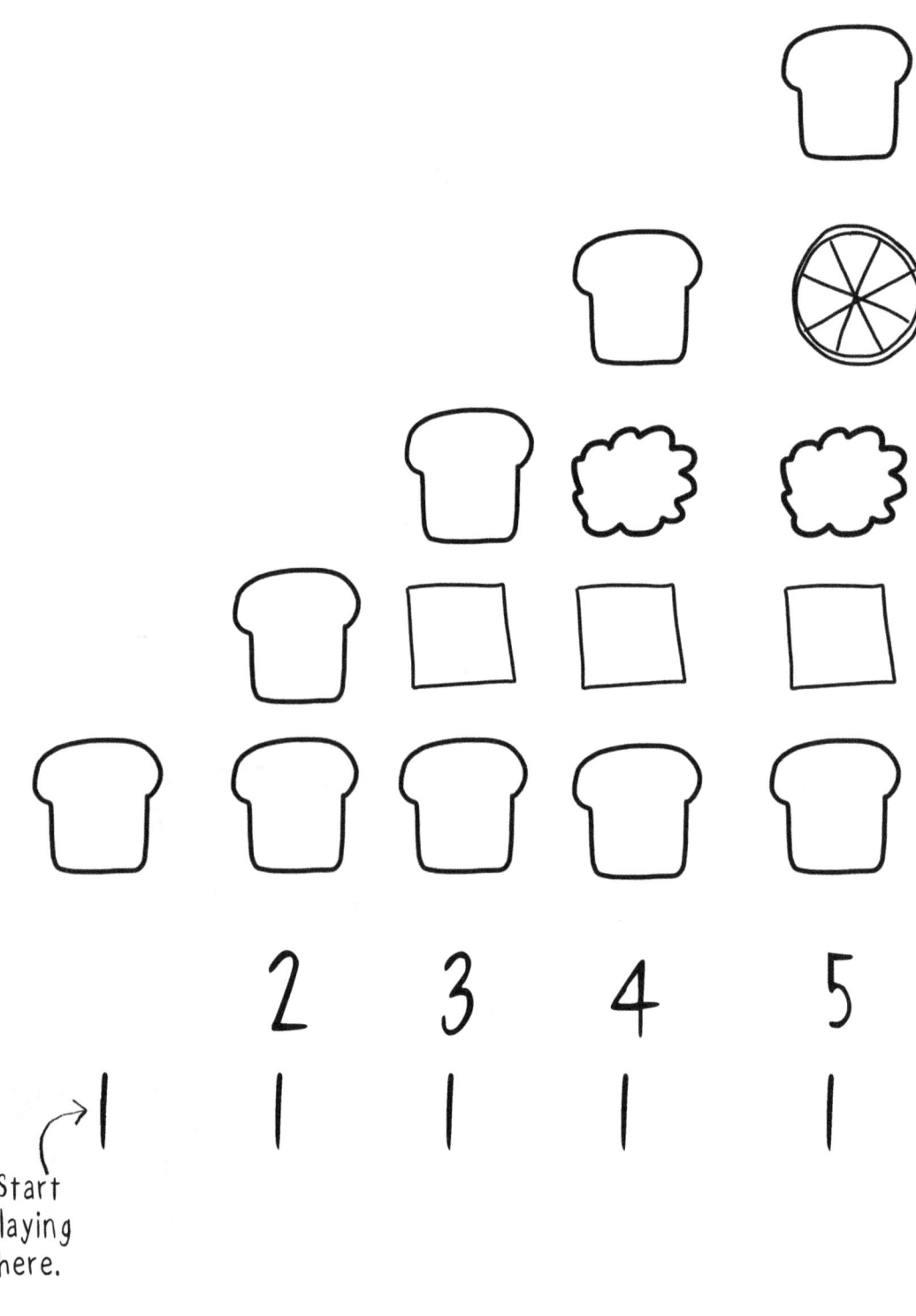

PB&J and What? SANDWICHES

Try these same sandwiches with different ingredients.

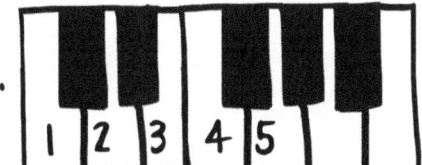

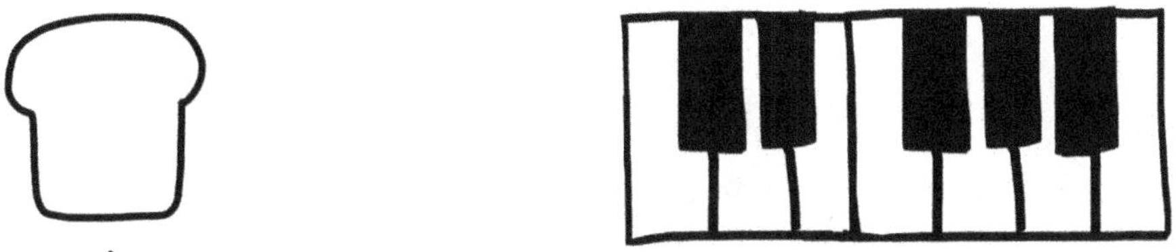

1

Now draw the first note dot.

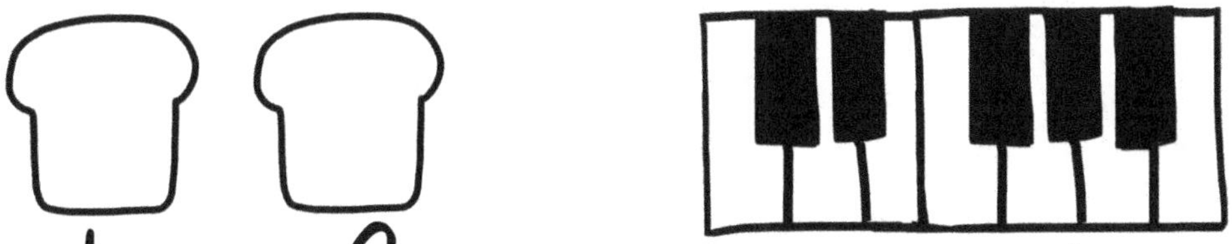

1 2

Draw a 2nd.

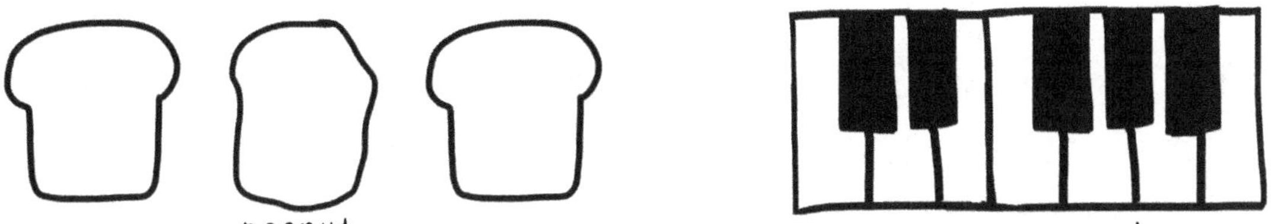

1 peanut butter 3

Draw a 3rd.

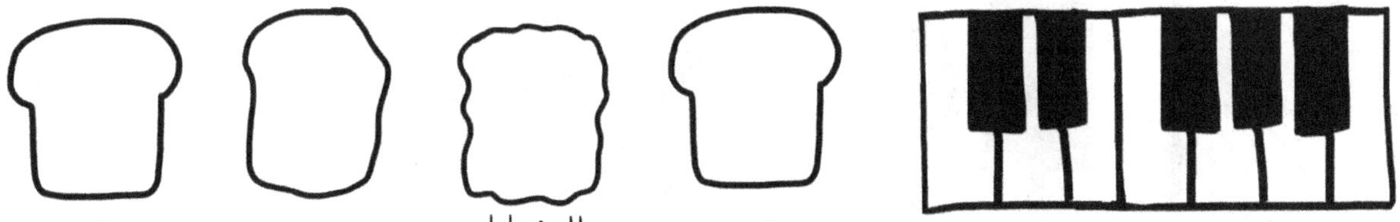

1 add jelly 4

Draw a 4th.

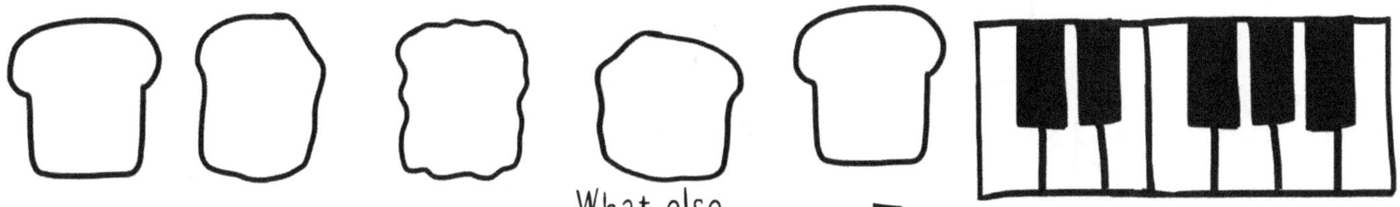

1 What else can you add? 5

Draw a 5th.

Double Decker SANDWICHES (TRIADS)

After you have played the basic sandwiches with only two notes (thirds), then you can do what I like to call **double decker sandwiches**. In music, we call them **triads** because there are 3 notes.

A TRIangle has how many sides? 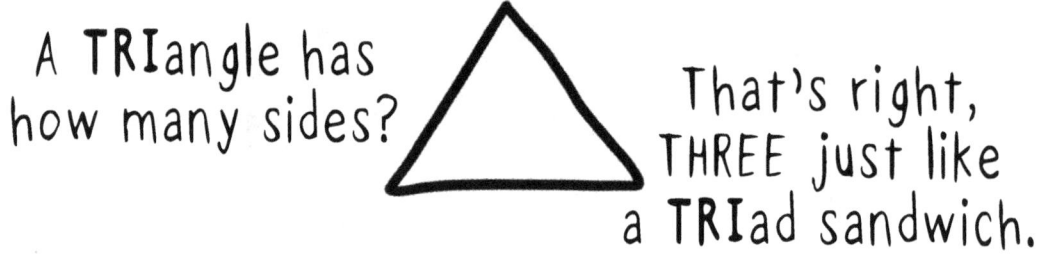 That's right, THREE just like a TRIad sandwich.

Start by making the first part of the sandwich with fingers 1 and 3, then, add one more piece of bread on top with finger 5 like this:

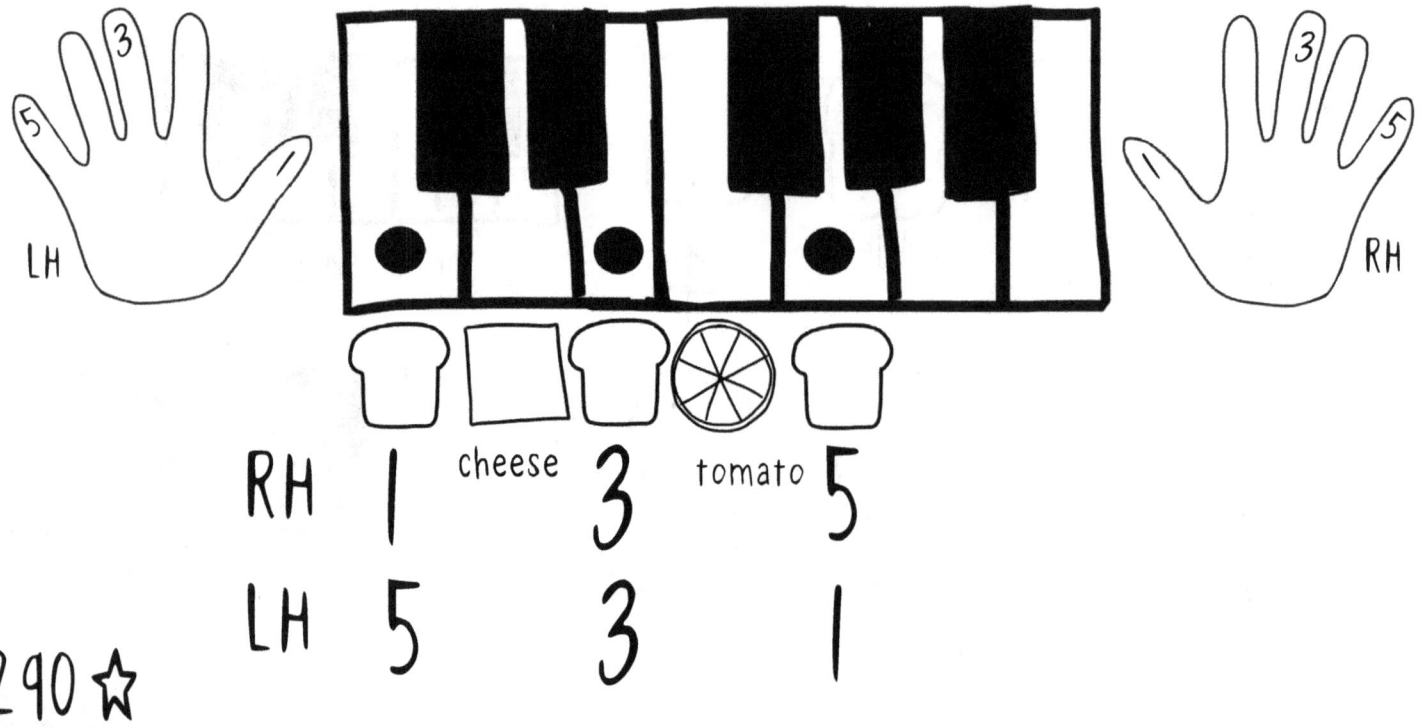

We can write these double decker sandwiches or triads like this.

5
3
1

Try playing ALL the triads on the white keys:

Can you draw the dots or color the notes yourself?

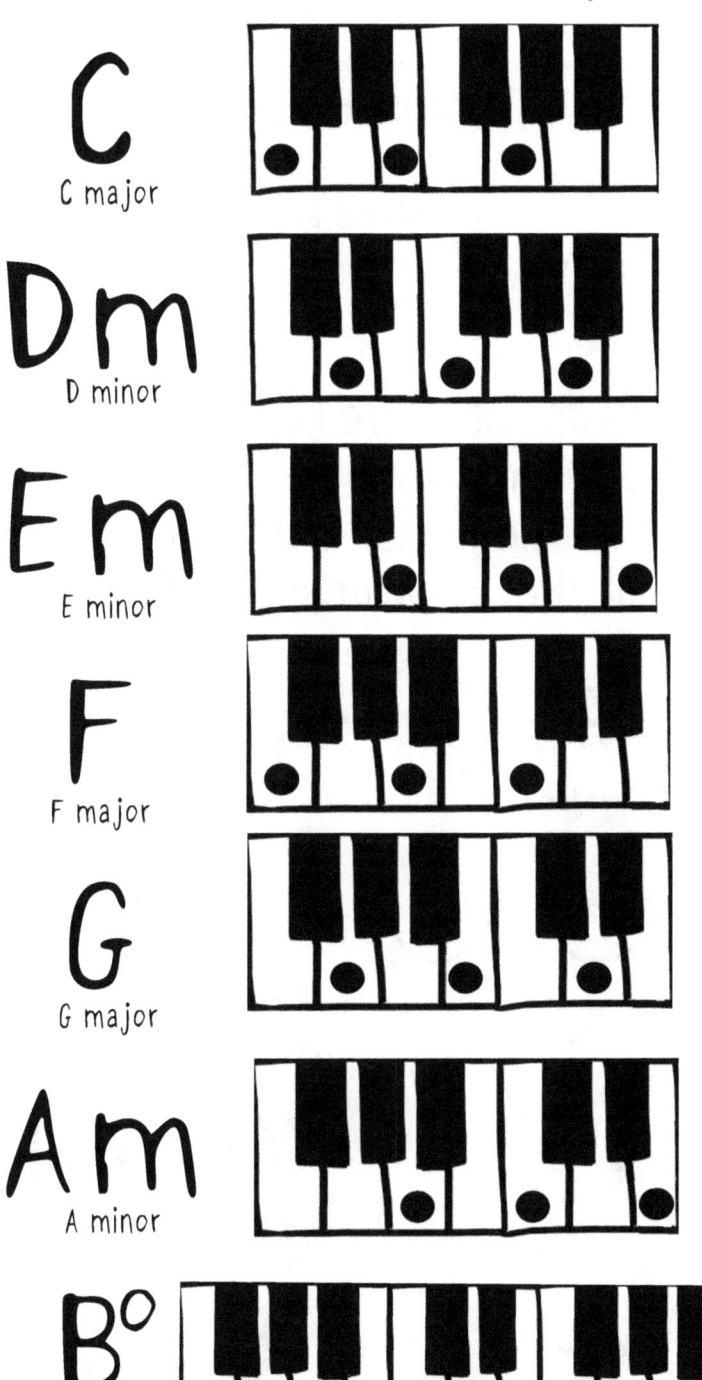
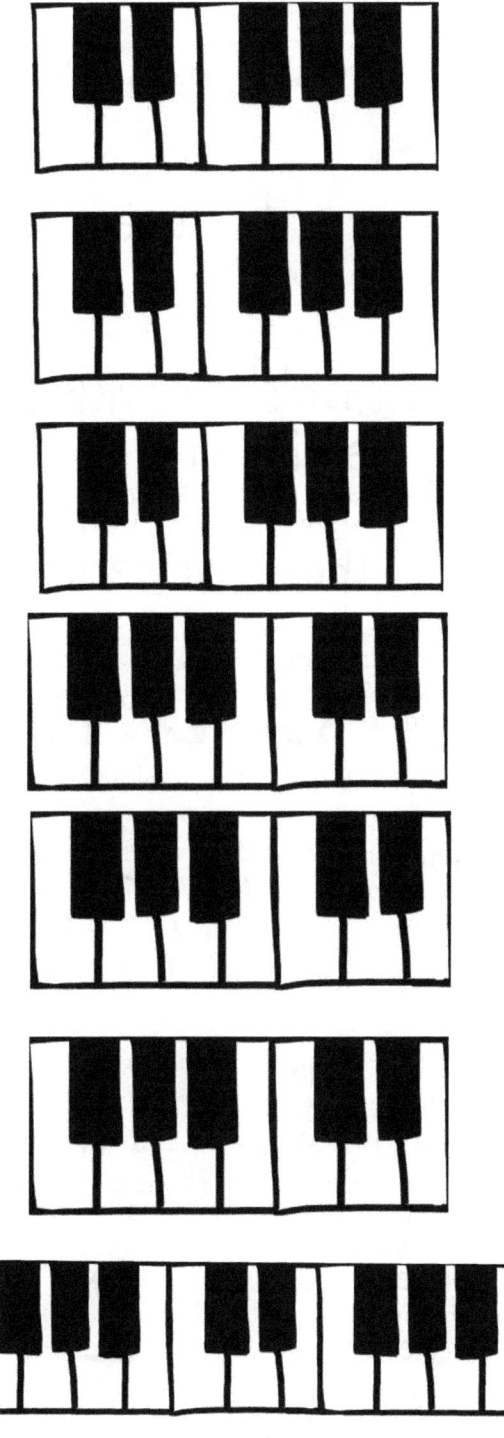

C — C major
Dm — D minor
Em — E minor
F — F major
G — G major
Am — A minor
B° — B diminished

♡ 291

How Do These Sandwiches Sound?

Listen to how they sound different:

Some sound **happy**. ⌣ These are MAJOR chords.

Some sound **sad**. ⌢ These are MINOR chords.

And one sounds **funky**. ∿ These are DIMINISHED chords.

These chords (sandwiches) can be placed on the white keys on the piano starting on C and they each have their own place in the C major scale (which are shown in the Roman numerals and these numbers below). We call these diatonic chords.

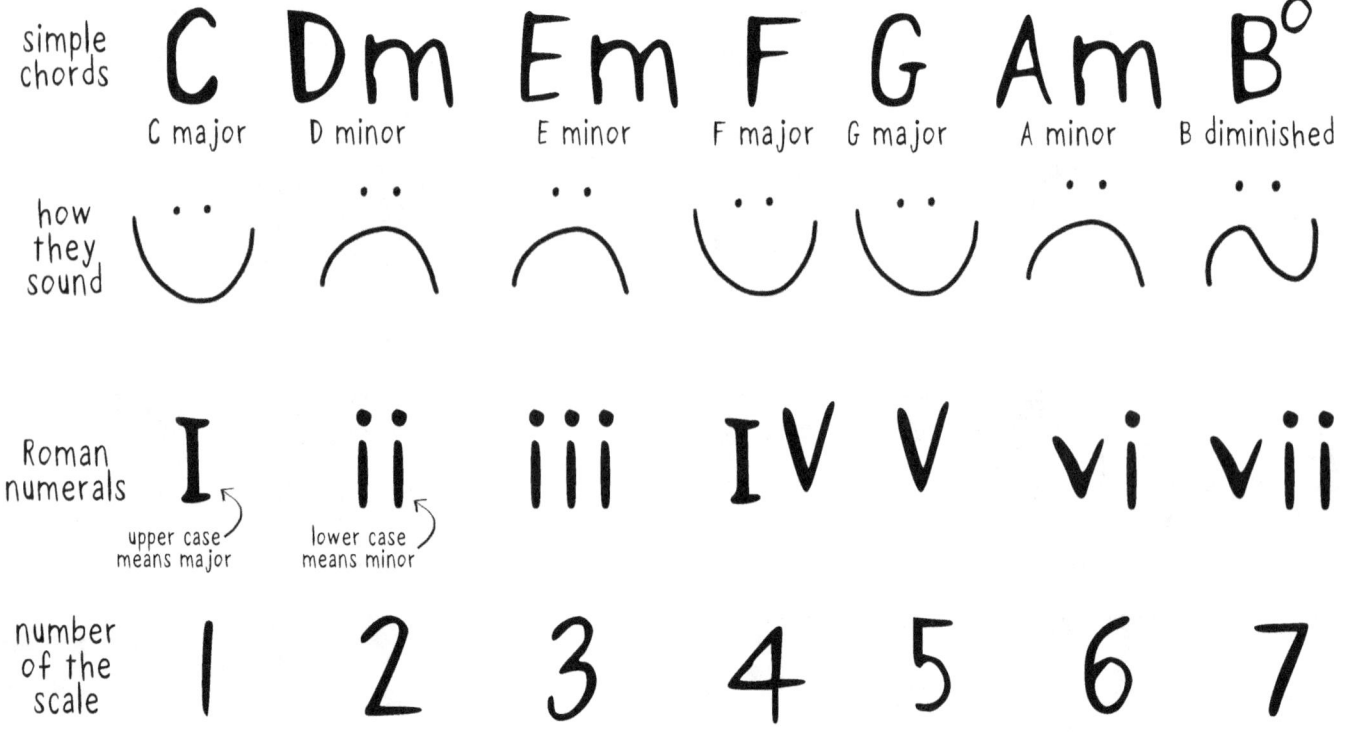

simple chords	C	Dm	Em	F	G	Am	B°
	C major	D minor	E minor	F major	G major	A minor	B diminished
how they sound	⌣	⌢	⌢	⌣	⌣	⌢	∿
Roman numerals	I	ii	iii	IV	V	vi	vii
	upper case means major	lower case means minor					
number of the scale	1	2	3	4	5	6	7

292 ☆

Where Do Diatonic Triads Go?

What's so great about these chords
is that you just have to know where to put
the first note (where to put finger 1),
make a double decker sandwich on it,
and then you can play them all in order.

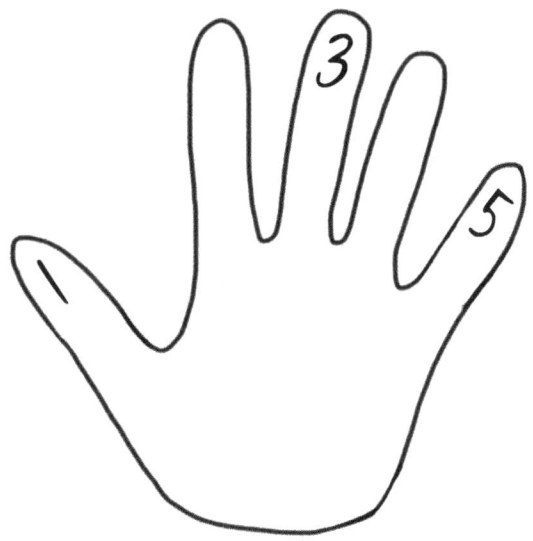

Try playing these diatonic triads based in the key of C major up and down the piano.

If you want ideas for other ways to play them, turn the page.

♡ 293

Left Hand Triad Rhythm Patterns

Here, you can play some different rhythm options like we did on pages 280-281 for thirds, but now with fingers 1, 3, and 5.

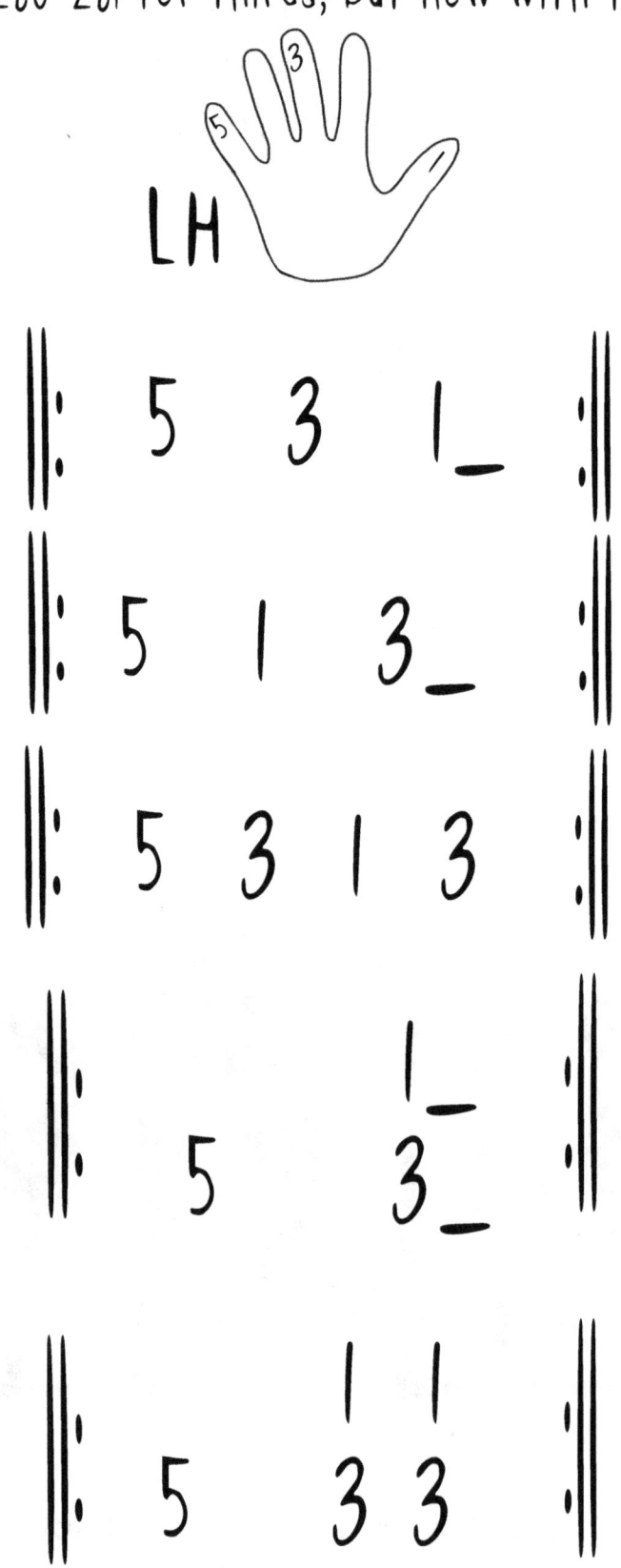

Right Hand Triad Rhythm Patterns

Give it a try with the right hand too.

RH

||: 1   3   5_ :||

||: 1   5   3_ :||

||: 1   3   5   3 :||

||: 1   5_ / 3_ :||

||: 1   5 5 / 3 3 :||

There are even more of these patterns in warm ups on pages 326.   ♡295

All Major Triads (Three Note Sandwiches)

Notice again, how these ones have FOUR steps inbetween the first two notes.
Then, there are THREE steps between the second two notes.
This is because a major triad is made up of a major third and then a minor third.

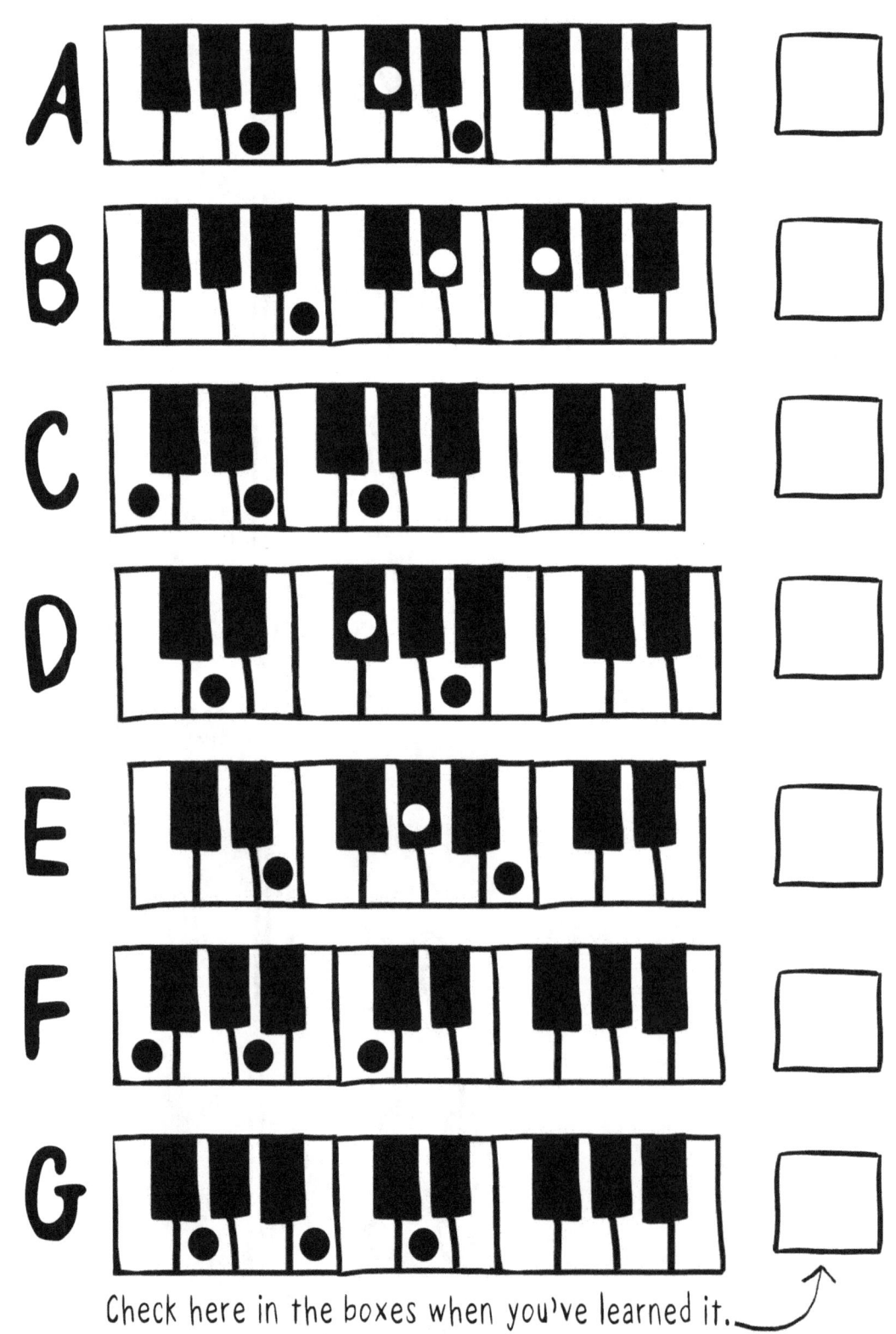

Check here in the boxes when you've learned it.

All Minor Triads (Three Note Sandwiches)

These ones have THREE steps inbetween the first two notes.
Then, there are FOUR steps between the second two notes.
This is because a minor triad is made up of a minor third and then a major third.

Am ☐

Bm ☐

Cm ☐

Dm ☐

Em ☐

Fm ☐

Gm ☐

Now, you can go back and play all the songs in the songbook,
but with these triads and not just small sandwiches.

♡297

How Can You Learn More Songs?

Now that you know all of these concepts for playing and singing songs, you can learn almost any song you want. All you need to know are what chords to play and what the melody notes are.

Here are FOUR METHODS for Learning Songs

If you wrote some of your favorite songs on page 9, but didn't get to learn how to play them yet, try one of these methods to learn how to play and sing them now!

Method 1 — Play by Ear

Listen to the song and pause it when you need to listen for the chord. It will most likely be one of the chords on pages 296-297 To learn the melody by ear, sing it until you find it on the piano.

Method 2 — Look Up the Chords on the Internet

If you're not up for the time it takes to learn by ear, or if it's just not your thing, other people have ALREADY done the work for you! Type into any internet search engine for the name of the song and piano chords. Searching for a website for guitar chords or tabs can also help you find the right chords.

Method 3 — Watch YouTube Tutorials

There are so many amazing piano tutorials on YouTube. Just type the name of the song and piano tutorial, and you'll get many amazing teachers and people helping to teach you how to learn the very song you want to learn.

Method 4 — Learn from a Music Teacher or Musician

Of course, while many teachers and musicians on YouTube do an amazing job, you might still want to have your own teacher either in person or virtually as well. See if you can find the right teacher for you to support locally, either in person or virtually. Also, you might have a parent, sibling, friend, or family member who can already play the piano! Ask them to share what they know and you can learn so much more.

An Introduction to the Musical Staff

The majority of the book uses a different, more simple, and non-traditional method for playing piano. So next, I will show you only a small preview of how to use these finger numbers to transition to **reading music in the traditional way** on the musical staff.

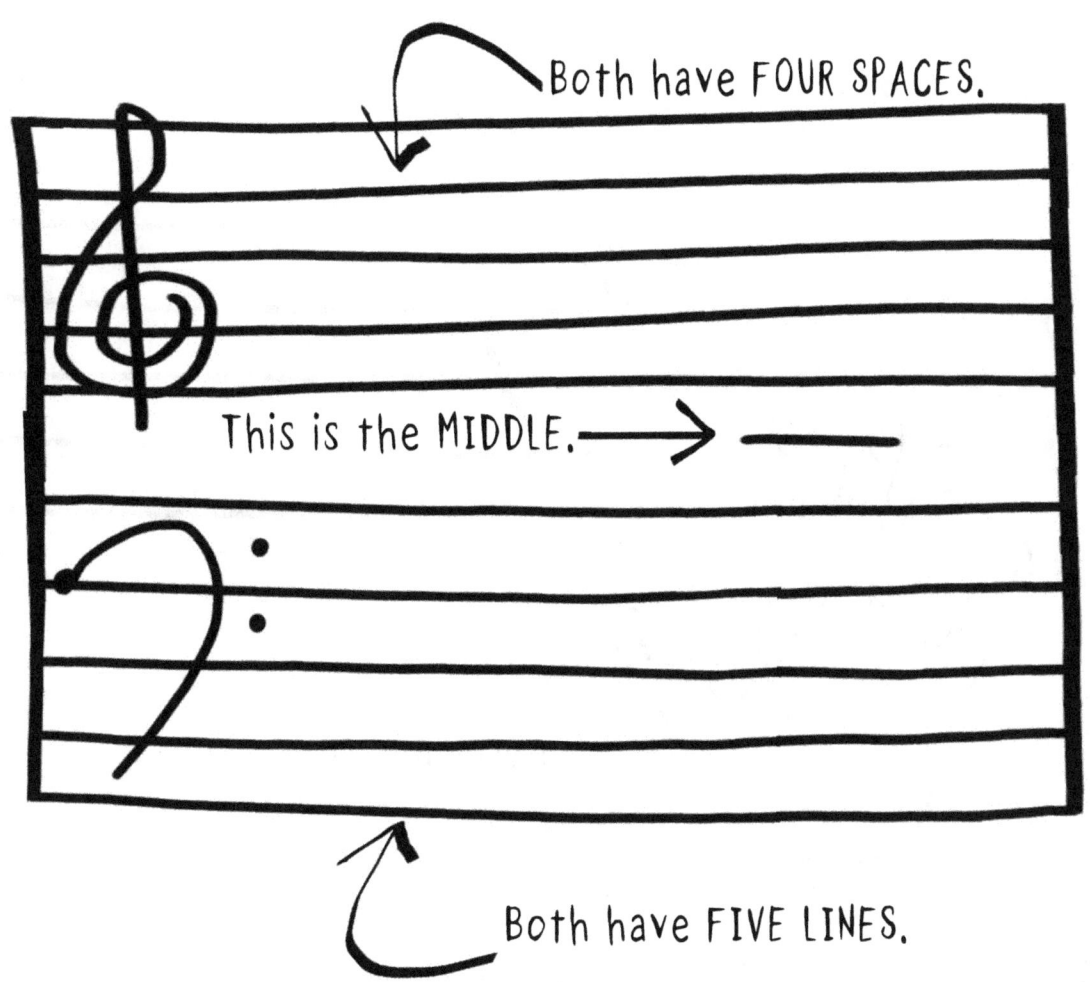

Both have FOUR SPACES.

This is the MIDDLE. →

Both have FIVE LINES.

♡ 299

Start at the Beginning

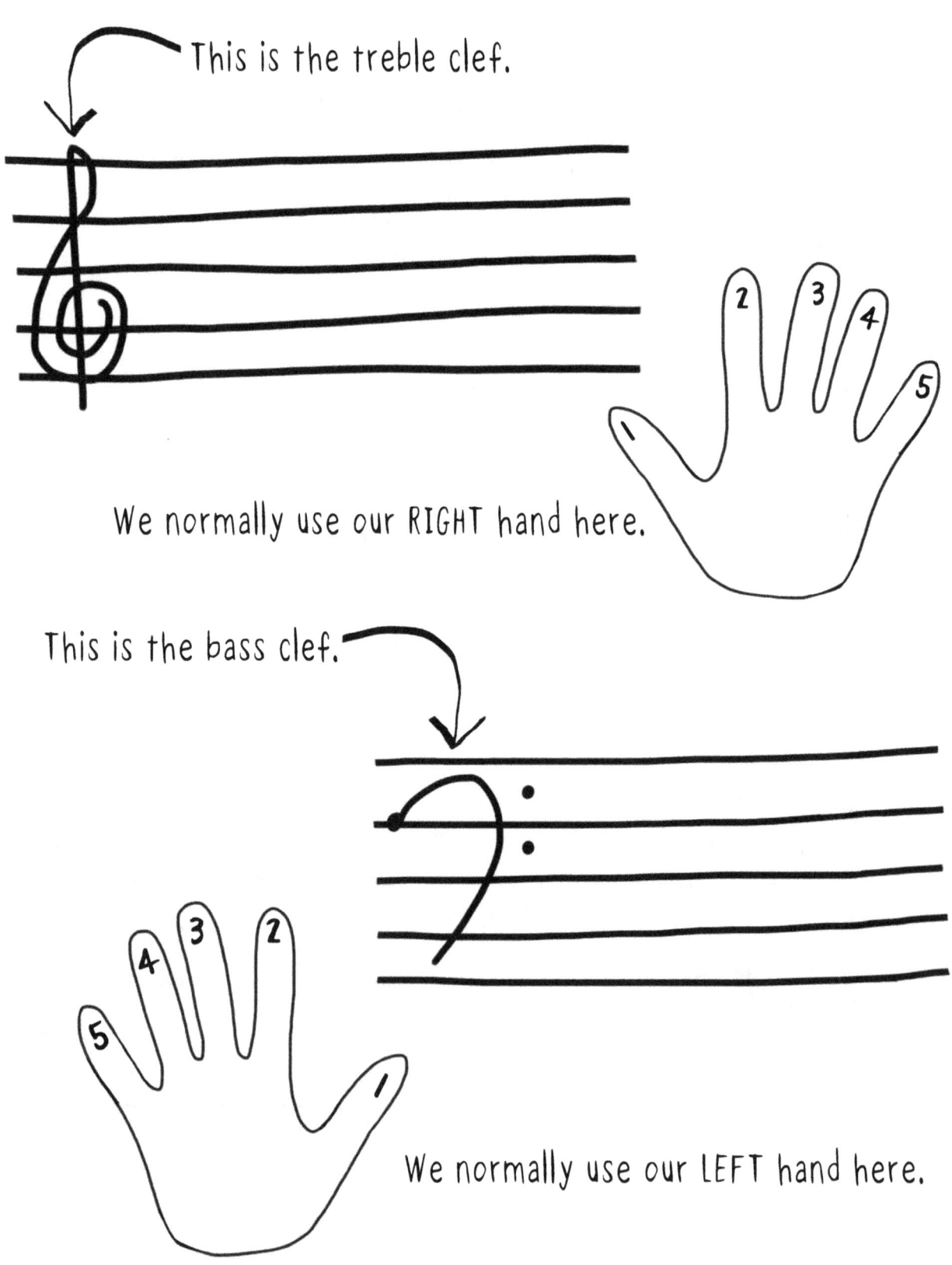

Just Follow the NUMBERS

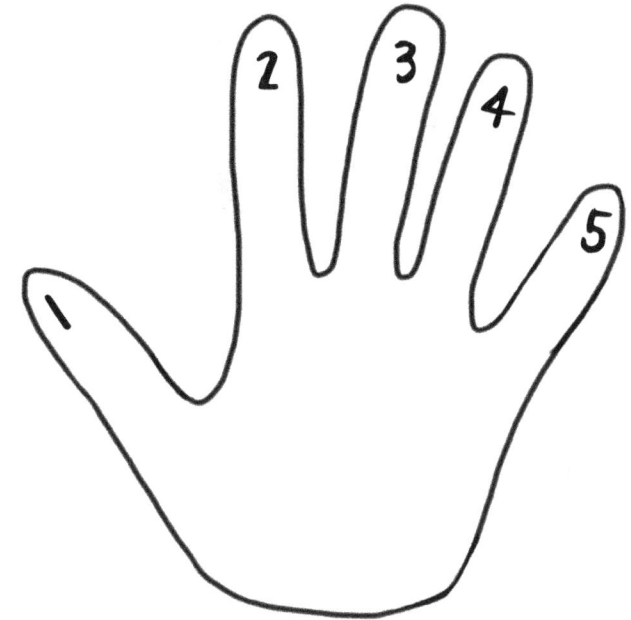

To use THESE finger numbers to learn how to read music, you only need to know where to put the thumb (finger 1) and then the rest will follow.

This is just like we did when I showed you where to put your finger number 1 on the piano.

Turn the page to see where these three finger positions that start on the notes C, F, and G would be on the musical staff.

♡ 301

Left Hand on C

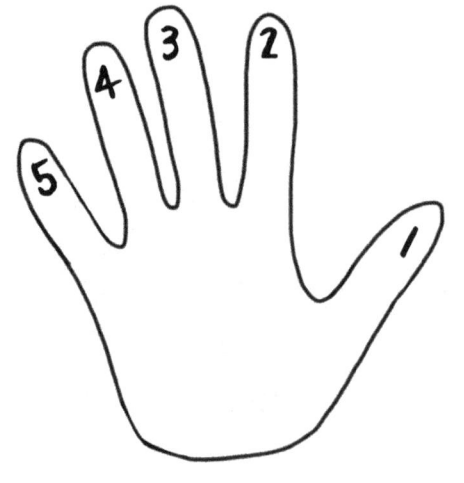

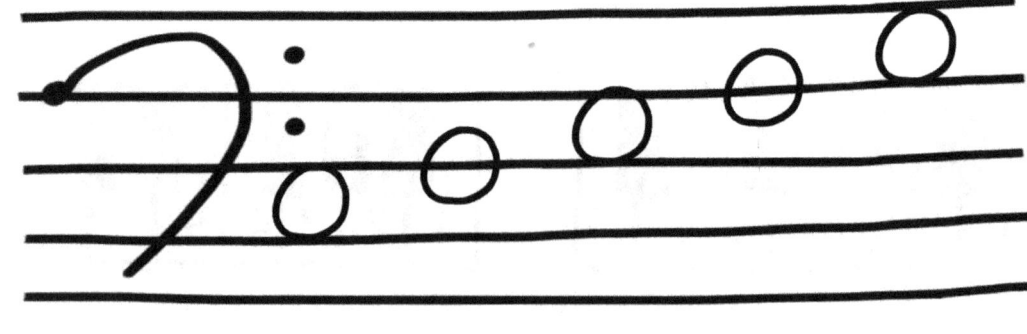

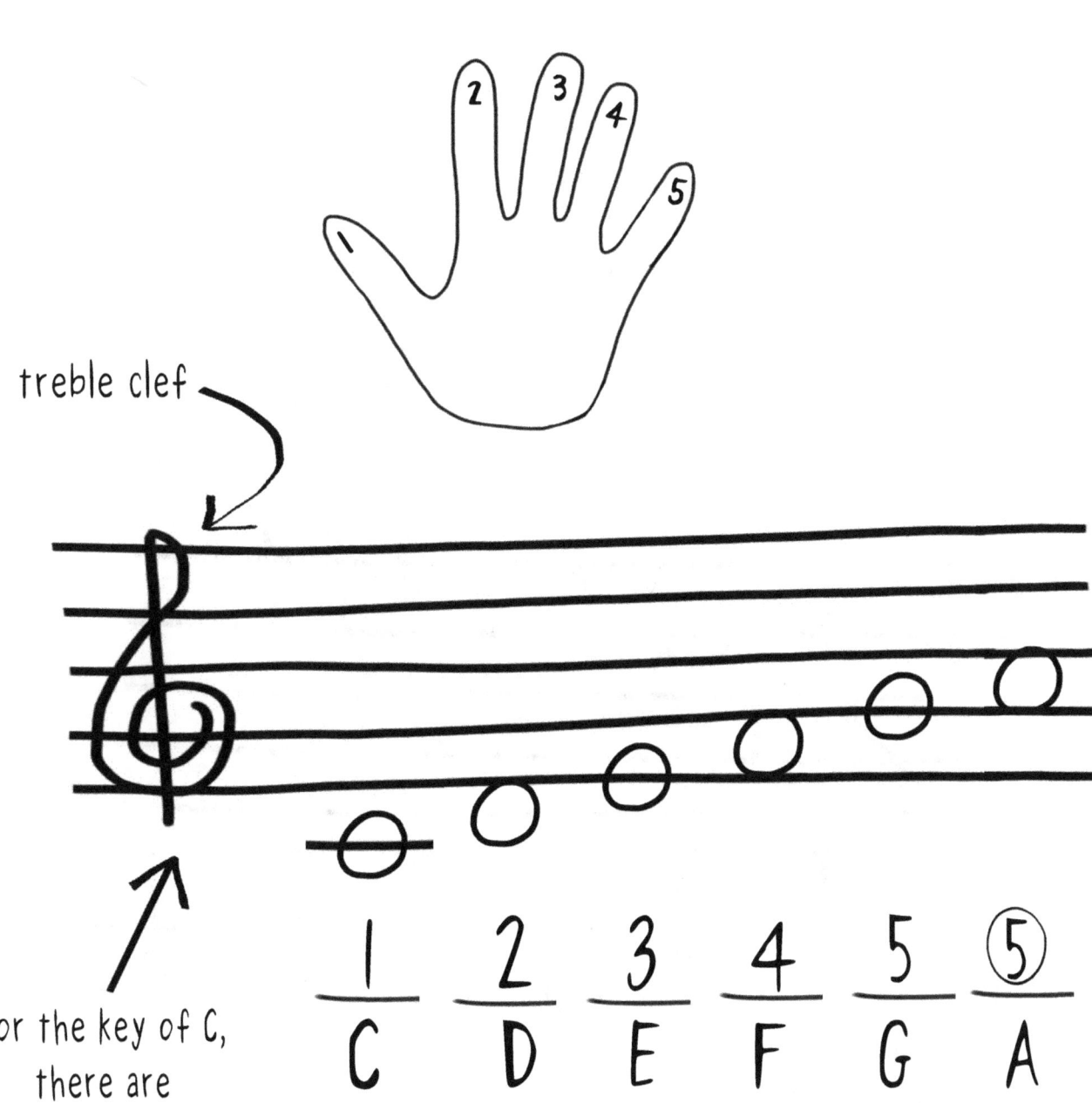

Left Hand on F

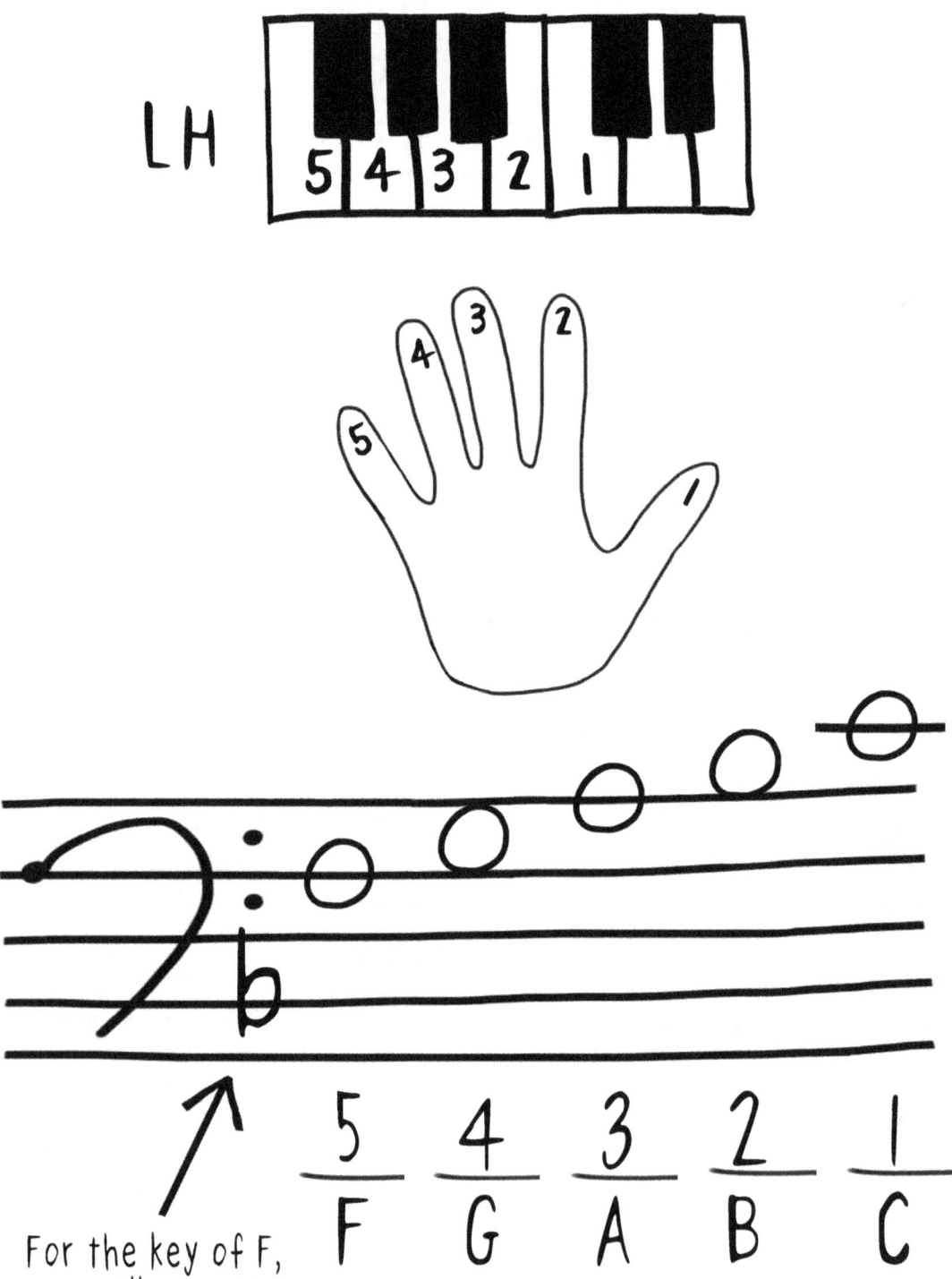

For the key of F, you will see this accidental B♭ on the second line in the bass clef.

5	4	3	2	1
F	G	A	B	C

304 ☆

Right Hand on F

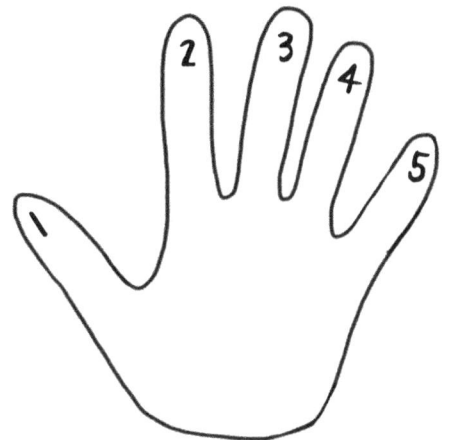

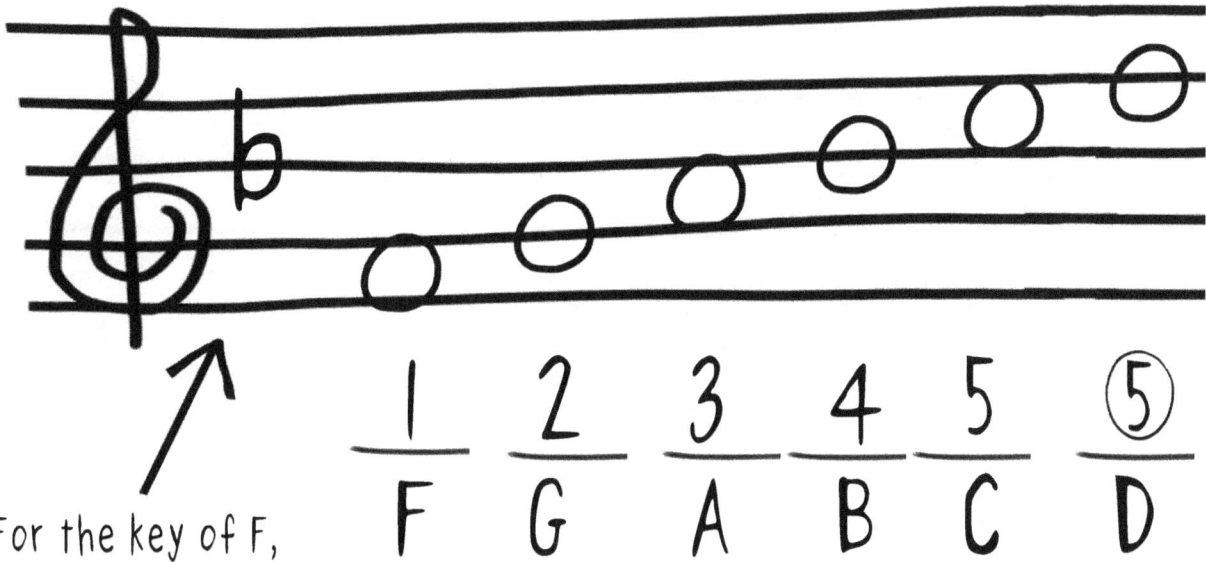

For the key of F, you will see this accidental Bb on the third line in the treble clef.

♡ 305

Left Hand on G

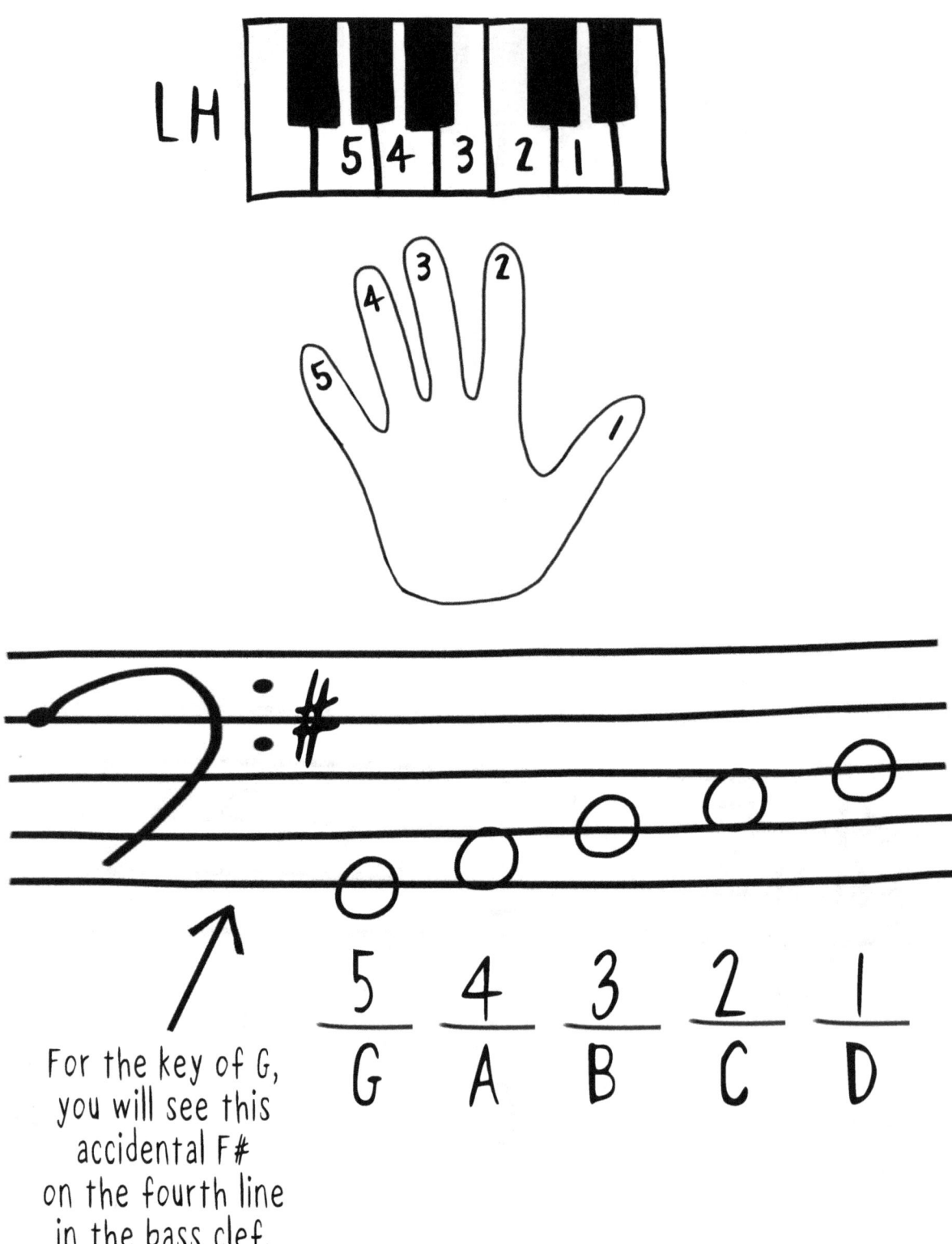

For the key of G, you will see this accidental F# on the fourth line in the bass clef.

Right Hand on G

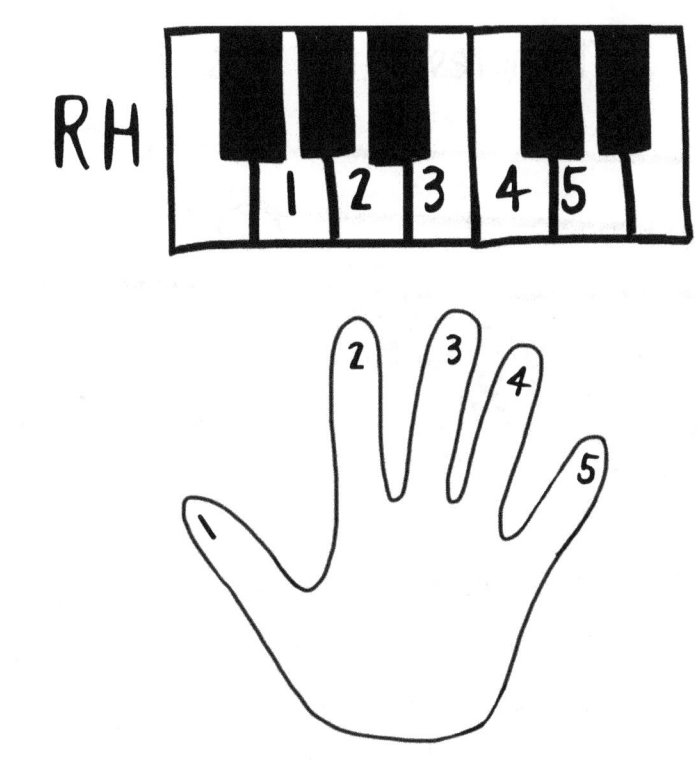

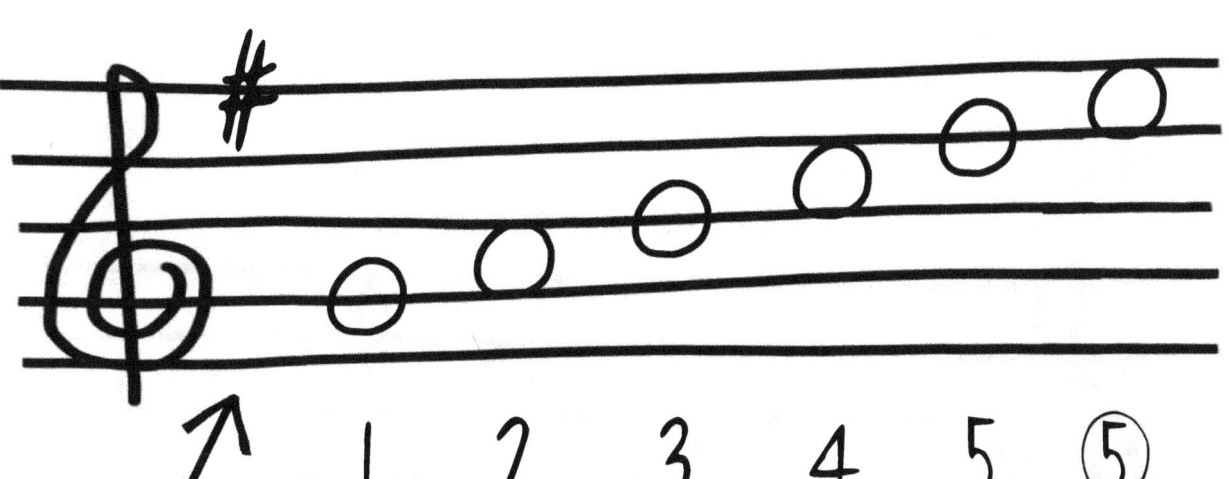

For the key of G, you will see this accidental F# on the fifth line in the treble clef.

♡307

The Musical Alphabet on the Treble Clef

The notes on the lines:

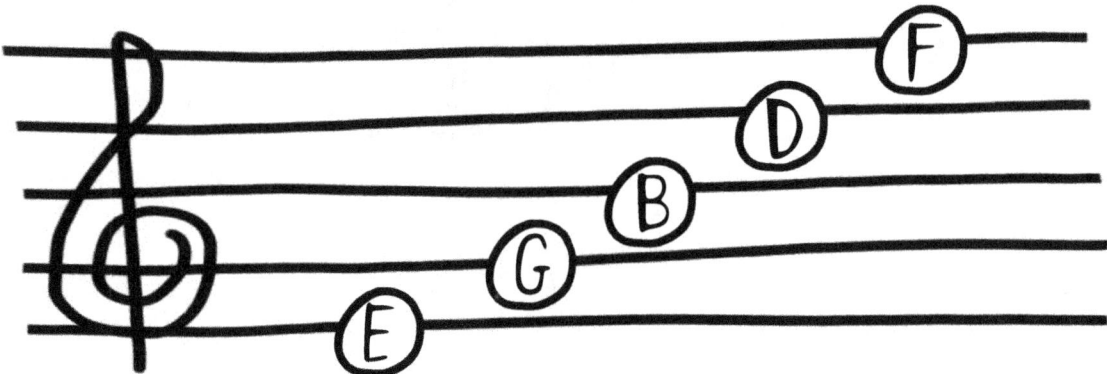

We can use some sentences to remember the alphabet on the treble clef lines. The most common one is
Every Good Boy Does Fine.
The one that I like is
Every Good Boat Does Float.

The notes on the spaces:

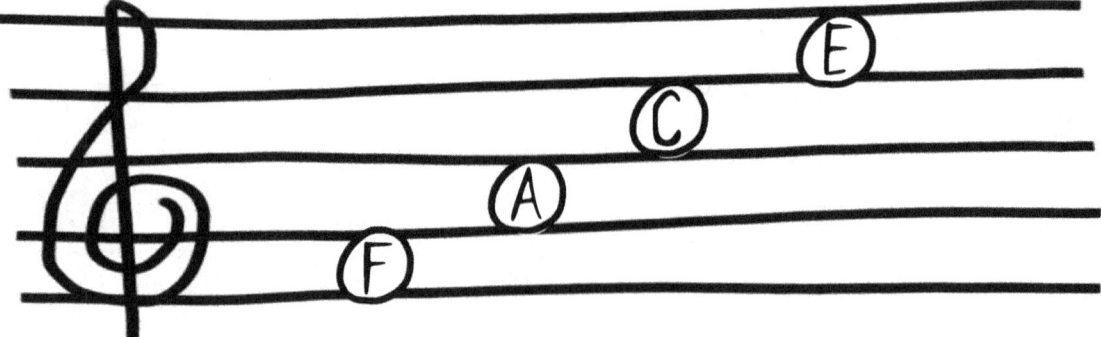

For the spaces of the treble clef, it is easy to see that they spell a word and that is FACE.

The Musical Alphabet on the Bass Clef

The notes on the lines:

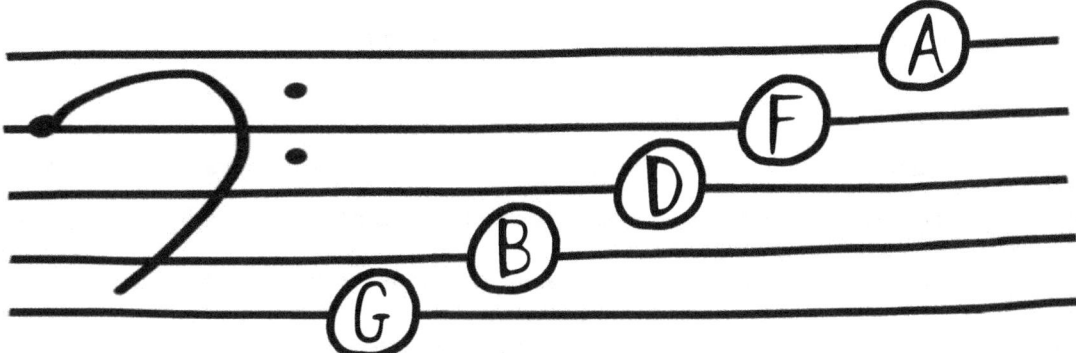

We can use some sentences to remember the alphabet on the bass clef lines. The most common one is
Good Boys Deserve Fudge Always.
The one that I like is
Girls Beautifully Dream For Adventure.

The notes on the spaces:

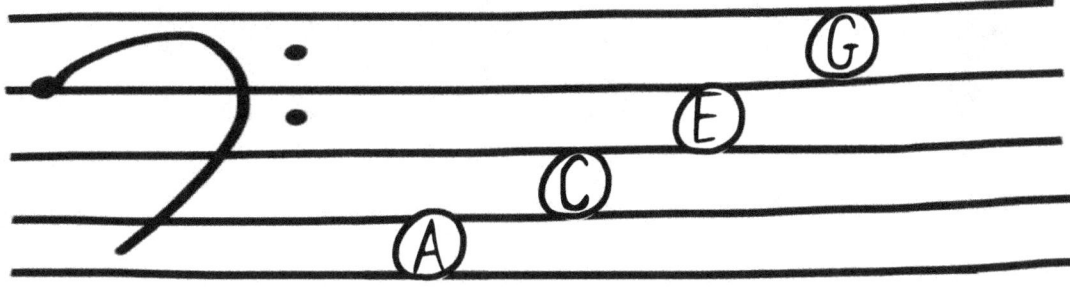

The spaces of the bass clef don't spell a word, so a common sentence is
All Cows Eat Garbage.
One that I also really like is
All Children Eat Groceries.

♡ 309

All Notes on the Bass Clef

Now, you can walk up the bass clef with the alphabet to see ALL of the notes on the staff!

Remember that these notes are the lower notes that are on the left side of the piano from middle C

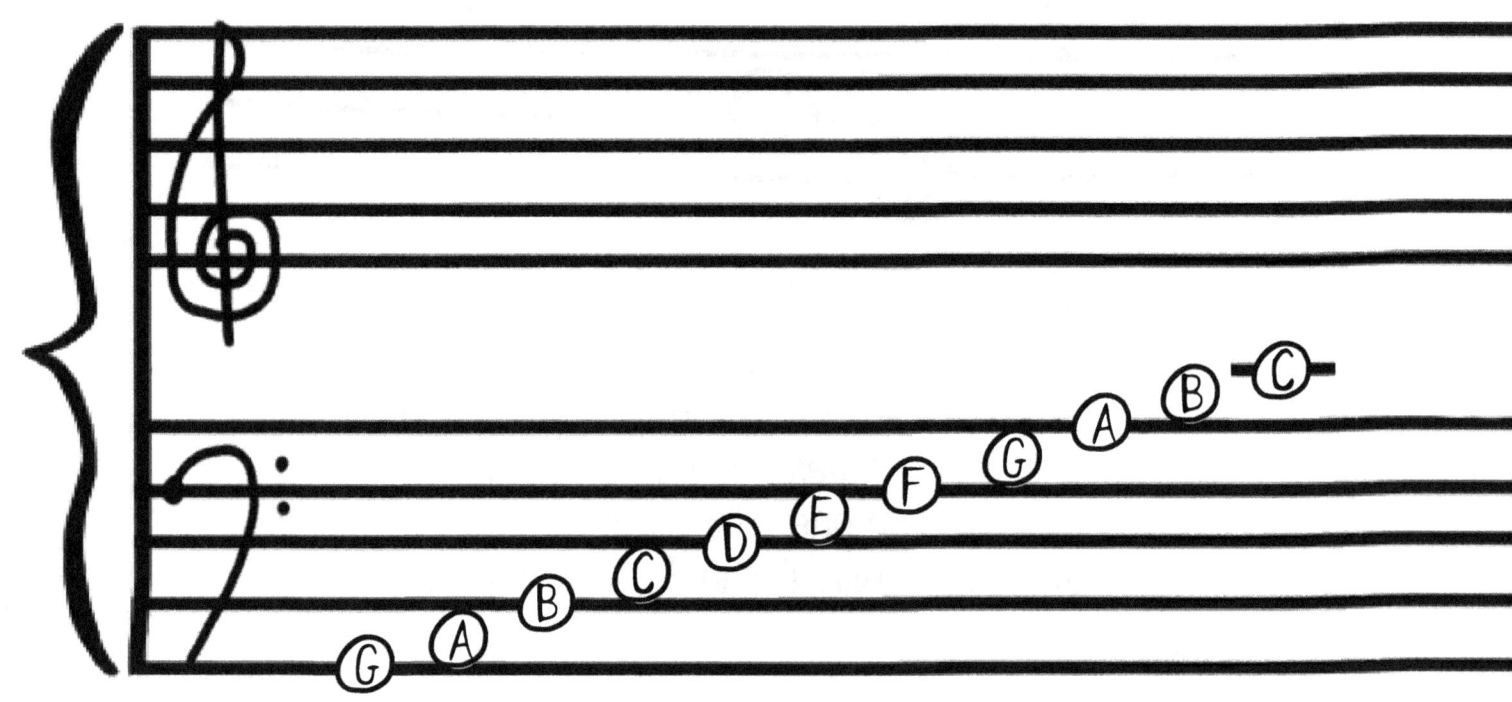

This C is called middle C. Find the C in the middle of your piano. That's the one.

Most of the time, but not always, the LEFT HAND plays the notes on the bass clef.

LH
LEFT HAND

310

All Notes on the Treble Cleff

Then, keep going to walk up the treble clef with the alphabet to see ALL of the notes on the staff!

Also, remember that these notes are the higher notes that are on the right side of the piano from middle C

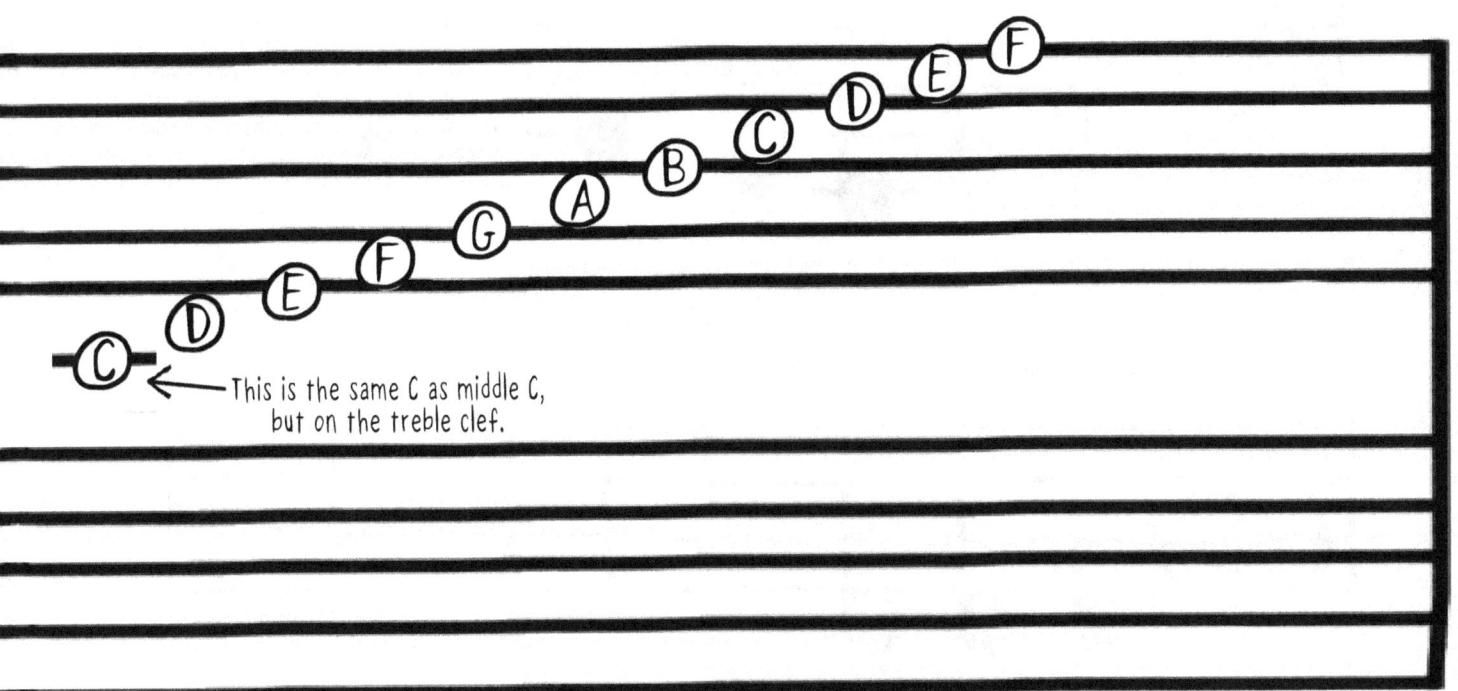

← This is the same C as middle C, but on the treble clef.

Most of the time, but not always, the RIGHT HAND plays the notes on the treble clef.

Give Reading Music a Try

Try one of the songs from this book using the actual written music! Use page 303 to see where to put your fingers and to reference the finger numbers. Can you guess what song it is?

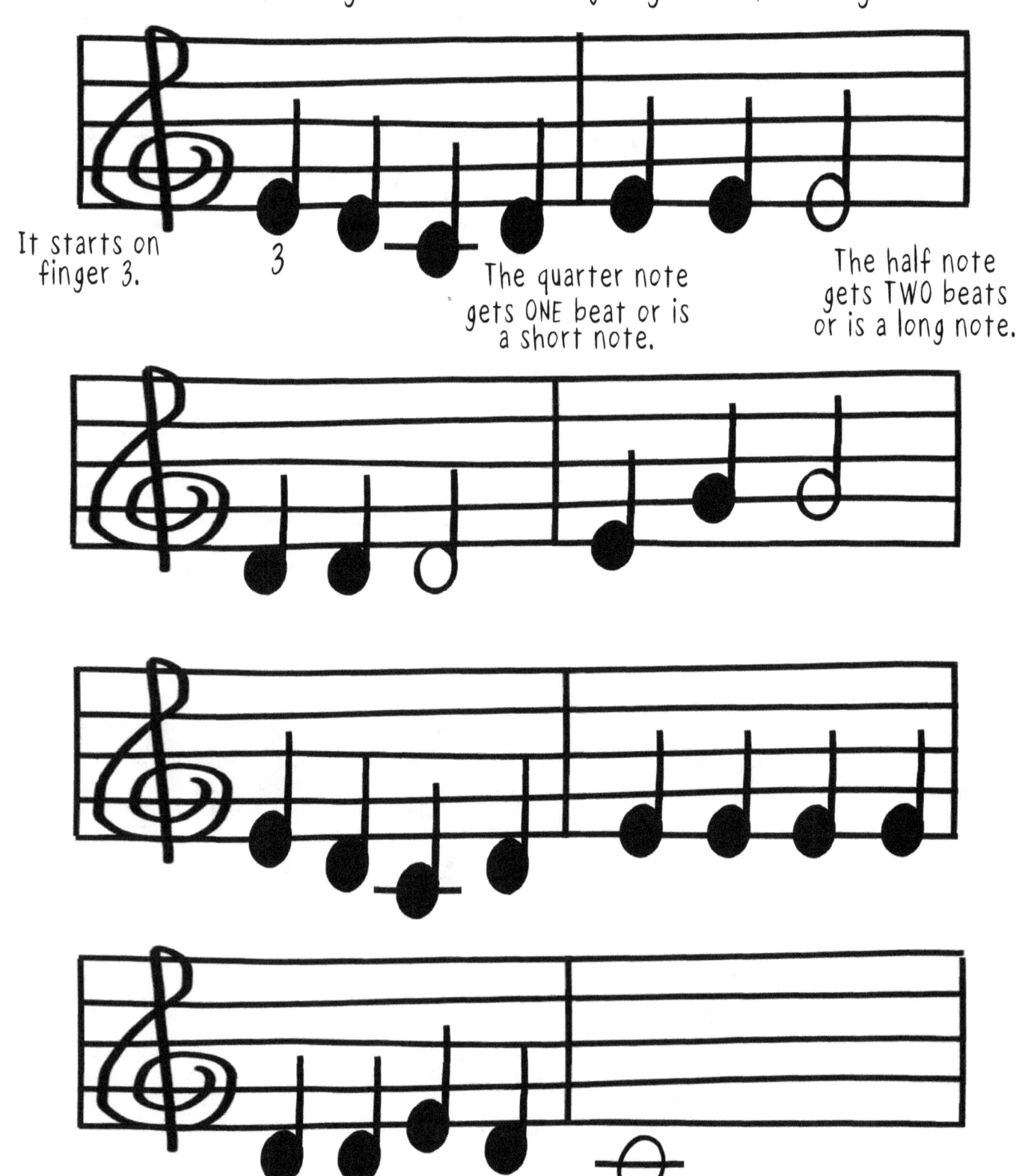

It starts on finger 3.

The quarter note gets ONE beat or is a short note.

The half note gets TWO beats or is a long note.

To see what song it is, go to page 126.

Warm Ups

On the following pages, you will learn what warm ups are on the piano (page 314) and how to play them (page 315). There are 103 warms ups on pages 316-333.

You don't have to go from warm up 1 to 103 in order. You can if you want to though. Also, you can use the circles to color in when you have done a warm up, but you might want to practice some of them more than once, especially if you're having a hard time with a certain concept.

You might even find a warm up that is your favorite.

Each page has a focus for the warm ups. I hope these help you practice playing and I hope you might even find these warm ups fun.

If you want a reminder of good finger technique (which is one of the reasons why we do warm ups), you can look at pages 17-20.

If you have practice time, it would be good to choose a warm up or two before you start playing other parts of the book.

If you are just looking for a challenge, a small repetitive exercise, or to fine tune your technique and music theory, then by all means, just come to these pages for those very things.

Carry on!

Warm Ups in Sports

Just like you might warm up or do stretches for a sport, you can do WARM UPS for playing the piano.

In **soccer**, you practice kicking a goal over and over.

In **basketball**, you practice shooting a basket again and again.

In **football**, you kick the ball over the goal post many times so you don't miss in the middle of the game.

In **dancing**, you might twirl, spin or do a move several times before you really master it.

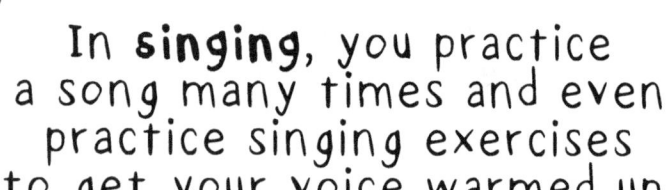

In **singing**, you practice a song many times and even practice singing exercises to get your voice warmed up.

So, with **piano**, we can practice lots of exercises and warm ups too!

Warm Ups on the Piano

The piano is a series of patterns which allows us to REPEAT and play things many times for warm ups.

For the groups of 2s and 3s, you can play them up and down the piano:

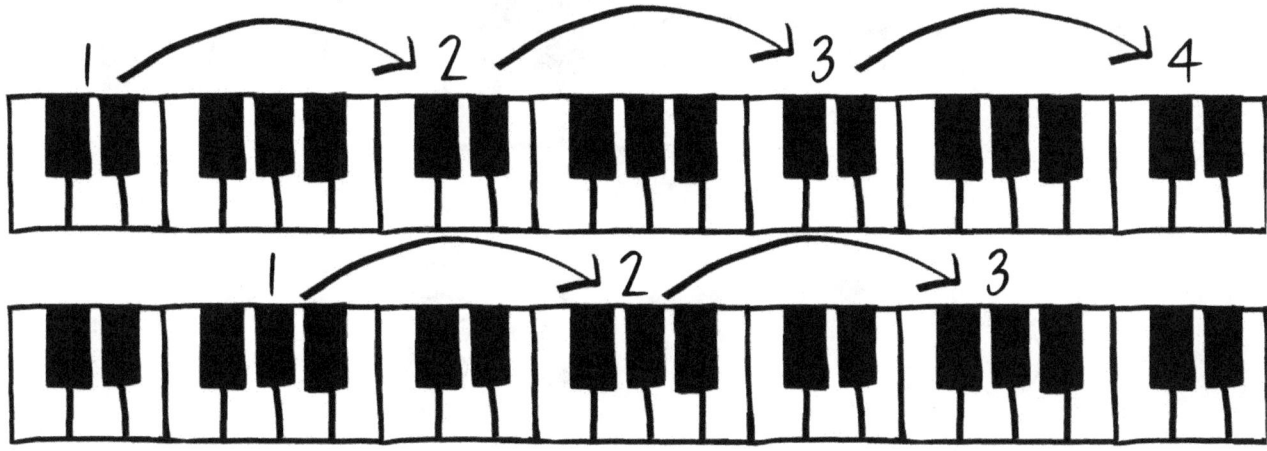

These are the options for white note warm ups:

You can play them all on the same note up and down the piano.

Or, you can start on one note and then move up by stepping note by note until you're at the same note again (that's called an OCTAVE). But for each time, you would put your finger 1 on the new note.

Here's an octave from F to F. You can also start higher and step down:

♡ 315

Groups of TWO Warm Ups
(RH & LH)

Remember to try these with your right hand and your left hand.

Use groups of 2  for these:

warm up ①   2 3

warm up ②   2 ⌐

warm up ③   ‖: 2 3 :‖

warm up ④   ‖: 3 2 :‖

warm up ⑤   ‖: 3 3 2 3 :‖

warm up ⑥   ‖: 2 2 3 2 :‖

Groups of THREE Warm Ups
(RH & LH)

Use groups of 3 [2 3 4] for these:

warm up 7) 3 〰

warm up 8) 3 ⌐⌐⌐

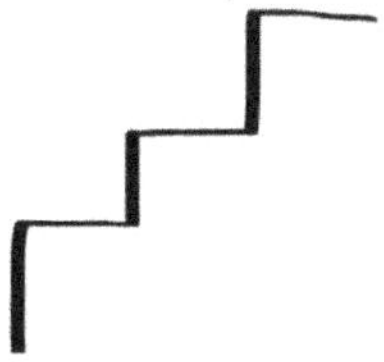

warm up 9) ||: 2 3 4 :||

warm up 10) ||: 2 4 3 :||

warm up 11) ||: 2 3 4 3 2 :||

warm up 12) ||: 2 4 2 3 :||

♡ 317

Warm Ups on White Notes
Using 2nds and stepping up and down (RH & LH).

Use one of the techniques on page 315 and repeat these patterns:

 ||: 1 2 3 2 1 :||

 ||: 3 2 1 2 3 :||

 ||: 1 1 2 3 3 2 1 :||

 ||: 3 3 2 1 1 2 3 :||

 ||: 1 2 3 4 5 :||

 ||: 5 4 3 2 1 :||

 ||: 1 2 3 4 5 4 3 2 1 :||

 ||: 5 4 3 2 1 2 3 4 5 :||

Patterns in Warm Ups
Using finger 1 as a base to jump and step.

 ‖: 1 2 | 3 | 4 | 5 | :‖

 ‖: 1 5 | 4 | 3 | 2 | :‖

 ‖: 1 2 | 3 | 2 | 4 | 2 | 5 | :‖

 ‖: 1 5 | 2 | 4 | 2 | 3 | 2 | :‖

 ‖: 1 5 | | 4 | | 3 | | 2 | :‖

 ‖: 1 | 2 | 1 3 | 1 4 | 1 5 | :‖

♡ 319

Keep Practicing Patterns

Watch carefully as these step and jump up and down.

 ‖: 1 2 3 2 3 4 3 4 5 4 3 2 1 :‖

 ‖: 5 4 3 4 3 2 3 2 1 5 2 1 ① 1 :‖

 ‖: 1 2 3 4 5 4 2 1 :‖

 ‖: 5 4 3 2 1 2 4 5 :‖

 ‖: 1 3 5 4 2 1 :‖

 ‖: 5 3 1 2 3 5 :‖

 ‖: 1 2 3 3 2 3 4 4 3 4 5 5 :‖

 ‖: 1212 2323 3434 4545 :‖

 ‖: 5454 4343 3232 2121 :‖

Warm Ups with Thirds

Jumping up and down thirds for warming up.

warm up 36 ‖: 1 3 2 4 3 5 4 2 1 :‖

warm up 37 ‖: 5 3 4 2 3 1 2 5 1 :‖

warm up 38 ‖: 1 3 1 3   2 4 2 4   3 5 3 5 :‖

warm up 39 ‖: 5 3 5 3   4 2 4 2   3 1 3 1 :‖

warm up 40 ‖: 1   3   5   3   1 :‖

warm up 41 ‖: 5   3   1   3   5 :‖

warm up 42 ‖: 1 1 3 5 5 3 1 :‖

warm up 43 ‖: 5 5 3 1 1 3 5 :‖

warm up 44 ‖: 1_ 3 5 5 3 1_ :‖

♡321

Warm Ups with Rhythm
Watch for long and short notes.

warm up 45 ‖: 1 2 3_1 :‖

warm up 46 ‖: 3 4 5_3 :‖

warm up 47 ‖: 1_2 3_2 1_ :‖

warm up 48 ‖: 1_1 2_2 3_3 4_4 5_5 :‖

warm up 49 ‖: 5_5 4_4 3_3 2_2 1_1 :‖

warm up 50 ‖: 1 1 5 5 4 4 3 3 2 2 1_ :‖

warm up 51 ‖: 1 2 3_2 3 4_3 4 5_ :‖

More Warm Ups with Rhythm

It's a question of which number is long.

warm up 52   ‖: 1_ 2 3 4 5 :‖

warm up 53   ‖: 1 2_ 3 4 5 :‖

warm up 54   ‖: 1 2 3_ 4 5 :‖

warm up 55   ‖: 1 2 3 4_ 5 :‖

warm up 56   ‖: 1 2 3 4 5_ :‖

warm up 57   ‖: 5_ 4 3 2 1 :‖

warm up 58   ‖: 5 4_ 3 2 1 :‖

warm up 59   ‖: 5 4 3_ 2 1 :‖

warm up 60   ‖: 5 4 3 2_ 1 :‖

warm up 61   ‖: 5 4 3 2 1_ :‖

If you want to practice more rhythm, go to page 47. ♡323

Warm Ups with Many Notes at a Time

With numbers in one line like this, you play
one note at a time or one finger at at time.

warm up 62   ‖: 1   2   3   4   5 :‖

But, if the numbers are stacked
like this, play them at the same time:

warm up 63   ‖: 2/1   3/1   4/1   5/1_ :‖

warm up 64   RH ‖: 3/1 :‖ ← This combination of notes can go up and down the piano. This is a third and is called a sandwich in this book.

warm up 65   LH ‖: 1/3 :‖

324☆

Keep Going! Keep It Up!

Here you see mixed single and stacked notes.

warm up 66 RH ‖: $\begin{smallmatrix}5\\1\end{smallmatrix}$:‖ ← This combination of notes can go up and down the piano. This is a fifth.

warm up 67 LH ‖: $\begin{smallmatrix}1\\5\end{smallmatrix}$:‖

warm up 68 RH ‖: $\begin{smallmatrix}5\\3\end{smallmatrix}$ 1 $\begin{smallmatrix}5\\3\end{smallmatrix}$ 1 :‖

warm up 69 LH ‖: 3 $\begin{smallmatrix}1\\5\end{smallmatrix}$ 3 $\begin{smallmatrix}1\\5\end{smallmatrix}$:‖

warm up 70 RH ‖: $\begin{smallmatrix}3\\1\end{smallmatrix}$ $\begin{smallmatrix}4\\2\end{smallmatrix}$ $\begin{smallmatrix}5\\3\end{smallmatrix}$ $\begin{smallmatrix}4\\2\end{smallmatrix}$ $\begin{smallmatrix}3\\1\end{smallmatrix}$:‖

warm up 71 LH ‖: $\begin{smallmatrix}1\\3\end{smallmatrix}$ $\begin{smallmatrix}2\\4\end{smallmatrix}$ $\begin{smallmatrix}3\\5\end{smallmatrix}$ $\begin{smallmatrix}2\\4\end{smallmatrix}$ $\begin{smallmatrix}1\\3\end{smallmatrix}$:‖

♡ 325

Triad Warm Ups (Fingers 1, 3, 5)

These are used with the double decker sandwich numbers.

warm up 72) RH ‖: 1 3 5 3 1 $\begin{smallmatrix}5\\3\\1\end{smallmatrix}$:‖

warm up 73) LH ‖: 1 3 5 3 1 $\begin{smallmatrix}1\\3\\5\end{smallmatrix}$:‖

warm up 74) RH ‖: 1 $\begin{smallmatrix}5\\3\end{smallmatrix}$ 1 $\begin{smallmatrix}5\\3\end{smallmatrix}$ 1 $\begin{smallmatrix}5\\3\end{smallmatrix}$:‖

warm up 75) LH ‖: 5 $\begin{smallmatrix}1\\3\end{smallmatrix}$ 5 $\begin{smallmatrix}1\\3\end{smallmatrix}$ 5 $\begin{smallmatrix}1\\3\end{smallmatrix}$:‖

More Triad Warm Ups

These are also used with the triad finger numbers.

warm up 76 RH ‖: 5 5 5 | 5 5 5 | 5 5 5 :‖
           3 3 3 | 3 3 3 | 3 3 3
           1 | 1 | 1

warm up 77 LH ‖: 1 1 1 | 1 1 1 | 1 1 1 :‖
             3 3 | 3 3 | 3 3
           5 | 5 | 5

warm up 78 RH ‖: 5 5 5 | 5 5 5 | 5 5 5 :‖
           3 1 1 | 3 1 1 | 3 1 1

warm up 79 LH ‖: 1 1 1 | 1 1 1 | 1 1 1 :‖
           3 5 5 | 3 5 5 | 3 5 5

♡327

Five Finger Scale Warm Ups

This is the five finger scale going **in the same direction** with both hands.

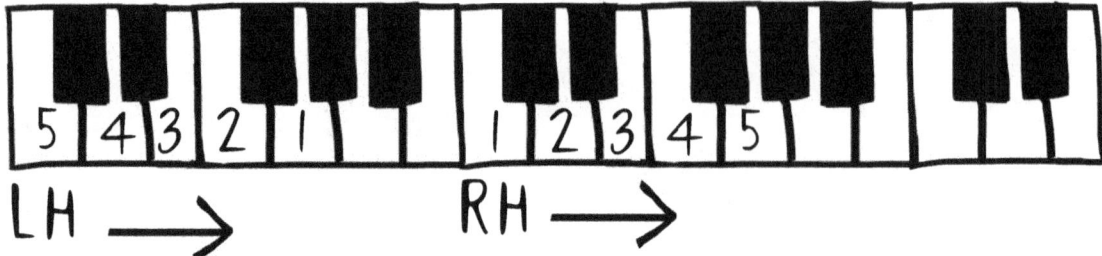

Play them separate, then try them together:

warm up 80

RH 1 2 3 4 5 4 3 2 1
LH 5 4 3 2 1 2 3 4 5

This is the five finger scale going **in different directions** with both hands. Keep your hands in the same position as above.

warm up 81

RH 1 2 3 4 5 4 3 2 1
LH 1 2 3 4 5 4 3 2 1

You can also try this by sharing the note C with finger 1 in both hands and going in opposite directions.

warm up 82

1 2 3 4 5 4 3 2 1 LH ☆ RH 1 2 3 4 5 4 3 2 1

Start here with both finger number 1's on C and go in opposite directions.

328 ☆

Over the Mountain Warm Ups

Practice going over one or two mountains, or maybe three.

Practice going down one or two mountains, or maybe three.

Here's a reminder of what that means:

♡ 329

Bridge Warm Ups LH

With your left hand (LH), you can play these three notes (3 2 1) going UP starting on finger 3. When you get to finger one (1), keep it where it is and CURVE finger three (3) over it to make a bridge over finger one (1) to travel up the piano.

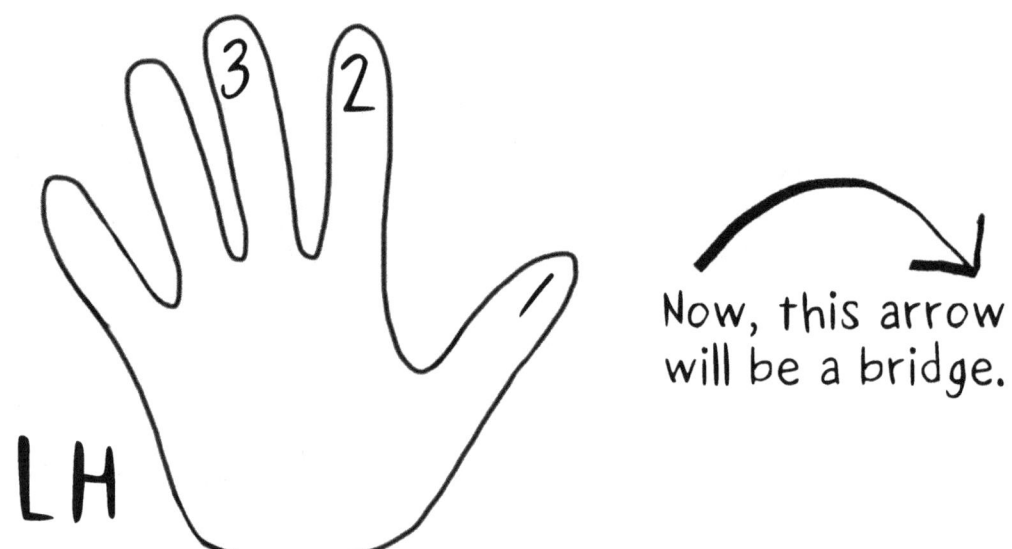

Now, this arrow will be a bridge.

Try going up the piano making a bridge with finger 3. Remember to curve it and go over finger one.

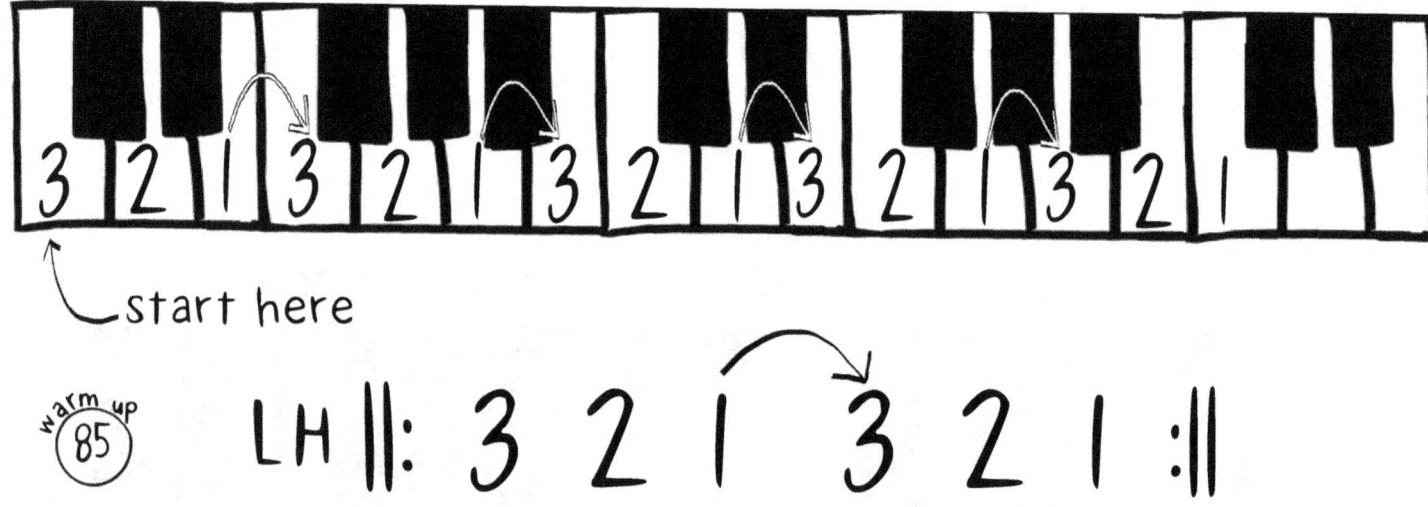

start here

warm up 85 LH ‖: 3 2 1 3 2 1 :‖

Next, try going down the piano and make finger 1 go UNDER the bridge that you make with finger 3.

warm up 86 LH ‖: 1 2 3 1 2 3 :‖

More Bridge Warm Ups RH

With your right hand (RH), you can play these three notes (1 2 3) going UP starting on finger 1. When you get to finger 3, keep it where it is and CURVE it making a bridge. Then, finger 1 can go under the bridge you made with finger 3 to travel up the piano.

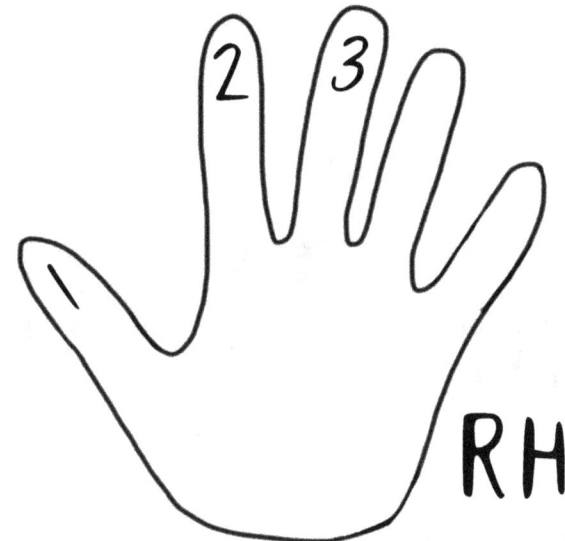

Try going up the piano making a bridge with finger 3. Remember to slide finger 1 under the bridge to play the next note.

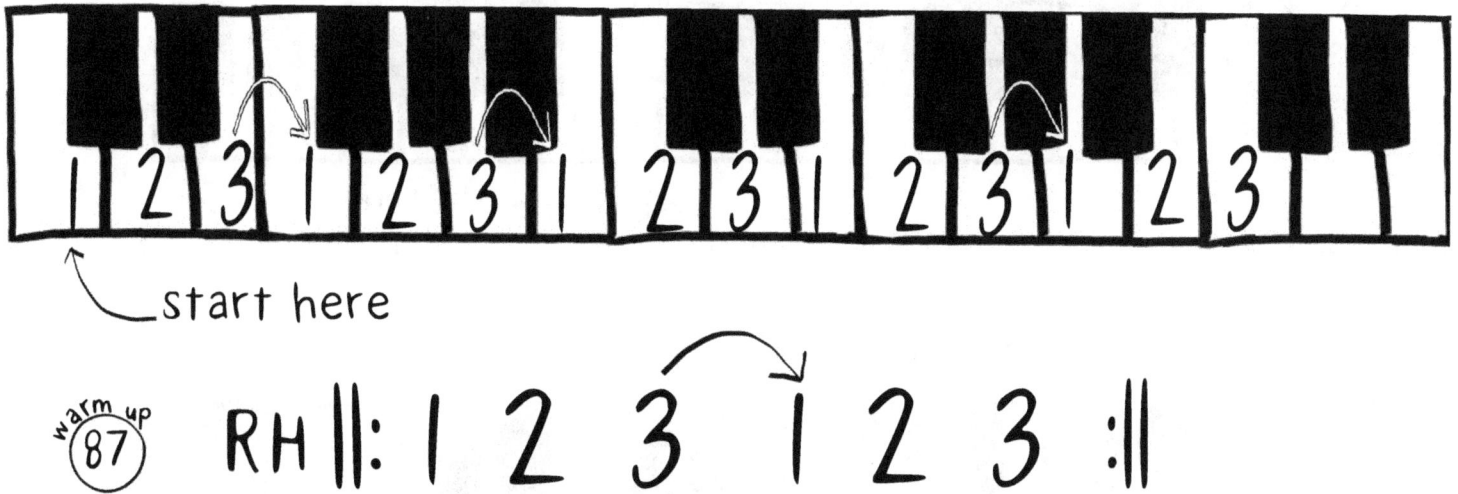

start here

warm up 87   RH ||: 1 2 3 1 2 3 :||

Now, try going down the piano starting with finger 3 then leave finger 1 where it is to make a bridge with finger 3 over it.

warm up 88   RH ||: 3 2 1 3 2 1 :||

♡ 331

Major Scale Warm Ups

Now, go over the bridge to try these C major scales:

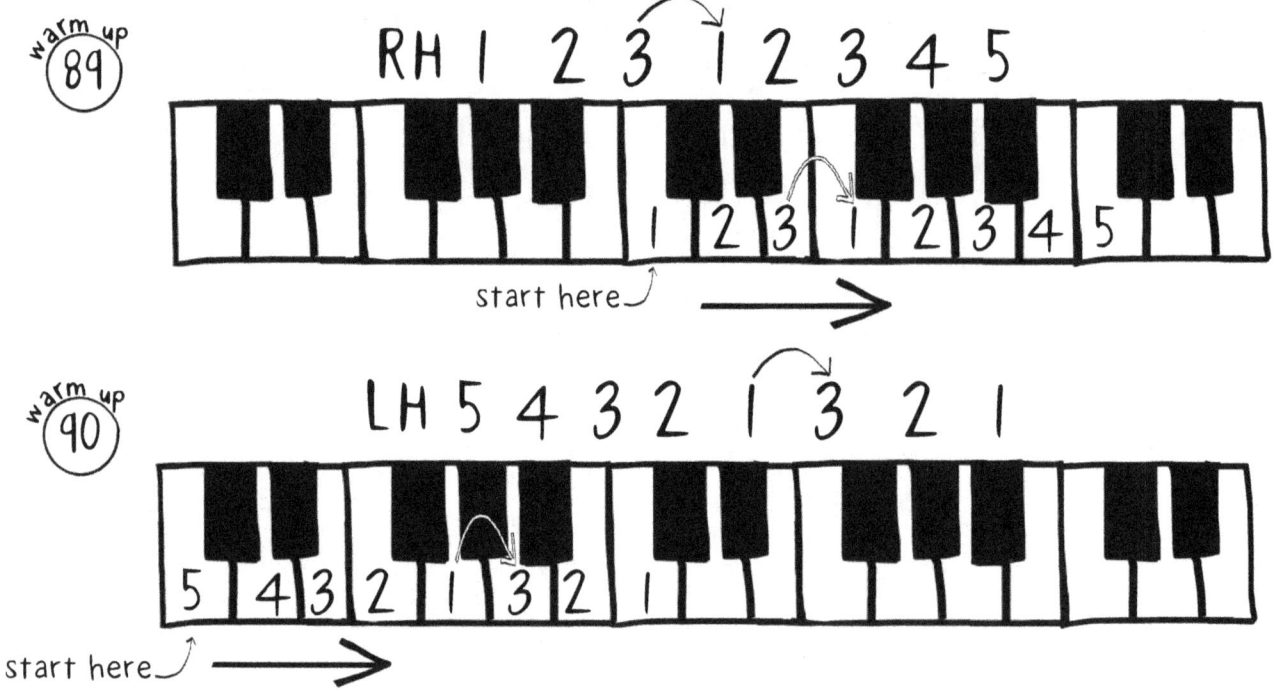

Now, play the C major scale going down:

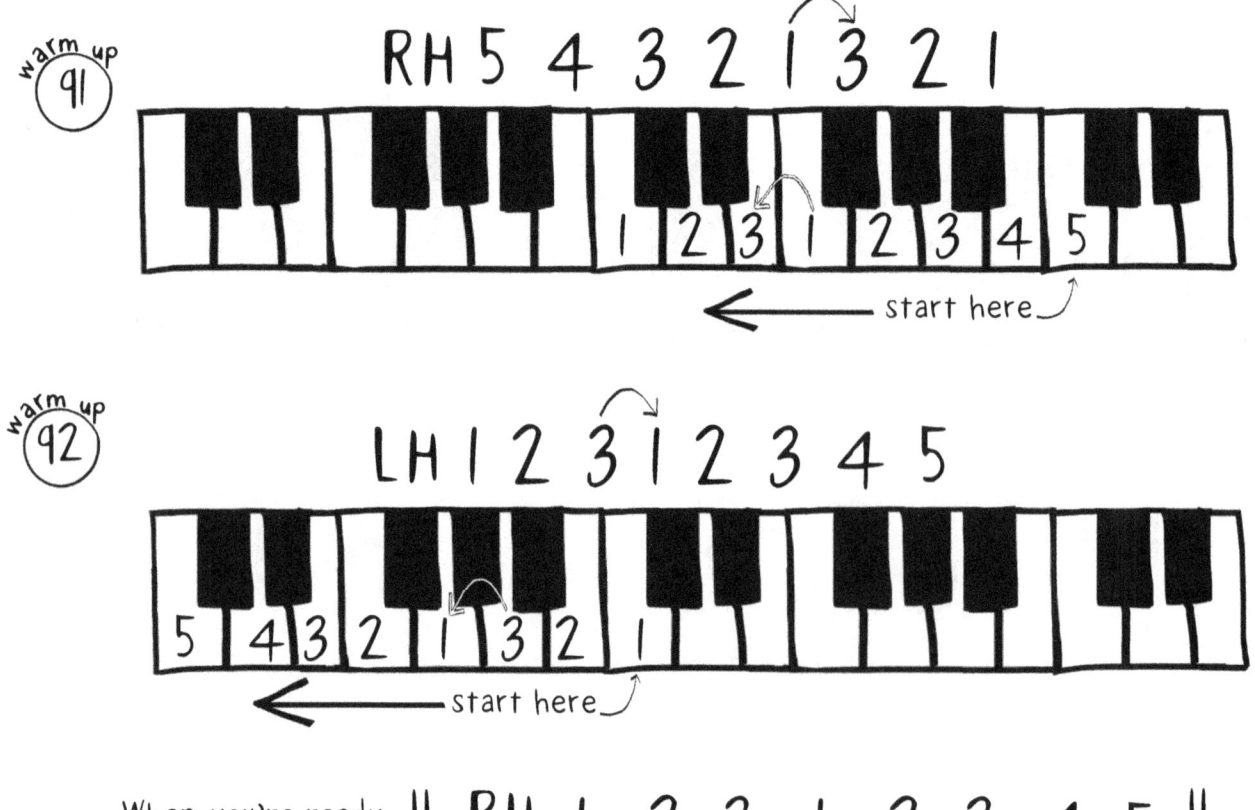

warm up 93 — When you're ready, try your C major scales with both hands together going up and down.

‖: RH 1 2 3 1 2 3 4 5 :‖
‖: LH 5 4 3 2 1 3 2 1 :‖

Every Day Warm Ups

If you only do a few warm ups regularly, do these ones:

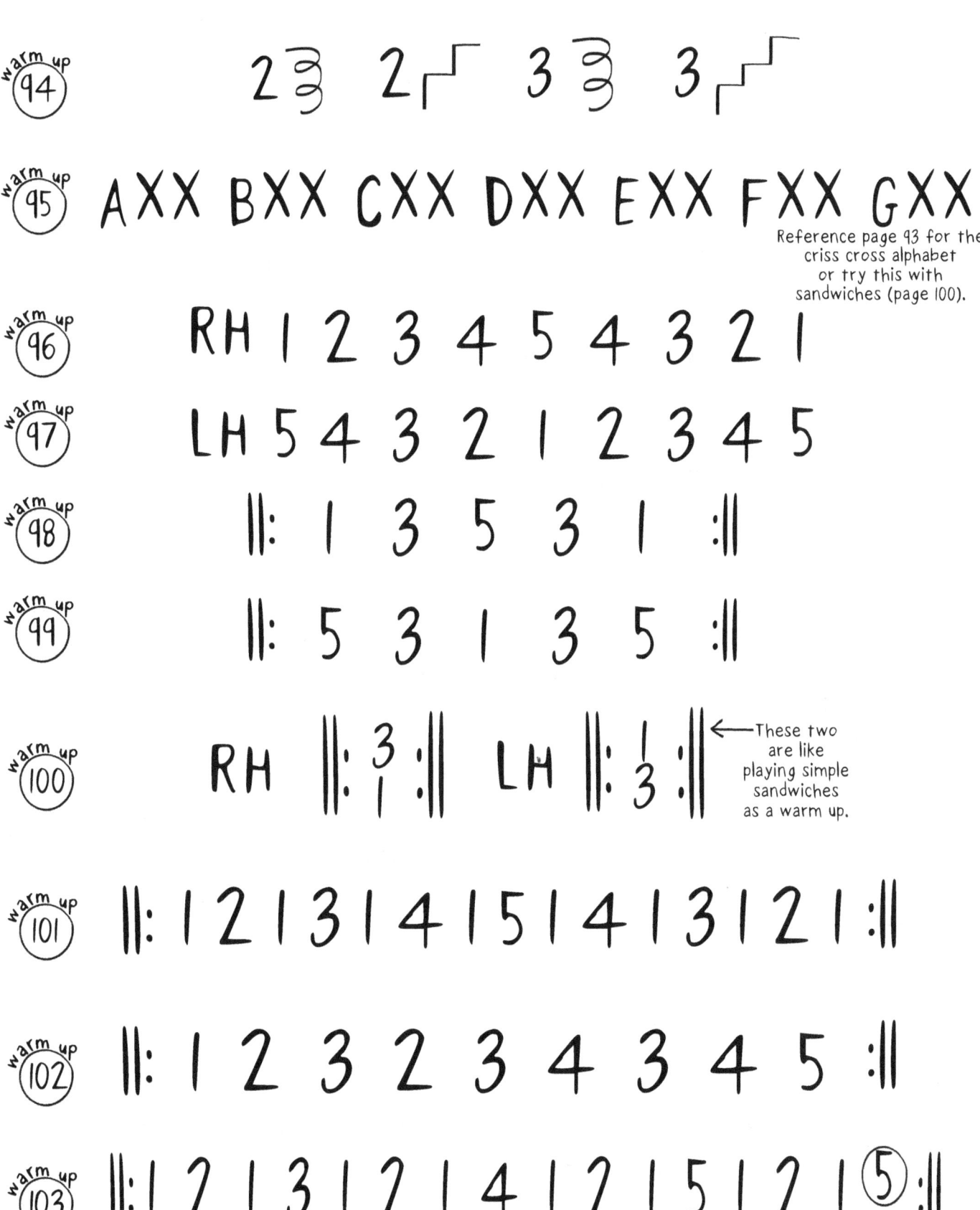

♡ 333

Way to Go!
You Did It!

Check what you did here in these boxes!

- ☐ You played songs!
- ☐ You sang songs!
- ☐ You made this book MORE COLORFUL!
- ☐ You learned musical sandwiches.
- ☐ You did warm ups.
- ☐ You made songs.
- ☐ You improvised.
- ☐ You had fun!
- ☐ You colorfully played the piano!

Now what?

- ☐ Go out and play more music!
- ☐ Learn new songs (look at page 248).
- ☐ Make new melodies.
- ☐ Write your name on your Certificate of Achievement on the next page.
- ☐ Continue to make the world more colorful and filled with music!

COLORFULLY PLAYING THE PIANO

Certificate of Achievement

TO CERTIFY THAT

your name here →

_____

SUCCESSFULLY COLORFULLY
PLAYED THE PIANO

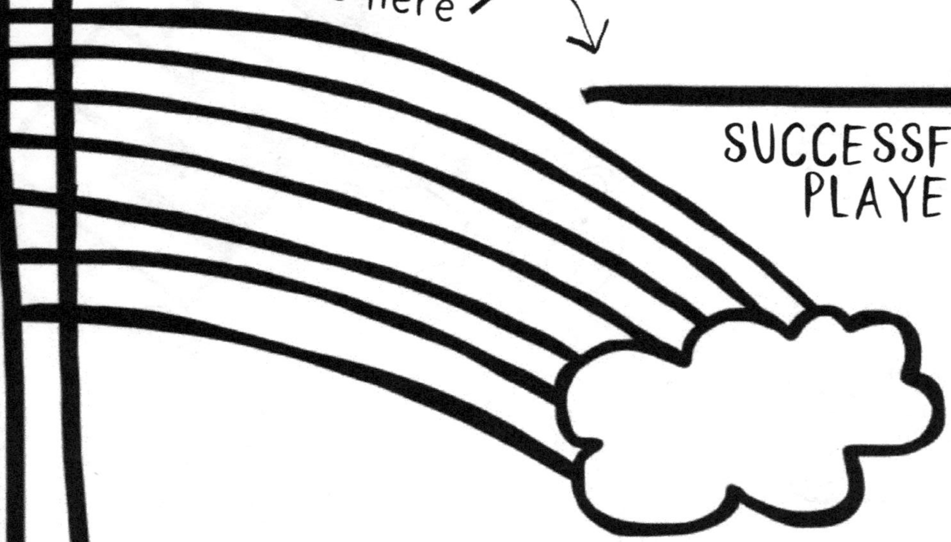

Jodi Marie Fisher
TEACHER